ARCHIVING THE PAST

FEMINIST MEDIA HISTORIES

Shelley Stamp, Series Editor

1. *Their Own Best Creations: Women Writers in Postwar Television*, by Annie Berke
2. *Violated Frames: Armando Bó and Isabel Sarli's Sexploits*, by Victoria Ruétalo
3. *Recollecting Lotte Eisner: Cinema, Exile, and the Archive*, by Naomi DeCelles
4. *A Queer Way of Feeling: Girl Fans and Personal Archives in Early Hollywood*, by Diana W. Anselmo
5. *Incomplete: The Feminist Possibilities of the Unfinished Film*, edited by Alix Beeston and Stefan Solomon
6. *Producing Feminism: Television Work in the Age of Women's Liberation*, by Jennifer S. Clark
7. *To Be an Actress: Labor and Performance in Anna May Wong's Cross-Media World*, by Yiman Wang
8. *Rated A: Soft-Porn Cinema and Mediations of Desire in India*, by Darshana Sreedhar Mini
9. *Undead: (Inter)(in)animation, Feminisms, and the Art of War*, by Karen Redrobe
10. *Archiving the Past: Women's Film History in France, 1927–1978*, by Aurore Spiers

ARCHIVING THE PAST

Women's Film History in France, 1927–1978

AURORE SPIERS

UNIVERSITY OF CALIFORNIA PRESS

University of California Press
Oakland, California

© 2026 by Aurore Spiers

All rights reserved.

A version of chapter 3, "Activists," appeared earlier as "My Name Is Alice Guy: The 'Musidora' Collective and Women's Film History," *Feminist Media Histories* 8, no. 3 (Summer 2022): 155–77.

Cataloging-in-Publication data is on file at the Library of Congress.

ISBN 978-0-520-40080-1 (cloth)
ISBN 978-0-520-40082-5 (pbk.)
ISBN 978-0-520-40083-2 (ebook)

GPSR Authorized Representative: Easy Access System Europe, Mustamäe tee 50, 10621 Tallinn, Estonia, gpsr.requests@easproject.com

35 34 33 32 31 30 29 28 27 26
10 9 8 7 6 5 4 3 2 1

To my grandmothers,
Marie Goury Spiers (1906–2007)
and
Monique Chaillier Masson (1925–2022)

The publisher and the University of California Press Foundation gratefully acknowledge the generous support of the Eric Papenfuse and Catherine Lawrence Endowment Fund in Film and Media Studies.

Contents

Acknowledgments ix

Abbreviations xiii

Introduction: On Women's Film History 1

PREMIER ENTR'ACTE: COLLECTION 15

1. Archivists 19

    DEUXIEME ENTR'ACTE: RECOLLECTION 63

2. Witnesses 67

    TROISIEME ENTR'ACTE: RECOVERY 107

3. Activists 111

    Epilogue: Toward Feminist Futures 149

Notes 153
Bibliography 187
Index 203

Acknowledgments

THIS BOOK would not exist without the film archivists and librarians who gave me access to countless precious materials over the years. I am particularly thankful for the staff of the Cinémathèque française, the Bibliothèque nationale de France, and the Archives Nationales, whom I encountered during my visits between 2015 and 2024. Their expertise was essential to the conceptualization and writing of this book.

I also wish to acknowledge the collective work of feminist film historians, several of whom have directly supported me. In addition to Jane Gaines, whose encouragement since my time as a master's student at Columbia University has sustained my research in more ways than I can tell, I would like to thank Jennifer M. Bean, Maggie Hennefeld, and Shelley Stamp, as well as the many contributors to the Women Film Pioneers Project. Their brilliance, kindness, and steadfast commitment to building a feminist future in the face of previously unimaginable challenges inspire me every day.

At the University of Chicago, where this book first developed as a dissertation, partly during the COVID-19 pandemic, I received incredible intellectual and moral support from my advisers, Allyson Nadia Field, Tom Gunning, and Jennifer Wild; from the entire faculty in the Department of Cinema and Media Studies, including Masha Belodubrovskaya, the late Robert Bird, Dominique Bluher, Katherine Buse, Jim Chandler, Kara Keeling, Tom Lamarre, Jim Lastra, Rochona Majumdar, Dan Morgan, Richard Neer, David Rodowick, Salomé Aguilera Skvirsky, AE Stevenson, Jacqueline Stewart, and Yuri Tsivian; and from my fellow graduate students, especially Sean Batton, Jenisha Borah, Dave Burnham, Tanya Desai, Matt Hubbell, Gary Kafer, Ritika Kaushik, Katerina Korola, Cooper Long, Cinta Pelejà, Jordan Schonig, and Amy Skjerseth. I am grateful for every class, workshop, screening, and conversation that we shared, and honored to count them as my colleagues and friends today. A special thank you to Sean Batton, Ritika Kaushik, Cinta Pelejà, and Amy Skjerseth for making Chicago home for my husband and me. I also want to thank the staff and administrators, Jane Bohnsack, Brianna Considine, Julia Gibbs, Mike Phillips, Shekinah Thornton, and Traci Verleyen Hope, as well as Nancy Spiegel from the Library and Bridget Madden from the Visual Resources Center, whose work made mine possible.

Many more film and other scholars have contributed to this book by sharing their work and engaging with mine in casual and formal ways, at the Society for Cinema and Media Studies conference and the Silent Cinema Scholarly Interest Group, at the Modernist Studies Association conference, Domitor, and more. Richard Abel, Grace An, Nicholas Baer, Leticia Berrizbeitia Añez, Amy Beste, Liz Clarke, Carolyn Condon Jacobs, Sandy Flitterman-Lewis, Tanya Goldman, Martin Johnson, Paul McEwan, Hayley O'Malley, Karen Ritzenhoff, Alejandra Rosenberg Navarro, Maya Sidhu, Anthony Slide, Matthew Solomon, Kim Tomadjoglou, Yiman Wang, and Tami Williams deserve special mention here. From Women and Film History International and the Women and Silent Screen conference, I thank Clara Auclair, Elyse Singer, Enri Moreno Ceballos, Kiki Loveday, and Kate Saccone, for their fierce feminist scholarship and comradery. At Texas A&M University, I am grateful to Matthew Campbell, Will Connor, Anna Holman, Daniel Humphrey, Francesca Marini, Justin Randolph, Miranda Sachs, Angie Spalink, Patrick Sullivan, and Emma Wingfield, and to the faculty from the Women's and Gender Studies Program, for being such welcoming and encouraging colleagues. Amid increasing threats against academic freedom and gender studies, I am particularly thankful for Anna Holman and Emma Wingfield for weathering the storm with me.

In book form, this project found the best home at the University of California Press. I wish to thank my editor, Raina Polivka, and my book series editor, Shelley Stamp, for their support, insights, and care, as well as Sam Warren and the rest of his team for their tremendous editorial work. My two peer reviewers, Eric Smoodin and Maggie Hennefeld, provided incredibly generous feedback for which I am forever grateful. I also want to thank my developmental editor, Megan Pugh, for offering thoughtful recommendations for revision. The illustrations in this book come from mostly French archives and libraries, whose staff I am indebted to for giving me and others access to that material. Sandra Laupa from the Cinémathèque française was particularly helpful, and I thank her for being such a wonderful interlocutor and collaborator throughout my research. My gratitude also goes to Valérie Vignaux, Yvon Dupart of Les Amis Musidora, and Dana Sardet, one of the members of the 1970s feminist film collective "Musidora," for their assistance in tracking down some of the images in this book.

On a more personal note, I want to acknowledge my parents, Isabelle and Gérard Spiers, as well as my sister, Catheline Modat Linsolas, and her family, Julien, Camille, and Alexandre, for supporting my choice to live and work thousands of miles away from France. My gratitude also goes to my in-laws, Denise and Steven Migliorini, and to my sister-in-law, Robyn Migliorini, and her family, Nick, Josephine, and June, for taking me in as their own. Thanks to my friends, Clara Auclair, Charlotte Arnautou, Brian Belak, Cyrielle Brunet, Clothilde Hennequin, Matt Jacobs, Karim Kattan, Violaine Morin, and Zack Silverman, for having me in their lives. Thanks to Carolyn Condon Jacobs and Kate Saccone, two brilliant scholars, for being my friends. And thanks to my husband, Kyle Migliorini, for loving me even more than the Boston Celtics. I can't wait for our next adventure together.

Abbreviations

THE LIST BELOW includes the abbreviations used for the institutions discussed at length throughout *Archiving the Past*. These abbreviations, arranged here in alphabetical order, are admittedly cumbersome, but their proliferation attests to the institutionalization of French and global film historiography in the period under study. Although some of these acronyms are accepted and commonly used, others—marked by an asterisk (*)—are employed here for the first time. This list also indicates the names of some relevant women, also in alphabetical order, associated with each institution. The goals are to help readers navigate the book and to make visible, in list form, how several women contributed to the production of film historical knowledge across times and places.

BAA* Bibliothèque d'art et d'archéologie (1909–18)
BC*   Bibliothèque du Cinéma (1927–29)
      Jeanne Moussinac

BiFi	Bibliothèque du Film (Film Library) of the Cinémathèque française (2007–)
BN	Bibliothèque Nationale (1792–1994)
	Michelle Seguin
BnF	Bibliothèque nationale de France (1994–)
CF	Cinémathèque française (1936–)
	Marie Epstein
	Lotte Eisner
	Eve Francis
	Mary Meerson
	Musidora
CN*	Cinémathèque Nationale (1932–39)
	Laure Albin-Guillot
CRH	Commission de Recherches historiques (Commission of Historical Research) (1943–66)
	Marie-Anne Colson-Malleville
	Marie Epstein
	Eve Francis
	Musidora
FIAF	Fédération Internationale des Archives du Film (International Federation of Film Archives) (1938–)
INA	Institut national de l'audiovisuel (National Audiovisual Institute) (1975–)
SAP	Service des Archives photographiques (Service of the Photographic Archives) of the Ministère de l'Instruction et des Beaux-Arts
	Laure Albin-Guillot
SPCA	Section photographique et cinématographique de l'armée (Photographic and Cinematographic Section of the Army)

INTRODUCTION

On Women's Film History

THIS BOOK is about two sides of women's film history: film history *about* women, and film history *by* women. It specifically addresses how feminist film historians conceptualize the archive and how women other than feminist film historians produce film history through multiple, varied forms of engagement with the archive. We feminist film historians tend to think about the archive in terms of absence and erasure, on the one hand, and presence and recovery, on the other, which ultimately perpetuates women's position as objects, not agents, of film historiography. This book argues instead—through examples from France between the 1920s and the 1970s—that women have long been active in the production of global cinema's history; they have served as *archivists* charged with collecting films and other materials, as *witnesses* tasked with remembering their past film careers, and as *activists* committed to recovering women's contributions to film history. By taking seriously how these women worked in, and with, the film archive across times and places, *Archiving the Past* recasts the film archive as a site of women's intervention. This book also contributes to a more complex understanding of how gender politics informs the production of global film history; it reflects on film history's biases, oversights, and erasures and models strategies for inclusivity, recuperation, and liberation within film historiography.

Just like cinema itself, the film archive doesn't have a specific date and country of birth; it emerged instead from a global set of ideas and initiatives that promoted, starting in the 1920s, the preservation of cinema's history as a necessary cultural enterprise. At the same time, there is no doubt that France, with its vibrant film culture dating back to the end of the nineteenth century, played a major part—if not real, at least imagined—in the development of the global film preservation movement, which explains why this book uses French film archives as case studies for rethinking the film archive more broadly. Early French filmmakers include the Lumière brothers, Alice Guy Blaché, Georges Méliès, Jean Durand, Louis Feuillade, Germaine Dulac, and Jean Epstein, among many others, whose critical works of non-fiction, narrative fiction, and experimental cinema propelled the new medium to the forefront of both mass popular culture and the arts around the world. Furthermore, from the 1920s on, French film archives, mainly the Bibliothèque du Cinéma (BC) (1927–29), the Cinémathèque Nationale (CN) (1932–39), and the Cinémathèque française (CF) (1936–), emerged, which counted among the earliest in the world; they were also highly influential for how other institutions dedicated to film preservation came about not only conceptually but practically. For example, not only did the founder of the CF, Henri Langlois, co-create the International Federation of Film Archives (FIAF; Fédération Internationale des Archives du Film) in 1938, but the CF and the Centre national du cinéma et de l'image animée (known as the CNC) remain, to this day, key FIAF members and powerful decision-makers when it comes to the preservation of the world's film heritage.

Much lesser known are the ways in which French film archives established women as significant agents of historical knowledge production. During (and since) the period under study, which begins in 1927 with the advent of sound cinema and ends in the late 1970s with the death of Langlois in 1977 and the FIAF Congress of 1978, French film archives were (and have been) staffed mostly by women, whose identities and experiences as gendered subjects often determined their job positions, work conditions, salaries, and career trajectories. The CF alone employed dozens of women administrators and archivists, including but certainly not limited to Suzanne Bidault (also known as Suzanne Borel, 1904–95), Yvonne Dornès (1910–94), Lotte Eisner (1896–1983), Marie Epstein (1899–1995), Mary Meerson (1900?–1993), and Musidora (1889–1957), all of whom were Langlois's closest collaborators.

In Eisner's case, for example, her skills and extensive knowledge of German and other national cinemas were instrumental in building the filmic and non-filmic collections of the CF.[1] Born to a Jewish family in Berlin, Germany, Eisner first established herself as a film critic for the influential trade journal *Film-Kurier*, whose regular contributors throughout the 1920s also included producer Erich Pommer and director Ernst Lubitsch.[2] After she was forced to escape Hitler's new Nazi regime in 1933, she then spent several difficult years in France, as a struggling expatriate taking odd jobs like babysitting, translating, and freelance writing, and, during World War II, as a fugitive in hiding from both the Nazis and the French police. Near the end of 1934, when she met the founders of the CF, Langlois and future director Georges Franju, for the first time, Eisner also began working without compensation to not only organize but also to safeguard the CF's growing film collections.[3] She indeed spent several months during the war looking after some films while hiding away at the Château de Béduer near Figeac in the Southwest of France.[4] After Liberation, she was officially hired by the CF, where she served as "chief curator" and, in her own words, *"bonne à tout faire,"* from 1945 through 1975.[5] Although she was

Figure 1. Lotte Eisner with a copy of *L'Ecran démoniaque* (*The Haunted Screen*, 1952) in her hands, date unknown. *Source:* Anonym © DR, Collection La Cinémathèque française.

mainly responsible for collecting non-filmic materials like scripts and set design drawings from filmmakers and movie workers whom she often knew from Germany, she handled many more jobs for the CF than her official title implied. She also published many essays and three major books on Weimar cinema—*L'Ecran démoniaque* (*The Haunted Screen*, 1952), *F. W. Murnau* (1964), and *Fritz Lang* (1976)—that sealed her status as a legendary figure of global cinema.

Many more women besides Eisner contributed to the development of film preservation and historiography, at the CF and other French film archives, but also, and very importantly, outside established institutions. Although French film archives came to rely on mostly women's labor early on, these institutions quickly became hotbeds for masculinist practices like cinephilia and auteurism, both of which center male directors as primary agents of cinema's history. Such practices are commonly understood as having to do with film reception and exhibition, rarely film preservation. Yet as this book demonstrates, French film archives contributed to the emergence of cinephilia and auteurism by producing historical knowledge—through acquisitions, cataloging, documentation, restoration, screenings, and other projects—that privileged the extant work of mostly male directors over women's input as editors, screenwriters, and colorists, among others. Meanwhile, women worked not only within, but also outside and against, established institutions dedicated to film preservation. Through their labor, which this book traces from the BC and the CN in the 1920s, through the CF between the 1930s and 1960s, to the "Musidora" film collective in the 1970s, these women not only initiated film archival practices; they also engaged in sometimes implicit, sometimes overt acts of feminist resistance against traditionally exclusive accounts of cinema's history. Specifically, as the film preservation movement continued to develop around cinephilia and auteurism, women's engagement with the film archive multiplied, expanded, and intensified in ways that often put pressure on the gender politics shaping the very object and site of their work.

Unlike Eisner, the women discussed in this book were admittedly never considered film historians. Nor were they ever trained as information and museum professionals, who in today's parlance include not only archivists, librarians, and curators, but also collection managers, catalogers, bibliographers, and many other essential workers. Jeanne Moussinac, who ran the short-lived BC from 1927 through 1929, was a writer who was married to the communist film critic Léon Moussinac and was close to the 1920s narrative film avant-garde (Louis Delluc, Abel Gance, Germaine Dulac). Laure Albin-Guillot was a professional photographer interested in the microscopic sciences and decorative arts before becoming the director of the first French national cinematheque from 1932 through 1939. By the 1940s, when Langlois asked Musidora to lead the Commission de Recherches historiques (CRH; Commission of Historical Research) at the CF, Musidora was a veteran actor and filmmaker with dozens of silent films under her belt.[6] The women she interviewed for the CRH were not only filmmakers and movie workers, but also the wives, widows, and sisters of so-called male film pioneers. In the 1970s, the feminist film group that took Musidora's name and organized the first women's film festival in France included some amateur film- and videomakers with day jobs outside the movie industry. However, all of these women served functions—as a result of chance and circumstance—that made them key but often invisible agents in the production of film historical knowledge.

My understanding of how such women's labor becomes invisible stems from feminist and postcolonial theories of the archive, as well as works from feminist film historiography. To start with, I am indebted to feminist and gender historians and to postcolonial thinkers, for whom the archive functions as an instrument and a system of white Western patriarchal power. Since at least the 1970s, feminist and gender historians committed to recovering women's lives and experiences—Antoinette Burton, Gerda Lerner, Kathy Peiss, Michelle Perrot, Joan Wallach Scott, and Bonnie G. Smith, to name just a few—have grappled with a dearth of archival material that they have found symptomatic of broader masculinist biases in patriarchal societies. Because women matter less than men in the public, official sphere, in other words, women's lives and experiences are less likely to have been recorded in the archive. It then follows that an important task for feminist and gender historians has been to identify extant primary sources scattered across collections and institutions. Women are not completely absent from the archive, but are buried under the weight of patriarchy as a form of archival power.

At the same time, the establishment of women's and feminist archives since at least the late nineteenth century, and with renewed intensity during the women's liberation movement and third-wave feminism, attests to another side of the relationship between feminists and the archive.[7] As Kate Eichhorn explains about twenty-first-century feminist archives like the Barnard Zine Library (2003–) and the Riot Grrrl Collection (2009–) in the United States, the archive also functions as a "space of possibility" for feminists to write a more inclusive history, and, in so doing, to revolutionize gender relations in the present.[8] The feminist archive—as document and institution—is, indeed, a central strategy of both women's history and feminist activism, one that serves as a corrective to archival power and to forms of historical erasure.

Following postcolonial thinkers like Michel-Rolph Trouillot, one must also recognize that the patriarchal impulses of the archive go hand in hand with colonial imperialism, and that feminist recuperative work should strive for decolonial approaches to the archive.[9] Although *Archiving the Past* isn't directly concerned with the preservation of colonial and ethnographic films, it nevertheless proves important to acknowledge that colonial imperialism has long informed the mission of French film archives—whether public or private—to amass collections that would promote cinema as national heritage on the local and global scale. Paula Amad and Katherine Groo have written about the "colonial impulse" behind Albert Kahn's Archives de la Planète (1908–31), dedicated to the production of photographs and films shot in mostly French colonies.[10] Yet few other scholars have discussed how French film archives more broadly intersect with colonial imperialism, even as calls for decolonizing museums and other cultural institutions grow louder in France.[11] In the absence of such scholarship, *Archiving the Past* can only briefly recognize that colonial imperialism has necessarily structured the film preservation movement since its emergence in France in the 1920s. One word in particular, "pioneer" (or *pionnier* in French), which many of the women and other people from *Archiving the Past* employ in its masculine form to describe early male filmmakers and movie workers, brings to the fore how both patriarchal and colonial impulses operate together within French film archives.[12] I use that word in this book as a historical term whose original connections to the exploitation of foreign lands and peoples should remain in our minds throughout.

That said, feminist film historians since the 1990s have conceived of the archive less in terms of colonialism and more in a way similar to feminist and gender historians, as both an instrument of patriarchal power and a privileged site for feminist recovery.[13] Therein lies the problem that this book takes as its starting point: by considering the archive as a site of oppression and/or liberation, as well as within a dialectic of absence and presence, we feminist film historians risk undermining the complex ways in which the archive also works to objectify women (as in, reduce them to the status of objects). As Kiki Loveday astutely remarks about the first woman to direct films in the world, Alice Guy Blaché (née Alice Guy, 1873–1968), the logic of feminist recovery, according to which what is "lost" from the past must be "found" again in the present, should raise suspicion when it comes to historical women filmmakers and movie workers. Loveday writes that "the problem with the rescue narrative as a framing device is that, however feminist its intentions, it functions by positioning the profoundly successful Guy [Blaché] as a damsel-in-distress."[14] But the problem that *Archiving the Past* addresses more specifically has less to do with historical narrativization than it does with archival labor. On the one hand, *Archiving the Past* demonstrates that women have been actively involved in the production of film historical knowledge—as archivists (see chapter 1), witnesses (see chapter 2), and activists (see chapter 3). On the other hand, this book deconstructs—through careful examination of various extant archival materials—how the archive, founded upon women's work, makes that work barely visible, legible, and knowable to historians in the end. It is by doing so, this book argues, that the archive ultimately transforms women from "makers" into "bearers" of film historical meaning.[15]

To reimagine the archive as a site of women's intervention, *Archiving the Past* casts a new look, attuned to the neglected traces of women's work in, and with, the archive. The women I examine in this book are neither entirely unknown to film historians nor completely undocumented in French archives and libraries. Scholars before me have gone to the same institutions—the CF, the Archives Nationales, and the Bibliothèque nationale de France (BnF), among others; they looked at the same collections and wrote about these women generally in works that either examined a different aspect of their careers or focused primarily on the career of someone else. In reevaluating these women, this book calls for a kind of feminist film history that attends not only to archival absences but also to archival oversights, whereby women are glazed over but rarely seen. Following Hannah Frank, whose "frame-by-frame" examination of animated cartoons reveals the non-creative labor of the women of the Ink and Paint Departments, I scrutinize documents line by line for the most minute and relevant details.[16] I also pay close attention to literal margins, scraps of paper, and random objects, on which women are likely to have left the marks of their sometimes ancillary work. In the end, such a forensic approach proves extremely productive, especially in chapters 1 and 2, dedicated to a limited number of collections about archivists and witnesses. These collections brim with important details, which, brought together, offer a better picture of women's historiographical work and a new path for women's film history.

Several adjustments about film historiography, on the one hand, and gendered labor, on the other, are required from us at this stage. To begin with, we must understand that film historiography, defined here as the production of film historical knowledge, is done by more people than just trained academic historians. Drawing on the work of David William Cohen, Marc Ferro, and Paul Thompson, Trouillot calls attention to "the fact that history is also produced outside of academia."[17] Several feminist and gender historians have made a similar argument, albeit with a different (this time feminist) goal in mind. In *The Gender of History*, for example, Bonnie G. Smith takes seriously the work of Germaine de Staël (*Considerations of the Principal Events of the French Revolution*, 1818), Margaret Fuller (*Women in the Nineteenth Century*, 1845), and Mary Ritter Beard (*America Through Women's Eyes*, 1933), whom she argues were amateur historians but also precursors of professional historiography.[18] Tangentially, yet perhaps even more importantly for *Archiving the Past*, Smith also remarks that male professional historians often "enlist[ed] mothers, wives, children, sisters-in-law, cousins, and other female relatives to do the work of researching, filing, editing, and even writing."[19] Some of these "helpers," as one tends to think of them, take central stage in *Archiving the Past*. This book further expands the boundaries of (feminist film) historiography by also considering librarians (whom Laura E. Helton calls, in a different context, "historian[s] who never wrote"), administrators, secretaries, curators, filmmakers, and movie workers as active participants to the preservation and writing of film history.[20]

Archiving the Past also proposes that we finally recognize women's work as both serious and valuable. This second adjustment is long overdue in film and media studies. Since at least the 1970s, feminist labor historians have challenged the ways in which Western patriarchal capitalist societies devalue women's work as cheap, menial, and unimportant. These historians have also clarified how ideas about women's work reinforce traditional roles assigned to women as wives and mothers, on the one hand, and traditional hierarchies between races and classes, on the other. Much has been written about, for example, the feminization of the clerical profession in the United States in the late nineteenth century, when young, educated, unmarried, mostly white, middle-class women were considered naturals at not only typewriting but also office management and client relations. These women, commonly portrayed as "secretaries" in many films and TV shows, provided a cheap but skilled labor force, which feminist historians have encouraged us to re-evaluate for their essential contributions to the US economy and social structure. Other female-dominated fields like social work, teaching, and librarianship, the last of which will prove particularly relevant to this book, have been the focus of a similar kind of reappraisal.[21] Understanding women's work in the past has certainly contributed to its growing recognition, or at the very least acceptance, in the present. Yet in film and media studies, women's work in the cinema has only recently garnered significant attention. The Women Film Pioneers Project, currently edited by Jane Gaines and Kate Saccone, and officially launched online in 2013, now features over 326 women (and counting) from the silent era, including producers, directors, screenwriters, and editors, as well as animal trainers, accountants, camera operators, and casting directors.[22] With their studies on the classical Hollywood studio system and the British film industry, respectively, Erin Hill and Melanie Bell have also reclaimed the importance of women movie workers to cinema's history.[23] *Archiving the Past* contributes to this emerging body of work by adding archivists, witnesses, and activists to the list of significant women in film.

In *Archiving the Past*, how women worked in, and with, the archive receives renewed attention. Each chapter in this book focuses on the function these women served (archivists, witnesses, and activists), on the one hand, and on the work they did (collection, recollection, and recovery), on the other. Between each chapter, a brief essay or "entr'acte" on Eisner elaborates on the type of work, understood as historiographical practice, done by archivists, witnesses, and activists, respectively. These essays aim to accomplish the following. First, they offer theoretical reflections on "collection," which designates how archival material is not only assembled but also organized through, for example, cataloging and indexing; "recollection," which refers to the act of remembering; and "recovery," which consists of producing a counter-narrative based on new archival findings and/or more speculative strategies. Second, they place the archivists, witnesses, and activists discussed in this book within a larger "constellation" of French and international women, one that includes not only Lotte Eisner but also Iris Barry,

Margot Benacerraf, Sophie El Goulli, Kashiko Kawakita, Aglaia Mitropoulou, Maria Adriana Prolo, Elena Sánchez Valenzuela, and Lia Van Leer, as well as the even lesser known figures from *Archiving the Past*.[24] As the first curator of the Film Library at the Museum of Modern Art in New York, and the founder of the Museo Nazionale del Cinema in Turin, respectively, Barry and Prolo are considered precursors of the film archival movement. Yet only a few scholars have discussed their work in detail.[25] The situation is even worse for Benacerraf of the Cinemateca Nacional de Venezuela, El Goulli of the Cinémathèque tunisienne, Kawakita of the National Film Archive of Japan, Mitropoulou of the Greek Film Archive, Sánchez Valenzuela of the Filmoteca Nacional de México, and Van Leer of the Jerusalem Cinematheque–Israel Film Archive, all six of whom remain virtually unknown outside the international community of film archivists.[26] By invoking Eisner in brief entr'actes, my hope is that *Archiving the Past* will inspire further research into these other women's work as archivists and more.

The rest of the book further emphasizes the breadth of women's contributions to film historiography. Within emerging or established film archives, women contributed to transforming film historiography into a serious field of study, one that aimed to produce film historical knowledge based on rationalized standards of organization, memory, and rediscovery. On the one hand, women archivists and witnesses adapted proven practices from other fields, especially modern librarianship, which developed in France in the 1890s. New social realities (increased literacy) brought forth new ideas about libraries (public access, collections management) that, in turn, influenced how film archives handled preservation. On the other hand, women archivists and witnesses helped establish new practices in response to new challenges having to do with the medium's specificities, for example, its materiality, as well as its modes of production, exhibition, and distribution. Outside film archives, feminist activists too became "makers" of film historical meaning. By organizing women's film festivals, among others, these activists even anticipated the work of feminist film historians committed to challenging traditional masculinist narratives about cinema.

The book's trajectory—and its structure—is, of course, linear, from the 1920s to the 1970s. Yet no real teleological progression exists from Jeanne Moussinac and Laure Albin-Guillot (chapter 1) to the women of the CRH (chapter 2) to the "Musidora" collective (chapter 3). For example, the archival practices discussed in chapter 1 did not necessarily influence those discussed in chapter 2, and the collective covered in chapter 3 had little to do with most of the women discussed in chapter 2. But while there is no direct causality from one chapter to the next, many incidental connections, overlaps, echoes, and repetitions emerge throughout the book that ultimately bring to the fore women's work in, and with, the film archive as a collective form of feminist resistance.

Significantly, I also see a lineage from the archivists, witnesses, and activists discussed in *Archiving the Past* to contemporary feminist film scholars, historians, and curators like Jennifer M. Bean, Giuliana Bruno, Jane Gaines, Maggie Hennefeld, Kiki Loveday, Karen Pearlman, Kate Saccone, Shelley Stamp, and Yiman Wang, whose radical reimaginings of the past similarly challenge traditional historiographical narratives and archival practices when it comes to the cinema.[27] Recent initiatives by the Women Film Pioneers Project (Jane Gaines and Kate Saccone), Cinema's First Nasty Women (Maggie Hennefeld, Laura Horak, and Elif Rongen-Kaynakçi), and Las Musidoras (Emilie Cauquy, Marién Gómez Rodríguez, and Elodie Tamayo), among others, provide a particularly valuable anchor point from which to interrogate women's and feminist modes of engagement with the film archive since the 1920s. Like some of the women from *Archiving the Past*, these initiatives have produced new works that repurpose archival footage and other archival materials and ultimately reimagine the film archive as an important site of creative feminist intervention.

At the same time, this book offers less a celebration of previously forgotten women than a reflection on the film archive as a paradoxical site of women's intervention and women's erasure. In the dark alleys and small offices of film archives and private apartments, women worked toward archiving the past. They did research, wrote letters, filed papers, and organized materials that would eventually make up the bulk of film historians' books. They also traveled to places near and far, tirelessly hunting down the remnants of cinema's historical past. But they did so *quietly, in the shadows, behind the scenes,* all of which metaphors describe less women's work than the power of the archive to objectify women in film historiography. By interrogating recovery, this book invites feminist film historians to rethink the film archive and, by the same token, to rewrite women's film history, both film history *about* women and film history *by* women.

PREMIER ENTR'ACTE

COLLECTION

IN 1928, Lotte Eisner wrote about her recent chance visit to the Prussian State Library in Berlin. "A rainy afternoon. Headlights flicker across *Unter den Linden*'s grey asphalt surface. To shelter from the rain, you escape into the *Staatsbibliothek*."[1] Yet in Eisner's account, the State Library becomes more than a refuge from the weather. As if mapping out an itinerary for the reader, Eisner discusses how to navigate the Library's collections for research on cinema's history. Featured prominently are the Library's architecture, employees, and catalogs, all three of which inform "collection" as historiographical practice.

First, enter the Library. Eisner's initial impressions of the State Library are far from encouraging. As she explained:

> Its towering atrium displays the patina of pastness considered obligatory in this country for official establishments. The clear implication is that there is no fun to be had in scholarship. On

this raw, sham-spring day, your visit proceeds up the unheated, draughty staircase; for knowledge must be hard-won. Cerberus stands at the entrance; you flash your admission ticket, and proceed to the catalogue room. In heavy rows stand hefty tomes, zealous readers skimming their pages, diligently filling slips of papers and notebooks.[2]

With this description of the building and its gatekeepers, Eisner offers a rather somber picture of the Library, which, founded in 1661, was at the time of her writing one of the largest libraries in the world. Although the Library's original building from the early twentieth century still stands in the historic center of Berlin, much of it has been rebuilt since World War II. When Eisner visited the Library in 1928, the neobaroque design was probably even more intimidating than today. It signified not only historicity ("the patina of pastness") but also bureaucracy (the "entrance" where "you flash your admission ticket," the "catalogue room" where you fill "slips of paper"), which designates, in this context, the various steps toward accessing the Library's collections. Paperwork, especially catalogs, is indeed central to Eisner's account of the Prussian State Library, wherein access to knowledge comes across as difficult and highly regulated. As a recent PhD graduate in art history and archaeology, Eisner was undoubtedly accustomed to such an environment. Yet here she sounds out of place, as if looking for material about film, which did not yet count as a serious topic of study, made her slightly uncomfortable.

Second, ask a librarian. Access to the Library's collections is only possible thanks to librarians. In Eisner's eyes, the first librarian she encounters looks like "the spitting image" of Werner Krauss in *The Trousers* (Hans Behrendt, 1927); the second is "friendly, if a little trepidatious at your inquiry"; the third, "Professor X," is a "friendly old gentleman with a full white beard [who] receives you amidst a sea of books."[3] Their gender, age, and demeanor project authority, wisdom, and willingness to help. Their expertise lies in their remarkable understanding of the library collections, specifically the ways in which these collections are classified based on subject and/or by alphabetical order. And their role, not only appreciated but entirely necessary, consists of directing Eisner to the right catalogs, in which she will find relevant titles and their locations.

Third, search the catalog. Eisner's first attempt proves unsuccessful. The Library's card catalog, which consists of a list of holdings arranged alphabetically by author's last name, is inadequate in this case. Its promise—to guide readers through the Library's collections to their objects of interest—remains unfulfilled, mainly because Eisner does not have book titles in mind. But the subject catalog next door yields better results. Dating back to the Library of Alexandria, where Callimachus, with the "Pinakes," organized papyrus scrolls into genres and sections, the subject catalog relies not only on alphabetical order but also on conceptual analysis. It is, in fact, a work of tremendous human labor, whereby librarians read materials, determine their topics, classify them based on content, and then assign them subject headings based on the appropriate classification system. Yet while perusing one of the three volumes in the State Library's subject catalog that contain entries on film, Eisner feels disappointed. "Everything is mildly muddled," she writes, "arranged as benevolent coincidence would have it, the serious and the silly, the good and the bad haphazardly intermingled.... Who was it who 'organized' material of much intrinsic richness, cheerfully jumbling together under 'film' whatever happened to arrive at the *Staatsbibliothek*?"[4] In a separate office, "Professor X" is currently working on a better card index for the "literature from 1915 to 1924."[5] But Eisner finds it quite limited when it comes to cinema, with many books still "on the shelves, out of order, uncatalogued,—worst of all, unavailable for loan."[6] The problem and its solution are clear for Eisner. As she phrases it, a "systematic, comprehensive film library and the longed-for film archive" would allow for books on film to be classified, organized, numbered, cataloged, and therefore accessible to the public. Order—in the form of systems, paperwork, and indeed bureaucracy—might be intimidating for Eisner, but it remains key to collecting as historiographical practice.

1

ARCHIVISTS

IN 1932, French film critic Lucienne Escoubé asked "what man, far-sighted and generous," would take on the urgent mission of preserving silent cinema.[1] As she and others expressed around that time, sound cinema, which had been introduced in France with the release of *The Jazz Singer* (Alan Crosland, 1927) in 1929, provoked anxieties not only about the medium's future but also about its fairly young past. On the one hand, film critics often discussed the many changes brought by sound cinema, including, for Lucie Derain, "a new source of prosperity," "the destruction, the abolition of outdated methods, and also the ruin of many people," especially actors and actresses with discordant voices.[2] On the other hand, even though silent films were still being produced, many feared that sound cinema would cause the complete obliteration of the (recently) established art of silent cinema.[3] What France needed, in Escoubé's words, was a cinematheque dedicated to collecting films and other materials and led by a man with both vision and resources.

In hindsight, some might say that Henri Langlois would be the providential man called for by the emergence of sound cinema in France in the 1930s.[4] Yet by the time Langlois co-founded the CF in 1936, two women—Jeanne Moussinac (née Lods, 1894–1975) and Laure Albin-Guillot (née Meifredy, 1879–1962)—had already entered the scene whose contributions to film preservation this chapter examines. Although Moussinac is perhaps best known as the wife of film critic Léon Moussinac, whom she married in the summer of 1916, and the sister of documentary filmmaker Jean Lods, she was a journalist, painter, and member of the Communist Party whose work for the BC also deserves attention.[5] Likewise, Albin-Guillot's efforts to build and sustain the CN during the Great Depression should be taken seriously, not only because the CN predated the CF by a few years, but also because Albin-Guillot—like Moussinac—shaped what film preservation would look like for years to come.

With this in mind, I consider Moussinac and Albin-Guillot as archivists whose "collecting" of film history sought to rationalize film knowledge in the 1920s and 1930s. These two decades are arguably foundational in this regard, for cinema began to count—through the type of work done by Moussinac and Albin-Guillot—as serious historical knowledge in France. Done by archivists, librarians, intellectuals, and fans, among many others, "collecting" may take various forms. Yet in this chapter, I consider "collecting film history" as a scientific practice that relies on access and collections management methods like cataloging and indexing, through which objects are taken out of their original contexts and reorganized and become the empirical evidence necessary for gaining—or rather, producing—film historical knowledge. It is, indeed, no coincidence that the BC and the CN were more or less directly connected to the Bibliothèque Nationale (BN), which was then considered not only the largest library in the world but also a training ground for the nascent (at least in France) field of library sciences (or *bibliothéconomie*, in French). Library sciences prove extremely valuable to understand the transformation of French libraries from the 1890s through the 1940s. Through a discussion of the concepts of bibliography, documentation, and *dépôt légal*, which were central to both modern librarianship and film preservation at the BC and the CN, we also begin to see how the creation of film archives like the BC and the CN had serious consequences for the dissemination of cinema's history in France. On the one hand, parts of the BC were compiled by Jeanne Moussinac in collaboration with Michelle Seguin from the BN, where a decent collection of publications about film was already classified following one of the BN's tested systems. On the other hand, the CN, in both name and spirit, was explicitly modeled after the BN. The BN's system of *dépôt légal*, which had required, since 1537, that any printed document published in France be deposited at the BN, was particularly important for the CN in its attempt to implement the same system for films produced in France. Although the CN was never successful when it came to the *dépôt légal*, ordering principles similar to those of the BN remained at the forefront of the CN's mission.[6]

Most of the primary material in this chapter comes from two collections in the French archives, which I consider through a double lens attuned to both textual meanings and traces of labor. First, the Fonds Léon Moussinac at the BnF-Arts du spectacle includes documents (letters and articles) concerning the BC, as well as documents (books, original scripts and scenarios, and photographs) that were assembled and organized by Jeanne Moussinac for the BC.[7] All these documents were donated to the BnF (then called the BN) by Jeanne Moussinac in 1964 and by her niece, Sabine Lods, in 1986. The Fonds Léon Moussinac is admittedly modest and incomplete. Its name also clearly indicates that the main focus is not Jeanne Moussinac but her husband Léon, and that anything related to Jeanne is there only for what it might reveal about him. Yet the Fonds Léon Moussinac remains our only entry point into Jeanne Moussinac's labor at the BC. In addition to the documents assembled by Moussinac, such as several manuscripts, photographs, scripts, and scenarios, the Fonds includes about fifty-five letters and invoices addressed to Moussinac and mailed between July 5, 1927, and March 12, 1929. On a few of these letters and invoices, handwritten notes by Moussinac herself indicate when she sent her responses and payments back, which allows us not only to establish a timeline for the BC but also to assess the extent of Moussinac's involvement.

Second, at the Archives Nationales (National Archives), the institutional paperwork of the Ministère de l'Education et des Beaux-Arts (the Ministry of Education and Fine Arts, now the Ministry of Culture), within which the CN existed between 1932 and 1939, informs us about the inception, organization, and legal creation of the CN.[8] Ranging from about 1931 to 1943, these documents consist of mostly internal communications between various employees of the Ministère, including Albin-Guillot, director of the CN, and Georges Huismans, director of the Beaux-Arts; copies of letters produced for the Ministère's records; various handwritten notes; and other documents unrelated to the CN. In addition to legibility and readability, the main difficulty with this collection is establishing with precision when letters were written, especially when it comes to letters that only survive in the form of the copies produced by the Ministère. On most of these copies, the date that appears at the top designates not when the letters were written but when the copies were made, which gives us an insight into both the activities of the CN and the administrative procedures of the Ministère. When the materials from the Archives Nationales prove insufficient, I also draw on discourses about Albin-Guillot and the CN published in the contemporary press and available in the digital collections of the BnF, the Cinémathèque de Toulouse, and the CF. Besides the Roger-Viollet archive, which holds about fifty-five photographs by Albin-Guillot, there is, to my knowledge, no archival collection in France dedicated to Albin-Guillot.[9] According to Albin-Guillot herself, much of her personal archive disappeared in flooding at her home.[10]

Whereas material documents constitute major historical evidence, as Moussinac and Albin-Guillot themselves demonstrated through their work, my emphasis on them in this chapter is to the detriment of other forms of mediation and communication between people and institutions. I think primarily of the conversations Moussinac might have had with her husband Léon, and with the filmmakers and film critics within her and Léon's circle of friends, either in person or on the phone. Agreements about donations might have been made in written forms that were amended or rescinded later in person, for example. And what about Laure Albin-Guillot's exchanges with various administrators, politicians, and artists during their visits to the Palais du Trocadéro, where the CN was set up? What remains in the archives reveals some but not all there is to know about the BC and the CN. Yet at the very least the material documents from the archives show that the collecting performed by Moussinac and Albin-Guillot for the preservation of cinema's history was scientific and rationalized, and therefore quite innovative for its time.

JEANNE MOUSSINAC AT THE BIBLIOTHÈQUE DU CINÉMA (1927–1929)

Started in 1927, the BC got its name from the Bibliothèque d'art et d'archéologie (BAA), which had been founded in 1909 by fashion designer and voracious collector Jacques Doucet for the use of art historians and scholars. Yet the BC inherited from the BAA more than its name. By the late 1920s, Doucet had already spent many years collecting books and artworks and supporting various artists from the Dada movement and the historical avant-garde more broadly. Doucet's biographer, François Chapon, tells us that Doucet wished to extend his book collections to philosophy, history, art, music, science, and, most importantly, cinema, when he first contacted Léon Moussinac (probably via famous bookbinder Rose Adler) in March 1927.[11] That Doucet thought of cinema as related to—but separate from—the other arts and sciences is significant in several respects. First and most obviously, Doucet, who had become a cinephile through his surrealist friends and was a loyal member of L. Moussinac's ciné-club, Les Amis de Spartacus, considered the cinema in a light similar to avant-garde filmmakers and many film critics: as a unique and modern art form whose history was worth preserving for future generations. In Jeanne Moussinac's words, "The cinema, against what one might think, should not be grouped together with the theater and the music hall. On the contrary, it is necessary to distinguish it, and in creating this library, we wish to emphasize that the cinema is a new art form."[12] Second, under Doucet's scrutiny, not only bibliophilia but also modern librarianship began to shape film knowledge in a new, more rationalized way.

What is a "bibliothèque du cinéma," or "cinema library"? Today, most libraries are community spaces where adults and children borrow books, magazines, DVDs, and video games, and where they attend readings and screenings, among other activities. For movies, and as a French native born and raised in the Paris area, I also immediately think of the CF, whose cinemas, Bibliothèque du Film (BiFi), and Musée du Cinéma (Museum of Cinema) I have visited many times. Yet in the 1920s and 1930s, the idea that such institutions should exist and then be open and easily accessible to the public was fairly new. Not only was film just entering such knowledge institutions as libraries, as Christophe Gauthier and others have shown, but libraries also went through some significant changes having to do with access and collections management.[13] Because of these changes, the term "library" used for the BC requires some unpacking.

To grasp the situation of French libraries before World War II from today's vantage point is not easy, in part because few secondary sources have discussed the matter in great detail.[14] However, based on primary sources like Eugène Morel's writings, the BN of the early twentieth century was complete chaos. Employed at the BN since 1892, Morel frequently discussed what he viewed as the disastrous state of French libraries in the early twentieth century, when the new demands of an increasingly literate and urban population were hardly met.[15] Mainly geared toward greater access, Morel's efforts were crucial in organizing the BN and other French libraries according to a rationalized system of cataloging that would help not only readers but also library employees. At the BN until at least the late 1940s, there was no freight elevator, no electricity, and, most importantly, no complete and workable catalog, which Morel defined as a "simple, convenient, and scientific system for organizing and finding books."[16] Collections were divided into series based on a coherent system (sometimes, but not always, the Dewey Decimal Classification), and titles in each series were given a call number that determined their location on the shelves. But Morel argued that, without a complete catalog, or when the catalog functioned like an inventory that simply listed titles alphabetically, only a limited number of readers could benefit from the BN's rich collections. In more concrete terms, readers were unable to do a bibliographic search and had to already know not only the titles they wished to consult but also their call numbers in the BN's collections. Readers filled out request slips, passed them on to librarians on duty (who then communicated with their colleagues in the stacks by shouting at them), and received the requested titles within a few hours at the earliest and the next day at the latest. While many titles at the BN were never actually requested, others could never be found in the block-long closed stacks.

To my knowledge, Morel never extensively discussed Doucet's BAA in his writings. Yet the BAA could have served as a counter-example to the inadequacy of French libraries that Morel so explicitly denounced.[17] From its methods of acquisitions to its commitment to public access, the BAA applied modern principles to the collecting of archival materials related to art history. André Joubin once explained that the BAA was not "an amateur's library," and that it compensated for the "paucity of resources that official institutions in Paris offered to art historians."[18] Furthermore, according to Joubin, "one of the main merits and the true charm of the library consists also in its practical organization. Each workroom, with books at hand, is devoted to a specific section of the history of art—museums, drawings, the Middle Ages, classical antiquity, the Far East, etc.—each contains methodically classified files, so that workers can immediately find the works they need. To the richness of the documentation is united the convenience of research."[19] Even under private ownership, that is to say before the BAA became the property of the University of Paris at the end of 1918, the BAA's collections were apparently organized based on topics, clearly indexed, and easily accessible to visitors in comfortable reading rooms.

Similar concerns over collections management and public access drove the creation of the BC in 1927. A close look at the Fonds Léon Moussinac in the collections of the BnF helps us further understand the BC, especially its ties to Doucet's BAA and to modern librarianship more broadly. Two sets of documents strike me as particularly relevant. To begin with, letters between Doucet and L. Moussinac reveal that Doucet's initial project was to produce a bibliographical inquiry entirely devoted to the cinema.[20] More specifically, in a letter from March 21, 1927, Doucet asks L. Moussinac for his help in tracking down periodicals and books dedicated to the cinema.[21] In the literary and arts newspaper *Le Crapouillot*, a "Bibliography of the 'Cinema,'" which Doucet suspects was L. Moussinac's doing, had listed twenty-four titles, ranging from books like Louis Delluc's *Charlot* (1921) and L. Moussinac's own *Naissance du cinéma* (1925), to periodicals like *Le Crapouillot* and *Schémas*.[22] Doucet indicated in his letter to L. Moussinac that he wished to use this bibliography as a starting point for his "petite enquête sur le cinéma" (little inquiry about the cinema). He then asked where he could acquire the books and periodicals from the bibliography, "for himself personally and for his little personal library," no doubt a reference to the BAA. The next day, on March 22, L. Moussinac replied that the staff at *Le Crapouillot* could find them for him, and that a few more titles could be of interest to his project, such as Pierre Albert-Birot's *Cinéma* (1920) and Ricciotto Canudo's *L'Usine aux images*.[23] Based on extant letters and invoices from the Office de Livres (Books Office) of *Le Crapouillot* to Doucet, Doucet then followed L. Moussinac's recommendation and ordered at least thirteen titles from *Le Crapouillot*, eleven of which had been cited in the "Bibliography of the 'Cinema.'"[24] Moreover, an invoice from the American bookstore Brentano's in the second arrondissement of Paris confirms that Doucet subscribed to the *Motion Picture Magazine* that L. Moussinac had mentioned in his letter to Doucet.[25]

Likewise, L. Moussinac's handwritten and typed manuscripts for "Sur la création d'une bibliothèque du cinématographe et son organisation" (On the creation of a library of the cinematograph and its organization) make it clear that the BC was first and foremost a bibliographical enterprise, with an emphasis on classification and public access.[26] Because the text of those manuscripts was later published without revisions in *Monde* on January 26, 1929, and in *Panoramique du cinéma* (1929), it may be thought of as not only the BC's blueprint but also its manifesto.[27] Its first four paragraphs are especially telling and worth quoting in full:

> The usefulness of a film library [*bibliothèque du Cinématographe*] is obvious, but its necessity needs to be demonstrated.
>
> Since the cinema has existed in practice, that is to say for some twenty years, a considerable number of articles, studies, and essays have been published, both from a scientific point of view and from an industrial or commercial point of view. These articles, studies, and essays have been scattered for the most part across journals or publications that are often difficult to find, a large number of these publications belonging to study groups or societies.
>
> Even today, where there are specialized journals, trade and others, many articles—often the most important ones—appear in literary, artistic, and scientific journals, and one must be already informed to discover them.

> A library dedicated to the Cinematograph, whose organization guidelines and organization itself would allow to gather and to classify methodically the greatest number of these writings—if not all of them—and to add to it an indispensable photographic documentation, would be for all those who are interested in it or were interested in it in any way, of an unquestionable usefulness.[28]

L. Moussinac's point is very clear: the rapid development of film criticism in recent decades had made it necessary to begin collecting—meaning not only acquiring but also classifying—published material in a designated institution open to anyone interested in the cinema. His emphasis on literature, art, and science attests to cinema's appeal across disciplines and to the scope of the BC's project to collect film history. In addition to books, articles, and periodicals, which would constitute the core of the BC's bibliography, L. Moussinac also mentions that a "photographic documentation" would be "indispensable" to future readers of the BC. The word "documentation," which L. Moussinac repeats several more times in "Sur la création," is notable, mainly because its use at the time was more or less limited to people involved in transforming librarianship in France. Although "documentation" is listed as a "neologism" in the *Dictionnaire de la langue française (Littré)* of 1873, it only appeared in the *Dictionnaire de l'Académie française* in 1935, about eight years after Moussinac used it to describe the collections of the BC.[29] According to the Académie française, "documentation" refers to a "collection of documents on one specific question," which implies that someone's meticulous work, their methods of both selection and classification, plays a major part in transforming documents into "documentation."[30]

In a letter to Jeanne Moussinac dated March 18, 1928, the leftist writer Henry Poulaille confirmed that the BC represented a fairly new development in French film criticism and historiography and a potential threat to the independence of authors like himself.[31] To Moussinac's request that he write an essay on Charlie Chaplin for the BC, Poulaille responded: "Dear Madame, I am delighted that you thought to ask me something about the cinema for M. Doucet's library, unfortunately I must ask you to explain the purpose of that type of work. Would it remain in the state of a manuscript? Do you and M. Doucet prohibit authors from using what they have submitted elsewhere? I am not interested in featuring only in an amateur's library, even less in being a number in a reading room at the Institute."[32] Through his tone, and his choice of the word "amateur" to designate the well-respected collector, Poulaille shows his contempt for the BC as the product of that collector's "collecting." Sharon Macdonald reminds us that many literary accounts since the nineteenth century have depicted the figure of the collector in a negative light. In John Fowles's *The Collector* (1964), for example, "collecting is contrasted with a genuine love of life and things," Macdonald explains, "and cast as a reprehensible 'deadening' activity in which mastery through possession dominates any kind of real sensibility to that which is collected."[33] In Poulaille's letter to Moussinac, a similar disdain for collecting as a form of ownership seems palpable. But Poulaille was also worried about the impact of the BC—especially what I have termed its rationalization of film knowledge—on his work and intellectual property. Although Moussinac ultimately convinced Poulaille to contribute a German essay to the BC, his initial reluctance about "being a number in a reading room" strikes me as particularly poignant in the context of modern librarianship.[34] At the modern libraries Morel and others envisioned, at the BAA, and at the BC, numbers were precisely the end goal; knowledge was to be synthesized and divided up into coherent and manageable chunks or series within which books, articles, periodicals, and other archival materials were attributed numbers for easy access.

When addressing the BC, scholars often hesitate to credit Moussinac for her work and to overemphasize the role of Jacques Doucet, Léon Moussinac, and Blaise Cendrars in organizing the BC's collections.[35]

Even Chapon, whose biography of Doucet contains one of the most detailed reviews of the BC, describes Moussinac as Doucet's "new assistant."[36] Chapon's tone is admittedly playful in that paragraph, yet the term "assistant" is so incredibly loaded when it comes to women's labor that it still undermines Moussinac to the benefit of the famous male collector. With that term, Chapon also contradicts his own statements regarding the amount of work produced by Moussinac for the BC. In citing Moussinac's notebooks and correspondence held in the Bibliothèque littéraire Jacques-Doucet and the BnF, yet calling her an "assistant," Chapon further contributes to Moussinac's erasure from film historiography.[37]

Details about Jeanne Moussinac's early life, education, and even interest in cinema are admittedly hard to come by, in both primary and secondary sources. On the one hand, Moussinac—like so many other women in cinema's history—usually appears as little more than a background character in the secondary literature devoted to male others. On the other hand, primary sources at the BnF are limited to a few love letters exchanged with her future husband, L. Moussinac, during World War I, and to a copy of her marriage certificate delivered by the city of Vesoul in eastern France on August 14, 1916.[38] Speculating about Moussinac based on the primary sources dedicated to her husband and brother seems therefore necessary. But doing so requires care and precaution. For example, Jean Lods once stated that he had gone to the movies when he was little, but that he became really acquainted with and interested in the cinema after he met L. Moussinac and fell under his influence.[39] Valérie Vignaux has shown that L. Moussinac thought of cinema not only as an art form and a national heritage, but also as a mass medium with great educational value.[40] L. Moussinac's conception of cinema was inextricably tied up with his communist engagement, in this regard. According to Vignaux, after his trip to the USSR in late 1927, "he now militate[d] for the deployment of a communist cultural policy for the emancipation of the working classes through access to arts and culture, which [led] him to participate actively in the creation, in March 1928, of Les Amis de Spartacus, a film club with a popular ambition, which, because it [was] located in the fifteenth arrondissement—a modest district of the left bank—[was] likely to attract workers but also intellectuals and aristocrats."[41] That Jeanne Moussinac—like her brother Jean—shared her husband's ideas is likely but also uncertain in the absence of further archival evidence.

By cross-checking secondary sources with primary sources, however, some biographical information about Moussinac may be gleaned from time to time. Born into a Protestant family in Vesoul in 1894, Jeanne Lods met Léon Moussinac before World War I, when she was about sixteen years old. Her brother Jean Lods explained in an interview that their "older brother [Pierre] was a corporal living in barracks in Besançon. On Saturday evenings, he would come spend his leave with us and then depart again on Sunday. One evening, he arrived with a man from Paris, a poet, all haloed by the prestige of the capital. . . . My sister was not at home that evening, but there was a photo on the piano. . . . Fifteen days later, Léon Moussinac was back. It was an evening of seduction. My sister was 16, he was 20 or 21."[42] Before the war ended, Jeanne Moussinac moved to Paris, where she worked as a secretary to a colonel in the air force, according to Jean Lods, who lived with her briefly while Léon Moussinac was still in the army. Married to Léon Moussinac until his death in 1960, Jeanne Moussinac was apparently never too far from her husband for the rest of their life together. Not only did she assist him in some of his projects, she also followed him on several trips to the USSR, where she was hired (with Paul Nizan's wife, Henriette) as a translator and editor of *Le Journal de Moscou*.[43] Yet Moussinac remained in the shadows so frequently that historians rarely dwell on her activities, with or without her husband.

Based on the extant archives from the BnF, however, there is little to no confusion regarding Jeanne Moussinac's role at the BC, which she spearheaded from spring 1927 until at least Jacques Doucet's death

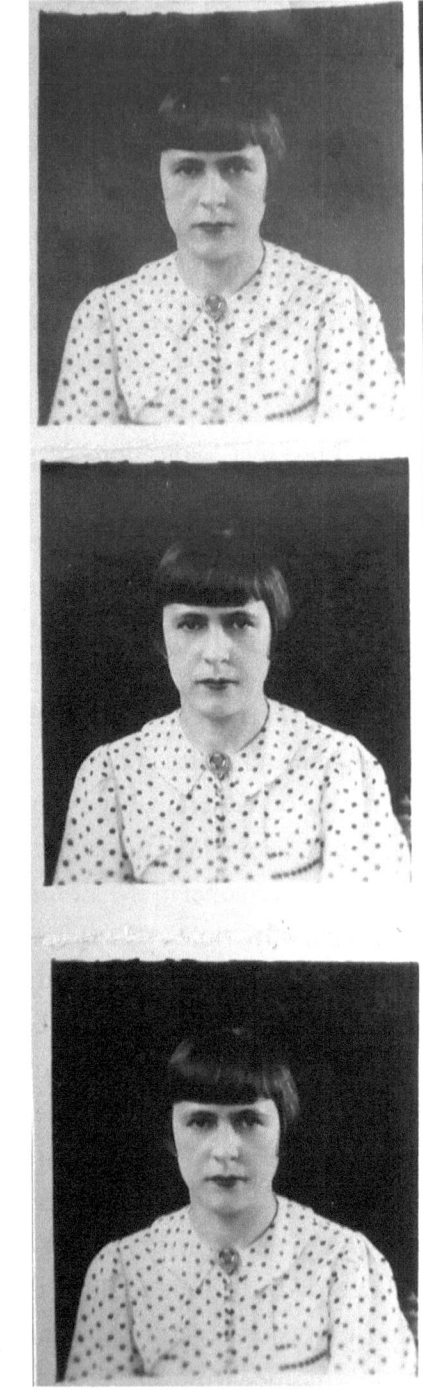

Figure 2. Photo booth portrait of Jeanne Moussinac, date unknown. *Source:* © Jean-Louis Lods.

on October 30, 1929. Jacques Doucet initiated and bankrolled the BC, Léon Moussinac helped conceptualize it, and Jeanne Moussinac did the rest, which consisted of reaching out to potential donors, elaborating bibliographies, requesting original studies from authors and film critics, and organizing the various documents in the collections of the BC. Drawing on Suzanne Briet's 1951 essay *Qu'est-ce que la documentation?*, whose second part deals with the work, skills, and methods of the *documentaliste*, I consider the following three categories to account for Moussinac's labor at the BC: *bibliography*, which Briet understands as the search for publications about a specific topic; *documentary production*, which designates, for Briet, all the documents produced by *documentalistes* themselves, including catalogs, bibliographies, index cards, summaries, dossiers, and so forth; and *classification*, which Briet says requires that the *documentaliste* follow either an existing system of numbering and ordering or a new system adapted to the *documentaliste*'s specific topic.[44] Because the BC ended rather abruptly upon Doucet's death, I choose to exclude some of the other categories Briet discusses, such as "dissemination" and "exhibition" (or *diffusion* and *exposition*, in French). I also wish to acknowledge here that the use of technologies that Briet argues is crucial to the work of the *documentaliste* does not seem relevant to Moussinac at the BC. Yet Briet's theorization of the *documentaliste* remains valuable. Not only does it help us understand how Moussinac's labor served the rationalization of film knowledge by the BC, but it also casts Moussinac in a new light. As the BC's only *documentaliste*, Moussinac finally takes center stage.

With its emphasis on exhaustiveness and accessibility, bibliographical work was, once again, central to modern librarianship as described by Morel and Briet, among others. At the BC, it certainly represented the starting point for Doucet, L. Moussinac, and Moussinac, who, for about two years starting in mid-1927, wrote letters to a number of film professionals whose book collections and archives she sought to acquire. Those film professionals included, among others, directors and screenwriters, who would donate their personal archives to the BC, and distributors and producers, from which Moussinac purchased publicity materials with Doucet's funds.[45] From September 1928 through February 1929, Moussinac also received from the Flammarion bookstore several lists of books about cinema's history, educational cinema, and Russian cinema, as well as invoices for various books, dissertations, and manuals on those and other topics.[46] Even without access to Moussinac's letters, one therefore understands through reading her correspondence that her goals—like those articulated by L. Moussinac in the BC's manifesto—were at least twofold. First was to add to Doucet's book collection, which Doucet himself had purchased from *Le Crapouillot* and Brentano's in March and May 1927. Second was to collect what L. Moussinac had called a "photographic documentation" and some other film production materials like shooting scripts (*découpages*) and scenarios.

Because Jeanne Moussinac would often meet with potential donors in person, or talk to them on the telephone, it is not always easy to determine whether all the parties mentioned previously ended up contributing to the BC based on their letters only. What seems quite evident, however, is that most of the people Moussinac contacted saw the BC in a favorable light. For example, on December 5, 1927, Germaine Dulac sent a "very big package" that contained the scenarios of *La Souriante Madame Beudet* (*The Smiling Madame Beudet*, 1923), with some negatives; *Ame d'artiste* (1924); *La Folie des vaillants* (1926), with photographs; *L'Invitation au voyage* (1927), with some negatives; and the script for *La Coquille et le clergyman* (*The Seashell and the Clergyman*, 1928), with some negatives.[47] In her letter attached to that package, Dulac also explained that she had her (female) secretary look for the scenario of *La Fête espagnole* (1920), which she would send as soon as possible. That scenario, together with the other documents from Dulac's package, remain in the Fonds Léon Moussinac at the BnF to this day.[48] In his letter dated July 5, 1927, director Léon Poirier also agreed to give Moussinac photographs from several of his films, mainly *Le Penseur* (1920), *Jocelyn* (1922), *La Brière* (1925), and *Verdun*, *visions d'histoire* (1928), whose production was still in process, as well as the two scripts for *Jocelyn* and *La Brière*.[49] Importantly, he also praised Moussinac's project and acknowledged its significance for himself and for cinema more broadly. "It seems very interesting to me," Poirier wrote, "that the cinema should enter, under your aegis, an important library. It is one more step towards its accession to the arts and I am furthermore very touched that you thought to save me a spot."[50]

Although Moussinac's interlocutors were generally enthusiastic about the BC, some wrote that their busy schedules prevented them from assembling their archives. Others like Jean Epstein and Léon Poirier explained that they could not part with their archives quite yet.[51] Indeed, due to the cinema's young history and ongoing developments, Moussinac was sometimes unable to secure all the archival materials she requested from film professionals. It is also worth noting here that Moussinac's interlocutors often mentioned Doucet in their letters, which certainly suggests that Doucet's name gave prestige to the BC. Furthermore, they referred to L. Moussinac often enough to reveal their respect and appreciation for his work. L. Moussinac himself wrote a few letters on behalf of Doucet to Paramount, *La Cinématographie*, and Jean Renoir, for example, no doubt because of L. Moussinac's stature in French cinema at the time.[52] Yet Jeanne Moussinac took on the bulk of the work alone, and extant evidence reveals not only her dedication but also her perseverance in collecting film history for the BC.

According to Suzanne Briet, what she terms "document production" (*production documentaire*) was one of the primary tasks of the *documentaliste*. She writes:

> The proper function of documentation centers is to produce secondary documents, derived from initial documents that these centers do not usually create, but which they sometimes preserve. Whether these centers constitute essential repositories or whether they act as simple users or relays for the benefit of a category of readers, *documentary production* is characteristic

of their work. We are at the heart of the documentary profession. These second documents are called: translations, analyses, documentation bulletins; files, catalogs, bibliographies, files, photographs, microfilms, selections, documentary syntheses, encyclopedias, orientation guides.[53]

The main secondary documents produced by the BC include the following: a "rough bibliography" assembled by Jeanne Moussinac and a librarian from the BN named Michelle Seguin, and at least one critical essay commissioned from the surrealist poet Philippe Soupault. Both responded to the BC's bibliographical mission, and both were Moussinac's initiatives.

Based on extant documents in the Fonds Léon Moussinac, Michelle Seguin first wrote to Jeanne Moussinac on August 7, 1928, after she had heard about the BC from a source Seguin did not identify.[54] Because Seguin herself had been working on a film bibliography at the Office de Documentation bibliographique (Office of Bibliographic Documentation) where she was employed, she now wished to seek Moussinac's expertise and compare notes: "I would be very grateful if, once I am done, you would allow me, Madame, to compare my documentation to that of your library. It is, indeed, possible that I missed some titles, and it would be very valuable to double check thanks to your specialized library." Although Moussinac's response is considered lost today, Seguin's following letter from November 5, 1928, suggests that Moussinac was extremely cooperative when they first met in person. Not only was Seguin able to make progress on her bibliography, thanks to Moussinac's help, but she also provided Moussinac with index cards for every title related to the cinema available at the BN.[55] That Moussinac connected with a librarian from the BN was, in fact, no coincidence. Not only were these two women working on similar projects, that is, film bibliographies, but they would also benefit from each other's expertise: Seguin in librarianship and Moussinac in the cinema.

The index cards mentioned earlier are worth describing in more detail. They were typed or handwritten on different-color papers, glued on brown sheets, and assembled together in several booklets that survive at the BnF today.⁵⁶ Some for France even included call numbers that would allow readers at the BC to go and find the titles they were looking for at the BN (often but not always in the Auguste Rondel collection). The rest, which referred to titles from Germany, Austria, the United States, Great Britain, Belgium, Spain, Hungary, the Netherlands, Scandinavia, Russia, and Switzerland, as well as titles about educational cinema, consisted only of the author's name; the original title; its translation in French; and the publisher, location, and date. Finally, a smaller set of index cards listed a few famous actors and actresses followed by titles of books on their careers, as well as those titles' call numbers at the BN when available.

Even though those booklets—with their mixed formats, colors, and handwritings—look amateurish at first glance, they attest to Seguin and Moussinac's rigorous bibliographical system, borrowed from the BN where Seguin worked. Take, for instance, the typed index cards for Luigi Pirandello's novella *On tourne* (*Shoot!*, 1916) and for Georges Demeny's essay *Les Origines du cinématographe* (1909), which read as follows:

Pirandello (Luigi).—On tourne. Traduction de C. de Laverière. 1°
édition.—Paris, aux éditions du "Sagittaire", Simon Kra, 6 rue Blanche.;
1925. In-16 p. et portrait.
Collection de 'La Revue Européenne'
   (8°Z. 22387 (19)
Demeny (Georges).—Les origines du cinématographe. Paris, H. Paulin
(1909). in-8°, 64 p. fig.
   (8°V. 33429⁵⁷

The call numbers under these two titles come from the BN's classification system, which librarian Nicolas Clément designed at the end of the seventeenth century to be highly efficient, consistent, and perennial, and which remains in use to this day for titles that entered the BN's collections before 1996. Following that system, titles are arranged by format and then subject, meaning that each call number indicates first the format, then the subject, and finally the number assigned to each title. For example, Pirandello's *On tourne*, whose call number reads "8°Z.22387(19)," is in Octavo format (8°) and within the series dedicated to "Polygraphies et mélanges" (Z). It is also the nineteenth title within the subseries numbered 22,387. Demenÿ's *Les Origines du cinématographe*, whose call number reads "8°V. 33429," is also in Octavo format (8°), but it belongs to the series dedicated to "Mathematics, Astronomy, Architecture, Military Art, Nautical Art, Mechanics, Fine Arts, and Mechanical Arts" (V), where it holds the number 33,429.[58] When entered into the online catalog of the BnF, these call numbers still correspond to the same two titles, which are now held at the BnF François-Mitterrand in the thirteenth arrondissement in Paris.[59] A digitized version of the same copy of *On tourne* by Pirandello is also available on Gallica.[60]

Less about classification and more about film history itself, the other extant document produced by the BC consisted of a sixty-page manuscript handwritten by Philippe Soupault and titled "Essai sur Charlie Chaplin" (Essay on Charlie Chaplin).[61] After Moussinac commissioned that manuscript from Soupault in March 1928, Soupault was paid, and he then submitted the manuscript just a month later.[62] As Soupault himself writes, he felt "passionate" about the project, which certainly had to do with his love for Chaplin.[63] Divided into two parts, "La Vie de Chaplin" (Chaplin's life) and "L'Art de Chaplin" (Chaplin's art), Soupault's essay first claims to "summarize the life and work of [the man] we tenderly call 'Charlot.'" But while readers are told about Chaplin's upbringing in London at the very beginning of the first part, they learn very little about his beginnings in the English music hall, his move to the United States, and his rise to global fame, for example. Although some information about Chaplin's production companies, divorces, and international travels may be found here and there, Soupault writes not a biographical account or a career overview but a personal essay relying on idiosyncratic memories and reflections. In the second part, Soupault's analysis of Chaplin's acting style, his screenwriting, his comic type, and his screen direction, among others, quickly gives way to Soupault's own thoughts on screen comedy and poetry. Drawing on Henri Bergson, whose work "Le Rire" (Laughter) had come out in France in 1900, Soupault argues that screen comedy follows the same logic as dreams, which poetry often emulates.

Once again, in the absence of Moussinac's letters, it remains impossible to say whether Soupault had fully satisfied the request for an essay on Chaplin. But Soupault answered—or rather, anticipated—Léon and Jeanne Moussinac's wish that the BC would eventually benefit cinephiles, writers, critics, scholars, and film professionals, in at least one aspect. When discussing whether Chaplin's films shared similar themes, Soupault suggests that his analysis relies not on the films themselves but on "photographs" from the films that he told Moussinac belonged to his private collection.[64] Based on a letter dated March 24, 1928, Soupault later donated these photographs to the BC, where others could use them in a similar way. The cycle of document production would repeat itself, in other words; the BC would continue to generate more film knowledge in the future.

While the organization of the BC was undoubtedly envisioned by Léon Moussinac, its classification remains more difficult to attribute to any one contributor. Nevertheless, the distinction between "organization," which designates the various sections of the BC, and "classification," which refers to the system of ordering and numbering used to arrange materials within these various sections, points once again to the specific kind of labor Jeanne Moussinac—or someone else—performed as *documentaliste*.

After Doucet's death in 1929, Jeanne Moussinac wrote an article about the BC that gives us some insight into the state—and perhaps even the classification—of the BC's collections at the time.⁶⁵ She not only mentioned donations from Jean Epstein, Germaine Dulac, René Clair, Léon Moussinac, and the Metro-Goldwyn Company, Paramount, and United Artists in Paris, but she also referred to materials she herself tracked down in France and during a trip to Germany. Whereas she suggested that the BC was still to be divided into (more or less) the same departments as L. Moussinac outlined in his proposal from 1927, she also indicated that a different kind of classification might have been used in the meantime. She wrote that, after the BC reached a certain point, "we then had to classify this documentation. A thousand index cards, which catalogued the books published in Europe and in the United States, will be completed soon. When M. Jacques Doucet died, the 'film repertoire' was about to be started. A solid basis for the library is therefore in place."⁶⁶ Furthermore, in describing the BC's collections, Moussinac made a distinction between different types of materials—film criticism, film photographs, scenarios and scripts, models for sets and costumes, original essays, and film prints—which might have served as a system of classification based on genres.

Although the BC relied mostly on Moussinac's labor, it apparently could not survive without Doucet's financial support. After 1929, the BC was acquired by Auguste Rondel of the Bibliothèque de l'Arsenal, from which it was later moved to the BnF-Arts du spectacle in the second arrondissement in Paris. The afterlife of the BC is documented via a series of letters between Jeanne Moussinac; Auguste Rondel; the publisher Jeanne Walter, who served as the president of Les Amis de la Bibliothèque Jacques Doucet; M. Guyot from the Université de Paris; and the writer Marie Dormoy, who was then director of the Bibliothèque littéraire Jacques Doucet.⁶⁷ Moussinac was apparently instrumental in transferring the BC to Rondel and in therefore preserving its collections after Doucet's death. However, because the BC survives not as an independent institution but as a subsection of the Fonds Léon Moussinac at the BnF today, it is like a "ghost archive" whose original classification escapes us. In other words, can we really say how the materials of the BC were classified based on how they are classified today within the collections of the BnF? How can we tell that the documentation of the BC was initially classified as it is today, into "film scripts and photographs," "various manuscripts," "various prints," "news articles," and "iconography"? Tracing the documents from their original owners to the BC proves rather difficult, and is probably quite impossible in some cases. But tracing those same documents within the different libraries they belonged to—mainly, the BC, the Bibliothèque de l'Arsenal, and the BnF—would require diving into administrative papers that only rarely survive. As mentioned previously, some of the books collected by Moussinac for the BC still bear the same call numbers in the collections of the BnF today. But as a ghost archive whose original classification may be considered lost, or at the very least faded, the BC haunts the BnF without ever quite materializing within its collections.

It remains quite obvious, however, that Moussinac's labor at the BC was geared toward collecting as a modern practice that began to rationalize film knowledge in France. Rime Touil argues that, compared to Auguste Rondel's library, which only included books and articles about the cinema, the BC aimed to collect a wider scope of archival materials. Yet Touil also admits that Rondel's library and the BC were in fact "complementary."[68] "It is ironic," she adds, "that Doucet's film library should join Rondel's library in 1932 following a donation from the Moussinacs, who were in charge [of the BC] since Doucet's death in 1929."[69] My analysis of Moussinac's labor as the BC's *documentaliste* suggests that the BC and the BN were perhaps less "complementary" than homologous, and that the fate of the BC was perhaps less "ironic" than logical, given the BC and BN's shared commitment to modern librarianship. A few years later, at the CN, similar principles having to do with systematization—mainly, the *dépôt légal*, which required that a copy of each title published in France be deposited in the collections of the BN—also shaped the work of Laure Albin-Guillot.

LAURE ALBIN-GUILLOT AND
THE CINÉMATHÈQUE NATIONALE (1932–1939)

Discussed as early as October 1932 in the general press, the CN was officially inaugurated in January 1933 and legally founded on March 24, 1934.[70] The CN is not to be confused with a number of regional, municipal, and private institutions dedicated to the preservation of educational films and actualités, especially the Cinémathèque de la Ville de Paris.[71] To be sure, the CN shared with these other institutions the idea that cinema's history was worth saving because of the documentary value assigned to most films. Yet in several other aspects having to do with modern librarianship, the CN was quite a novel enterprise that marked a significant shift in film preservation in France. Not only did the French government get involved, which suggested that the idea of a national film heritage was, at the very least, advancing, but the CN was also designed with the BN as its model, especially the BN's system of *dépôt légal*. Based on extant archives, the *dépôt légal* was apparently never officially considered at the CN. Yet the CN's focus on implementing a clear and regulated system of acquisitions and collections management, and on organizing a safe and appropriate storage facility, compares well with that of the BN around the time of its modernization. The CN was also publicly perceived as the equivalent of the BN for films, which speaks volumes about the affinities between the two.

To associate the *dépôt légal*, which dates from the Great Library of Alexandria and which had been practiced in France since 1537, with modern librarianship might seem far-fetched and even inadequate at first glance. In France, however, it was not until Morel and others pushed for public libraries in the early twentieth century that the *dépôt légal* became systematic. It remains unclear to me whether the new law of May 19, 1925, was a direct consequence of Morel's advocacy. Yet an article by Morel on that law reveals his support for the changes to the *dépôt légal*, which could improve, for him, the content of—and access to—library collections.⁷² Whereas only printers (*imprimeurs*) had been required to submit copies of their books to the *dépôt légal* before, the new law bound both printers and publishers (*éditeurs*) to do so. According to Morel, "the success, when it comes to books, is unexpected. Most publishers have accepted to conform to the new obligations. . . . At the end of August, the deposited volumes amounted to more than 1,200. . . . If one thinks of the strongest years, even before the war, the number of such books at the *dépôt légal* never went beyond 5,000 per year, and went as low as 3,000 these last few years."⁷³ This *double dépôt légal*, as historians often call it, guaranteed that the collections of the BN be more exhaustive, better organized, and ultimately cataloged more consistently.

Importantly, the new law of 1925 also expanded the list of documents covered by the *dépôt légal* to include not only "printed materials of all nature (books, periodicals, brochures, prints, engravings, illustrated postcards, geographical maps, etc.)," but also "musical works, photographic works sold publicly or reproduced, cinematographic and phonographic works and all the graphic arts productions in general."⁷⁴ As Frédéric Saby explains in his brief historical overview of the *dépôt légal* in France, the idea that sounds should be recorded and preserved had already led to the creation—with the help of Pathé Frères—of the "Archives de la parole" charged with collecting phonograph discs of various spoken languages between 1911 and 1914.⁷⁵ That same idea was then officialized with the new law of 1925 and eventually implemented upon the foundation of the Phonothèque nationale in 1938. When it comes to films, the *dépôt légal* provided for by the new law would take even more time to take effect. While several of the major French film studios—mainly, Gaumont, Pathé, and Lux—had deposited typed scripts and paper prints at the BN between 1906 and 1926, it was not until 1977 that a true *dépôt légal* for films existed de facto.⁷⁶

Yet the idea of the *dépôt légal* was associated with the CN from the very beginning, most likely as a result of the 1925 law. From April 11 through July 21, 1932, the French newspaper *La Liberté* published a series of articles written by René Chavance and Raoul D'Ast and dedicated to the new CN. This "investigation," as the authors called it, aimed not only to inform readers about the creation of the CN in the basement of the Palais du Trocadéro, but also to collect the opinions of film professionals like Charles Delac, Marcel L'Herbier, Germaine Dulac, Jean Benoit-Lévy, and Léon Gaumont, regarding the CN. Because the idea of a national cinematheque had been in the air for some time, no doubt as the result of the transition from silent to sound cinema, film professionals already had fixed ideas about the project, especially the *dépôt légal* for films. On the one hand, they responded quite favorably to the CN, which they thought would preserve the French national film heritage.[77] According to Dulac, who considered film to be "the living documentary of history," "the creation of a national cinematheque under the control of the State necessarily follows in my opinion from the need to preserve films. The negative [print] and the last complete positive [print], that is to say, similar to the original version [*version-mère*], of a film at the end of its exploitation, should also always be offered to the national cinematheque before being destroyed." L'Herbier likewise responded favorably to the CN, whose contributions to "science and history" he compared to those of the BN. On the other hand, film professionals often expressed their hesitations and concerns over the *dépôt légal*, which they imagined would be the principal mode of acquisition at the CN. For Delac, for example, the *dépôt légal* would be both impractical and financially impossible, mainly because of the inflammable nature and production costs of positive film prints.

I wish to emphasize here that I have found no archival evidence indicating that the CN ever considered implementing the *dépôt légal*. One of the earliest documents about the CN at the Archives Nationales, a "note concerning the construction of a cinematheque" from March 4, 1931, suggests instead that film production companies would "donate... films which had lost their commercial value but were interesting from a historical and documentary point of view."[78] The first article of the

1934 decree made the CN's policy official: "The cinematographic films deposited by producers at the Service des Archives photographiques et cinématographiques of the Beaux-Arts administration are preserved in a cinematheque, called 'cinémathèque nationale', where they [those films] will be available to scholars (film authors, directors, historians, etc.)."[79] Although this article is (perhaps deliberately) ambiguous, the rest of the decree confirms that film production companies were asked, but not lawfully required, to donate at least some of their films to the CN.

Even without the *dépôt légal*, the CN established a system of acquisitions, collections management, and storage that calls to mind the system of the BN during and after its modernization. In one of the articles cited previously, Chavance described the CN as follows:

> On the side of the Palais [du Trocadéro] opens the modest entrance of this new institution. But past the narrow door the premises look clean and reassuring. In the semicircular bays, reminiscent of some ancient monument, very modern vaults have been built, all clad in reinforced concrete, lined in the center and on the sides with steel or cement shelves that divide them into two aisles, each controlled by an iron door; they are separated from each other by thick partitions to ensure their isolation in case of fire. In addition, Greenel appliances are mounted on the ceiling, ready to spread water in abundance if necessary, and powerful vacuum cleaners, activated by a dynamo, catch the flammable emanations of the films to send them outside. The electric lighting, skillfully distributed, does not contravene these safety measures. The upstairs floor contains the offices, a projection room, and a laboratory for handling the films. The film library can hold . . . three million meters of film and its surface will eventually be doubled.[80]

At the Archives Nationales, several documents further attest to the CN's commitment to preservation and safety. For example, a three-page report on the "preservation of valuable films," which is unfortunately unsigned and undated, explains how to "protect valuable films without increasing the risks [of fire] for neighbors."[81] Many letters also discuss the relocation of the CN from the Palais du Trocadéro to the Parisian suburbs, where

Figure 3. Studio portrait of Laure Albin-Guillot, 1941. *Source:* © Laure Albin-Guillot/Roger-Viollet.

the CN would be farther away from residential areas. Finally, as I explain in more detail later, Laure Albin-Guillot was committed to making the CN into a "modern, practical, new, [and] very avant-garde" institution, where the French national film heritage would be easily accessible to film professionals and scholars.[82] Like Moussinac, Albin-Guillot therefore participated in the CN's rationalization of film knowledge.

Among Albin-Guillot's many photographs, only a few directly evoke the cinema. One of them is a photomontage with a completely dark area on the left, a woman's hands holding a filmstrip in the center, and the empty hallway of the CN on the right.[83] Used on the letterhead of the Association des Amis de la CN, which advocated for the CN to receive better funding, this photomontage might represent cinema's two fates: darkness, destruction, and oblivion, on the one hand, and the CN, preservation, and survival on the other. In my eyes, and because of my interest in Albin-Guillot, it also functions as a powerful image of Albin-Guillot's role at the CN. With the woman holding the filmstrip in the center, as if protecting it from the darkness on the left, the photomontage makes that woman central, both literally and metaphorically. Our focus is on her hands in action, on her labor safekeeping cinema's history at the CN.

Whereas Moussinac lived and worked in her husband's shadow, Albin-Guillot was a world-famous photographer who remains fairly well-known within the field of art history today. Albin-Guillot began her career in the 1920s, when her first fashion photographs and microphotographs were noticed in French magazines and exhibits organized in Paris. Until her husband's death on June 12, 1929, Albin-Guillot collaborated with him on microphotographs that often ended up adorning such decorative art objects as room screens and lamps.[84] It was after his death, however, that Albin-Guillot's practice exploded. According to Christian Bouqueret, Albin-Guillot became one of the most fascinating representatives of "New Vision Photography," which consisted of a moment in the 1930s when avant-garde photographers sought to capture the impact of emerging technologies on life and culture through formal experimentation.[85] On the occasion of a retrospective at the Musée du Jeu de Paume in Paris in 2013, Delphine Désveaux and Michaël Houlette likewise emphasized that Albin-Guillot was an "eminent member of the new French photography of the interwar years, alongside [André] Kertész, Man Ray, Lora [Webb Nichols], and [Dora] Maar."[86] In discussing Albin-Guillot's portrait photography, nude photography,

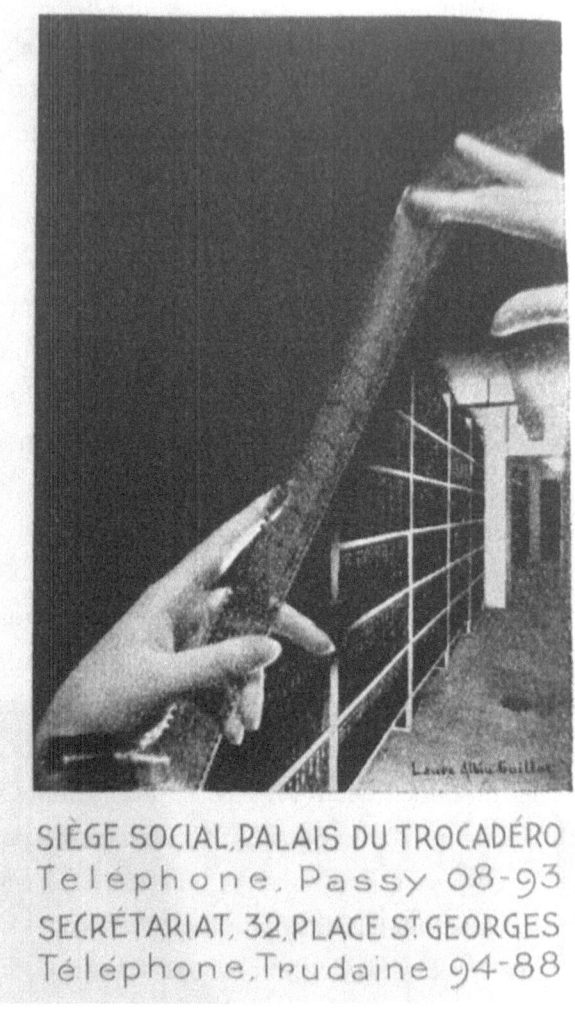

Figure 4. Photomontage by Laure Albin-Guillot. *Source:* F/21/8671, Archives Nationales.

and illustrations, as well as her contributions to advertising and the decorative arts, Désveaux and Houlette also revealed the impressive breadth of her work across various forms and media.

Yet Albin-Guillot's stint as the director of the CN, which Bouqueret, Désveaux, and Houlette mention only in passing, remains largely unexplored. Her connection to the cinema is admittedly oblique, which might explain (in part) why film professionals were hesitant to give the CN their support and why historians have not paid much attention to Albin-Guillot's role in film preservation. No doubt the result of a general preference for Langlois and his CF, which overlapped and even competed with the CN for some time, the place accorded to Albin-Guillot in French film historiography means that very little is actually known about her work for the CN. One way to make sense of that work is to invoke timing and the vagaries of public institutions and to say that Albin-Guillot might have become the director of the CN *because* she was already in charge of the Service des Archives photographiques (SAP; Service of the Photographic Archives) under which the CN existed. Following this line of thought, Albin-Guillot landed at the first French national cinematheque by chance, and the tragic fate of the CN was due to what *Le Cinéopse* once called Albin-Guillot's "ignorance" of the cinema.[87] Raymond Borde, who co-founded the Cinémathèque de Toulouse in 1964, likewise blamed Albin-Guillot for the failure of the CN to get off the ground. In his words, "On January 10, 1933, [the Beaux-Arts] create a 'Cinémathèque Nationale' that they set up in the basement of the Palais du Trocadéro and entrust to a woman of the world, an amateur photographer [*photographe à ses heures*], Mrs. Laure Albin-Guillot. . . . She's given a historic role about which she understands nothing. . . . Nothing happens. Once again, in France, history knocks at the wrong door. Mrs. Laure Albin-Guillot ruins everything. Whatever her artistic merits, she's completely inefficient. She's inert."[88] Not only did Borde undermine Albin-Guillot's professional career as a photographer, of which he apparently knew next to nothing, but he also misidentified the cause of the CN's failure. While film professionals were hesitant to fully support the CN, the CN also lacked funding for its development.

By digging deeper into Albin-Guillot's life and career and by examining the extant archives concerning the CN at the Archives Nationales, we find that she was deeply committed to the preservation of film history and, more specifically, to the CN's mission not only to *acquire* but to *collect* extant films according to a clear and regulated system. Albin-Guillot did not do the work of a *documentaliste*, however. As the archivist, director, and curator of the CN, all of which appear as her official titles in various extant documents, she performed a different kind of labor having to do with advocacy and promotion. More specifically, based on the materials at the Archives Nationales, Albin-Guillot dealt with budget allocation, acquisition, relations with film professionals, and the search for an adequate location. Because she was never officially nominated director of the CN, she apparently remained unpaid for most of her work.

As a photographer, Laure Albin-Guillot was at once unique and representative of the post–World War I era she lived and worked in. Unique, because she was a kind of transitional figure between pictorialism and New Vision photography, and because she gained enough notoriety to pull herself up to the highest echelons of the French administration. Representative, because she counted among the many white bourgeois women for whom photography became accessible after the war and because she got involved in the same genres of photography—art photography, nude photography, studio portraits, microphotography, publicity, and the decorative arts—as many other avant-garde photographers of the 1930s.[89] In reconstructing Albin-Guillot's career, I have also found numerous connections between her and well-known figures of the film avant-garde, including Germaine Dulac, Léon Moussinac, Jean Painlevé, and Man Ray. It is, in fact, astounding how many names came up during my research that placed Albin-Guillot within very close range of intellectual and artistic circles deeply interested and/or involved in cinema. To cite but a few examples, both Albin-Guillot and L. Moussinac were involved in the decorative arts; Albin-Guillot once exhibited her microphotographs with Painlevé, whose science films also relied on microphotography; and Albin-Guillot sometimes collaborated with Dulac in committees and feminist groups like the Soroptimist Club.[90]

According to at least one journalist, René Micquel, in 1934, Albin-Guillot was also an amateur filmmaker whose documentaries Micquel cited alongside the films of well-known amateurs like Raymond Bricon, Jacques Henri-Robert, and Georges Gronotayski (aka Géo Grono).[91] Gilles Ollivier argues that "the typical portrait of the French amateur filmmaker is as follows: a man between 35 and 40 years old, rather a doctor or a shopkeeper [commerçant], who, for financial reasons, makes films in 9.5mm and then, from the end of the 1940s, in 8mm. . . . As for his films, when they are fictions, they often crudely imitate the feature films of the time; when they are documentaries, they most often appear as vacation souvenirs."[92] Although she was a woman, Albin-Guillot shared similarities with amateur filmmakers of the 1930s. Not only was she a member of the Société française de Photographie, out of which came many amateur filmmakers, but she also belonged to the same social milieu. Although no other record of Albin-Guillot having made her own films apparently survives at this point, the possibility that she might have done so is nonetheless important. Not only does it suggest that Albin-Guillot was perhaps directly involved in filmmaking, but it also further emphasizes the ties between photography and cinema that Albin-Guillot's professional career already brings to the fore, and, most importantly for us here, Albin-Guillot's close interest in the film medium.

Whether Laure Albin-Guillot was truly destined to become the head of the first national film library remains somewhat unclear. Extant materials suggest instead that Albin-Guillot was designated to direct the SAP at the Ministère de l'Instruction et des Beaux-Arts, on May 15, 1932, which most likely explains why she found herself in charge of the CN.[93] In addition to collecting existing photographs of the national monuments of France, the employees of the SAP were commissioned to create and archive photographic records of paintings, sculptures, and other artworks from French national museums. But most importantly for the CN, the SAP was also home to a small collection of films produced by the French Army during World War I. The Etablissement de Communication et de Production Audiovisuelle de la Défense (ECPAD; Institute of Communication and Audiovisual Production of Defense), which now groups together most of the French Army's photographs and films from the 1880s through today, claims that the archives of the Section photographique et cinématographique de l'armée (SPCA; Photographic and Cinematographic Section of the Army) were scattered in September 1919, when the SPCA was itself restructured.[94] It was probably around then, or shortly after, that the SAP at the Ministère de l'Instruction et des Beaux-Arts inherited from the SPCA about 120,000 photographs and 200 kilometers of film footage produced by the French Army during World War I.[95] By the time Albin-Guillot was nominated director of the SAP in 1932, the CN already existed de facto if not de jure under the SAP's jurisdiction, and Albin-Guillot became the director of the SAP and the CN at the same time.

A brief note regarding the discourses about the CN in the contemporary general press may be helpful here. On the one hand, the press made few comments about Albin-Guillot's nomination at the SAP (and the CN), except to say that she was the very first woman to occupy that position. Her nomination was, according to Henriette Chandet in *L'Echo de Paris* and to the feminist newspaper *La Française*, among others, a new "success" or "victory" for women in France.[96] On the other hand, journalists from the general press wrote about the CN fairly regularly throughout the 1930s, and they even clearly identified Albin-Guillot as the CN's main driving force. (They often quoted her to introduce the CN, for example.) But journalists remained rather vague concerning Albin-Guillot's exact duties and responsibilities. The only photograph of Albin-Guillot at the CN that I have found in the general press appeared in *La Volonté* of January 23, 1933 and showed her "inspecting some films before their classification."[97] (The caption failed to mention the male film technician, perhaps "Mr. R. Dupoux," holding the other end of the film reel on Albin-Guillot's left.) Yet that photograph, which was clearly staged for promotional purposes, tells

Figure 5. Photograph of Laure Albin-Guillot and film technician printed in "Les Archives du cinéma," *La Volonté*, January 23, 1933, 2. *Source:* Retronews.

us very little about Albin-Guillot's actual work at the CN. Furthermore, even though the CN had just been inaugurated in the presence of the undersecretary of the Beaux-Arts, Jean Mistler, the caption—like so many other contemporary press reports—suggests that the CN remained in early stages.

If not in the contemporary press, information about Albin-Guillot's contributions to the CN may be found in the administrative papers of the Ministère de l'Instruction et des Beaux-Arts at the Archives Nationales, which include original letters, copies of letters, memos, notes, and invoices. A good portion of these papers is admittedly difficult to go through. On the one hand, copies of letters produced by the Ministère are usually handwritten and postdated. On the other, memos and notes mostly consist of internal communication between Albin-Guillot and other administrators of the Beaux-Arts, which is necessarily brief and elliptical.[98] These memos and notes might be slightly opaque too, mainly because of hierarchical relations at the Ministère. (Albin-Guillot was technically under the authority of such higher-ranked administrators as Georges Huismans, Emile Bollaert, and René Godave, for example.) Yet the importance of Albin-Guillot's labor for the CN, especially its rationalization of film knowledge, emerges quite clearly in the few documents either mentioning Albin-Guillot or signed by Albin-Guillot herself.

As the CN's archivist, director, and curator, Albin-Guillot was both the Ministère's representative to the public and the most vocal advocate of the CN within the Ministère itself. Film professionals were concerned about the *dépôt légal* that they thought the CN would implement, mainly because of financial costs. But the biggest problem had to do with the CN's budget, which was virtually nonexistent from the very beginnings in the early 1930s through the end, around 1939. Most likely because of the Great Depression hitting France in 1931, the Ministère was unable to allocate funds to the CN, which meant that Albin-Guillot was never compensated for her work, few employees were hired, and no storage facility was rehabilitated or built for the CN's collections in the end. Although the CN relied on donations from film production companies, it apparently acquired very few new films, and the small original war film collection from the Ministère constituted the majority—if not all—of the CN's film repository.

Albin-Guillot's efforts focused instead on advocating for the CN within the Ministère and on finding a permanent home for the CN's film collections, which the Ministère ultimately never approved.[99] Whereas the Palais du Trocadéro seemed like a good location for the CN at first, Albin-Guillot later considered the Château de Vincennes and several military forts administered by the French Army outside Paris. She also commissioned architect Robert Mallet-Stevens, with whom she had worked before, to draw up plans for a new building near the Tour Eiffel. Attached to a letter dated May 4, 1934, a note explains that the CN, which Albin-Guillot planned to transform into a "musée national de la photographie, du cinématographe et du disque" (national museum of photography, the cinematograph, and the phonograph) at that point, was to include exhibit rooms, a screening room, film laboratories, and, most importantly, a film library that Albin-Guillot described as follows:

> In the offices of the film library [*filmathèque*] will be classified all contemporary films and all films since the origin of cinema. This classification, in order to allow an easy documentation, must be done under about fifteen headings: titles, dates, authors of the scenario, composer, decorator, main actors, genre (comedy, vaudeville, war, sports, science, history etc. etc.), represented sites, time period, action, production company, sound recording, etc. Electrical devices will allow you to instantly find the number [*numéro d'ordre*] of a film by asking for one of the headings. Small screening rooms will be available for scholars. Others will be reserved for filing. One, finally, will be put at the disposal of the censorship. Meeting rooms will be reserved for the different commissions: propaganda etc. Some offices will classify the records, rooms will be dedicated to their preservation. Small auditoriums for studying. Moreover, the schools of photography and cinema will be set up in this establishment.[100]

Based on this note, Albin-Guillot's plans for the CN are clear. In classifying films in at least twelve categories ("titles, dates, authors of the scenario, composer, decorator, main actors, genre . . . , represented sites, time period, action, production company, sound recording"), all of which would be easily searchable, the CN was to make film history accessible to film professionals, students, and scholars, among others. Budget notes further indicate that Albin-Guillot wished to hire at least eleven additional employees, including a typist, an operator, a female editor [*monteuse*], a photographer, a fire chief [*brigadier*], and three guards.[101]

None of Albin-Guillot's recommendations would be followed up on, however. In a letter addressed to the director of the Ministère de l'Instruction et des Beaux-Arts on November 16, 1935, Albin-Guillot expressed her frustration with the Ministère's slow workings:

> I come to appeal to your benevolence and to remind you that for more than three years I have been working on the establishment of the National Cinematheque, the Museum of Cinematography, Photography, and the Record. I will not remind you of the difficulties of all kinds which, until now, have prevented me from achieving a positive result. I make daily efforts; you know my devotion to and my lack of financial interest in this beautiful cause of the preservation of film treasures. I have come to ask you, if not for an immediate appointment, at least for an exchange of letters or for a provisional appointment, giving me the assurance that, having done all the preliminary work voluntarily, I will have the conservation of this film museum.[102]

After reading this and several other letters at the Archives Nationales, it seems rather difficult to accuse Albin-Guillot of being "inert," as Borde once did. The CN's failure may be attributed instead to the Ministère's reluctance, or perhaps its inability, to finance the CN in the midst of the Great Depression.

Starting around 1936, Langlois's CF also quickly became a viable and better option for the preservation of cinema in France. Although Langlois and Albin-Guillot met several times, and the CN even briefly housed some of the CF's collections, Langlois probably never intended to forfeit some of the CF's responsibilities to Albin-Guillot's CN. With the support of many film professionals behind Langlois, the CF soon overpowered the CN to become virtually the primary film archive in France in the late 1930s. In any case, even though Albin-Guillot's efforts to get the CN off the ground were evidently thwarted by the Ministère and by the CF, she remained the CN's best advocate, and a film archivist deeply committed to the collection of film history as a scientific practice.

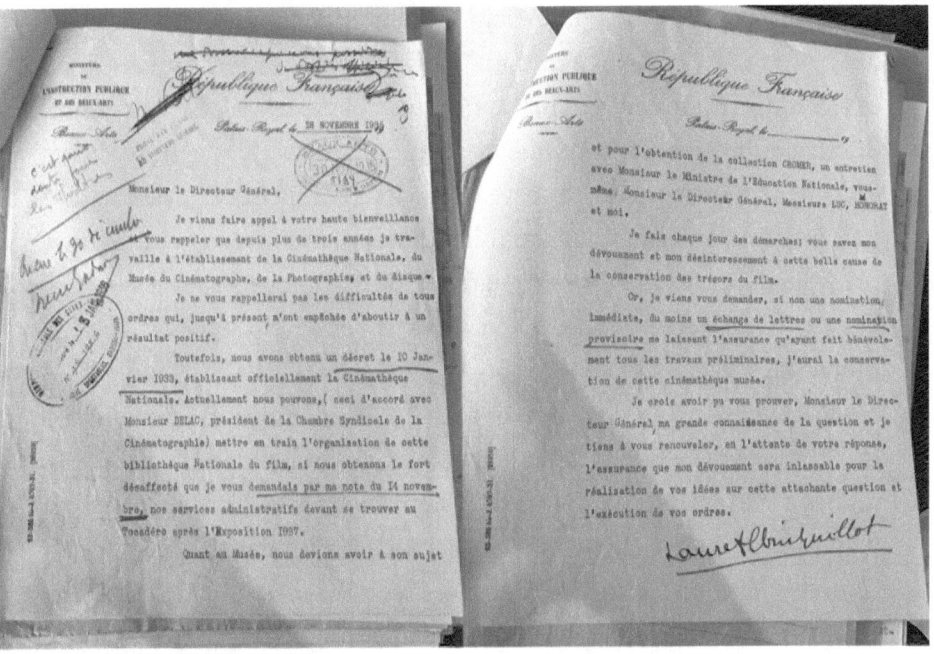

Figure 6. Letter from Laure Albin-Guillot to the director of the Ministère de l'Instruction et des Beaux-Arts, November 16, 1935. *Source:* F/21/8671, Archives Nationales.

CONCLUSION: (IN)VISIBLE LEGACIES

Most visitors to French and other film archives have likely experienced firsthand, yet unknowingly, the legacies of Moussinac's and Albin-Guillot's work for the BC and the CN. Often dismissed completely, or relegated to the margins of film preservation and historiography, Moussinac and Albin-Guillot nevertheless contributed to shaping what many film archives look like today, from their collections management practices to their public access and outreach policies. Moussinac and Albin-Guillot had different lives and careers; they arrived at the BC and the CN from vastly different routes, and they experienced different levels of success in their efforts to collect film history. Whereas Moussinac and her husband Léon were chosen to establish the BC by Doucet, who trusted their expertise and connections to the film avant-garde of the 1920s, Albin-Guillot might have been selected as head of the SAP and then of the CN as a reward for her career as one of the most prominent photographers of the 1930s. It is also worth noting that Albin-Guillot continued to exhibit new work at gallery shows and international salons, to serve on various competition juries, and to give lectures, among other activities, during her entire appointment at the Ministère and the CN. By contrast, Moussinac was a far less public figure whose name was (apparently) rarely cited in the press. Finally, Moussinac accomplished far more in two years at the BC than Albin-Guillot ever did in seven years at the CN. While the collections of the BC survive at the BnF today, albeit as a ghost archive, those of the CN probably never amounted to more than the small war film collection it started with. Yet these two women's commitment to the rationalization of film historical knowledge—through collecting practices like cataloging and the *dépôt légal*—have had a long-lasting impact on the ways in which most global film archives function to this day.

In France, the CF may be seen as one of the sites where the legacies of Moussinac and Albin-Guillot remain most visible today. It was, under Langlois's leadership, a notorious mess. In a bathtub belonging to Langlois's parents, Gustave and Anne-Louise, metal film canisters were piled up to the brim and above, precariously stacked, randomly thrown together during the chaos of World War II. For film scholars, cinephiles, and regulars of the CF, this photograph of the Langloises' bathtub by Denise Bellon captures Henri Langlois's passionate dedication to the preservation of film history. It also signifies—in hindsight—his notorious exuberance, which has played a major part in the mythology built around him as providential savior of cinema since at least the 1950s. Yet what some would see as an admirable rescue mission, others might consider an archival nightmare wherein fragile and highly flammable nitrate prints are stored in the functioning bathroom of a private apartment. By contrast, the extant photographs of the CN

Figure 7. La Baignoire des Langlois, 1945. *Source:* © Denise Bellon/akg-images.

are at once dull and comforting. Often published in the general press, these photographs show a long corridor lined with sturdy shelves of organized film cans, in what appears to be a concrete basement. They sometimes include a male technician (perhaps Mr. R. Dupoux) in a white blouse, serious-looking and alone.[103] Yet this opposition—between the boisterous chaos of Langlois's CF and the quiet order of Albin-Guillot's CN—is misleading. Since at least the late years of World War II, the growing body of administrators and employees working

Figure 8. Photograph of the Cinémathèque Nationale printed in René Chavance, "Après l'enquête de 'La Liberté': La Cinémathèque nationale va être instituée," *La Liberté*, January 11, 1933, 2. Source: Retronews.

at the CF strove to implement more rigorous collections management practices, including a complete catalog of the CF's film holdings, which certainly call to mind both the BC and the CN.

Today's CF in fact strangely resembles both the BC and the CN as the two were constituted by Moussinac and Albin-Guillot, respectively. Like the BC, the CF—especially, its BiFi—aims at collecting not only films but also any other archival materials related to the history of French and international cinemas. And, like the CN, which was once supposed to have a film library, a museum, and a screening room, the CF—with the BiFi, the Musée du Cinéma, and four movie theaters (named after Langlois, Franju, Jean Epstein, and Eisner)—forms a large hub for Parisian film culture. Finally, the CF too became the site of many women's contributions to film preservation and historiography; as archivists and more, these women walked in the footsteps of Moussinac and Albin-Guillot.

DEUXIEME ENTR'ACTE

RECOLLECTION

MORE THAN TWENTY YEARS after visiting the Prussian State Library in Berlin, Lotte Eisner found herself writing about mostly Weimar cinema in France. Not only did she have access to the film collections of the CF where she served as head archivist, but she also benefited from personal connections with several major German and Austrian filmmakers of the 1920s. As a result, her publications, which included three monographs—*L'Ecran démoniaque* (*The Haunted Screen*, 1952), *F. W. Murnau* (1964), and *Fritz Lang* (1976)—as well as numerous articles, provide rich, detailed accounts of the style and working methods of Fritz Lang, Paul Leni, F. W. Murnau, G. W. Pabst, and Paul Wegener, among others. But what perhaps most characterizes Eisner's work is a sustained reflection on the archive, already started, as it were, in her writings from Berlin.

"Recollection," in the form of personal conversations and formal interviews, features prominently in that reflection. In addition to extant films and paper archives like catalogs, newspapers, magazines, posters, programs, and photographs, which she argued film historians should examine with scrupulous attention to detail, Eisner often insisted on the importance of oral history for reconstructing cinema's recent past. For example, in "Comment écrire l'histoire du cinéma" (How to write cinema's history), published in the French magazine *Positif* in April 1953, she explained that interviews with living filmmakers and movie workers should supplement archival research:

> And above all, we need to turn to the still living witnesses of a bygone era that seems to us emerging from the mists [of time]. So, we need to question the old actors, the old directors, the scriptwriters, cameramen, and set designers of yesteryear. They will always be happy to enlighten us, correct our mistakes, give us confirmations or denials. It will be a chance for them to reminisce about the "good old days," to draw on their often still infallible memory.[1]

As Eisner made explicit in the rest of the article, she had in mind the interviews with the so-called pioneers of silent cinema that Langlois—and Musidora, Marie Epstein, and Eve Francis—organized at the CF starting in the 1940s. These interviews, Eisner emphasized, were reliable sources for "historians worthy of the name."[2]

Although she never took part in the CF's interviews, Eisner actively contributed to the legitimization of recollection as a practice central to film historiography. On the one hand, Eisner knew many filmmakers from her time as a journalist in Berlin in the 1920s and reconnected with them as she worked for the CF after the war. In her previous life, right before exile, she was indeed witness to the vibrant cultural effervescence of the Weimar Republic; she attended private parties and salons with "le tout Berlin"; went to the theater and cinema several times a week; and visited the sets of many German expressionist films at UFA's studios where she met Lang, Pabst, and others for the first time.[3] After World War II, she reached out to some of her past acquaintances again, asking them to give time and material to Langlois's new

CF. Eisner became particularly close to Lang, with whom she met several times and exchanged many letters throughout the 1950s, 1960s, and 1970s. Their conversations, about Lang's decade-long career in the cinema, informed Eisner's book on his German and Hollywood films at both micro- and macro-levels; Lang provided not only factual information but also line and copy edits, most of which Eisner likely included in the final manuscript published in English in 1976. Similar to many of her writings on Weimar cinema, Eisner's *Fritz Lang* is the result of recollection as a form of collaboration.

On the other hand, Eisner sought the assistance of secondary witnesses with family or professional ties to silent filmmakers and movie workers. As she made it very clear in the prefaces to both *F. W. Murnau* and *Fritz Lang*, for example, interviews with the collaborators and relatives of Murnau, who had died in 1931, and whom Eisner had never met, proved essential to the accurate description of his cinema in her book. "As to his working methods," she wrote, "my approach was to interview his surviving collaborators, the designers, cameramen, and others from his film units. I also had the great good fortune to meet Murnau's brother, Robert Plumpe Murnau, who entrusted me a number of scripts annotated in Murnau's own hand, among them the shooting script of *Nosferatu* [1922] itself, reproduced in translation at the end of the book."[4] The acknowledgments list the names of additional relatives, including Robert's daughters, Ursula Plumpe and Eva Dieckmann, both of whom became Murnau's rights holders in the early 1960s.[5] In the article cited previously, Eisner clearly rejected the idea that first-person accounts were untrustworthy, emphasizing instead the "infallible memory" of the "old actors, the old directors, the scriptwriters, cameramen, and set designers of yesteryear."[6] With *F. W. Murnau*, she extended her trust to witnesses with potentially more indirect experience of the cinema. In doing so, she not only validated these witnesses, but she also contributed to developing recollection as a legitimate and collaborative historiographical practice.

2

WITNESSES

IN THE SPRING OF 1936, a few months before the CF was officially founded, Henri Langlois started acquiring his first films, which he then entrusted to his friend and early filmmaker Georges Méliès in Orly, about seven miles south of Paris. By then Méliès, whose film career had ended around 1913, had already been rediscovered by journalists, historians, and young filmmakers who often visited him, his second wife, Jehanne d'Alcy, and his granddaughter, Madeleine Fontaine (later known as Madeleine Malthête-Méliès), at the castle where they lived in Orly.[1] According to Malthête-Méliès, it was director René Clair who introduced Langlois and Georges Franju to Méliès soon after the creation of their ciné-club, Le Cercle du Cinéma, in late 1935.[2] When Langlois received films from Pathé Frères, Albatros, Pierre Braunberger, Germaine Dulac, Gaston Modot, and others, he asked to store them in the small warehouse located on the castle's grounds. Méliès thus became the first gatekeeper to

Langlois's collection, or as Franju said, the "first 'curator' [*conservateur*] of the Cinémathèque française."[3]

This anecdote, I believe, illustrates rather well Langlois's dedication to preserving silent films, his admiration for early filmmakers like Méliès, and, indeed, his vision for the CF and for the CRH that this chapter examines. A brief article announcing the creation of the CF in late 1936 explains that "guided by directors [*metteurs en scène*] and cinephiles who participated in the evolution of French film, supported by producers and the press, the Cinémathèque will finally be able to make possible the history of cinema through cinema,"[4] which I understand to mean two things. First is that the CF would rely on filmmakers—like Méliès—to write film history, and second is that extant films—like the ones Langlois entrusted to Méliès—would be placed front and center of the CF's historiographical project.

Although seemingly paradoxical, for running films through a projector degrades them over time, public film screenings were always crucial to, and inseparable from, the CF's film preservation practices. The institutional history of the CF, which Laurent Mannoni has written about extensively in *Histoire de la Cinémathèque française* (History of the Cinémathèque française, 2006), lies beyond the scope of this chapter.[5] Yet it is important to note at this point that the CF originated in Langlois and Franju's ciné-club, Le Cercle du Cinéma, which hosted weekly screenings as a way to "search for, showcase, and preserve the classics of cinema," shortly after French cinema had transitioned from silent to sound.[6] As Langlois wrote in *La Cinématographie française* on August 24, 1935, "Because the talkies have stopped the production of silent films for a while, silent cinema can't evolve anymore and it now belongs to the past," which made it all the more urgent for Langlois to find copies of extant silent films and screen them to a public of Parisian cinephiles.[7] Newspapers and film magazines published between 1936 and 1947 reveal that the Cercle du Cinéma showcased mostly silent films, particularly German expressionist films; Hollywood comedies featuring Charlie Chaplin, Buster Keaton, and Harold Lloyd; Hollywood dramas; Soviet films; and French films by Méliès and the "first French avant-garde (1919–1925)," which Langlois often acquired from retiring producers, exhibitors, and distributors, and from filmmakers themselves.[8] The concept of the ciné-club was itself a throwback to the 1920s, when Louis Delluc, Ricciotto Canudo, Léon Moussinac, Germaine Dulac, and others established the first French ciné-clubs in Paris, mainly the Club des amis du septième art (CASA) and Amis du cinéma. But whereas the 1920s ciné-clubs aimed to "encourage, first of all, an informed audience that would support advances in film art and, only secondarily, real social change," according to Richard Abel, the Cercle du Cinéma looked toward establishing an appreciation of film's historical past among young filmmakers and cinephiles.[9] Importantly, it also honored early French directors, whose films remained a staple of the CF's programming for many years.

If the CF grew out of a cinephilic impulse, then the project that best exemplifies the CF's ambitions was, without a doubt, the CRH. Founded in 1943, the CRH had very clear objectives: First was to interview so-called French film pioneers and/or their living relatives about the early French film industry, which the CRH divided between the "heroic times" (*temps héroïques*, before 1914) and the "silent art" (*art muet*, after 1914). Second was to identify the extant films that the CF had already acquired. And third was to collect film prints and other archival materials—including production photographs, film programs, catalogs, scripts, administrative documents, and correspondence—that would enrich the collections of the CF.

Organized at irregular intervals between 1944 and 1966, and each lasting approximately one and one-half hours, the CRH interviews are not only rich in anecdotes and gossip but also informative when it comes to the so-called pioneers' start in cinema, their work methods, and the dates of their films, for example. In addition to individual careers, the CRH was interested in the pioneers for what they could remember about cinema's first decades more broadly, that is, the size of film crews; the role of directors and camera operators; the use of artificial lighting, pre-written scripts, and close-ups; and the construction of sets. Perhaps not incidentally, the focus of the CRH on French national cinema also had the effects of diminishing Hollywood's historical significance in the development of film as a technical and artistic practice and of contributing to the collective memory of cinema as a French invention.[10] Yet there are many instances in which pioneers contradicted each other and failed to remember names, dates, or events, meaning that the issues of interest for the CRH were not always illuminated. In the short term, however, Langlois hoped that the CRH would provide enough information and archival materials that the CF could organize some exhibits dedicated to cinema's history. Mannoni tells us that, before Langlois's Musée du Cinéma (Museum of Cinema) officially opened at the Palais de Chaillot in 1972, the CF had inaugurated two exhibition galleries dedicated to the birth of cinema and to Méliès, respectively, in November 1948.[11]

This trajectory—from the Cercle du Cinéma to the CRH to the Musée du Cinéma—explains the motives behind the CRH as a historiographical and archival project spearheaded by the CF. But it also closely associates the CRH with Langlois, which is both relevant and insufficient. Relevant, because Langlois's vision for the CF to write "the history of cinema through cinema" shaped the CRH interviews, even when Langlois was not physically present in the room. Insufficient, because the CRH was driven not only by Langlois but also by members and guests, many of whom were women, and by mostly female employees, whose collective labor of "recollection" should be accounted for.

Specifically, the more than seventy meetings of the CRH were organized first by Musidora between 1944 and 1952, and then by Marie Epstein and Eve Francis in 1956 and 1966, respectively, during which these three women, Langlois, and other members of the CRH—mainly Marie-Anne Colson-Malleville, Henri Ménessier, Jean Mitry, and Georges Sadoul—talked to so-called film pioneers and/or their living relatives and collaborators about the early days of French cinema, while a female typist stenographer transcribed what they said. Guests of the CRH, including many women, were received in groups at the apartment Colson-Malleville shared with Germaine Dulac before Dulac passed away, and starting in 1948, at the CF, where films were occasionally screened. At other times guests met with members of the CRH one on one, at their homes, which often allowed for more targeted interviews about their individual careers. In any event, women performed multiple functions that made them key, yet rarely acknowledged, agents of the CRH.

With the CRH serving as a focal point, this chapter thus argues that many women—including, but not limited to, Musidora, Francis, and Epstein—served as important witnesses whose labor, professional experience, film knowledge, dedication, and personal connections to early filmmakers made possible the first oral history project dedicated to the cinema in France. This chapter indeed considers the CRH an oral history project relying on "shared authority" between interviewers, interviewees, and even secretaries, whom I place in three different but related categories: witness interviewers, narrators, and stenographer typists.[12] (While the first two categories are inspired by oral history scholarship, all three are my own inventions.) Unlike memoirs written by and credited to a single author, for example, the CRH interviews were a collaboration of early filmmakers with the interviewers, other guests, and stenographer typists hired to do the *actual* (mechanical) writing of film history. Their "shared authority" is therefore crucial to understand the specificity of the CRH interviews as historical sources, their value for rethinking historiography as collective and collaborative, and women's engagement with the film archive as witnesses of cinema's historical past.

Unlike many archival collections, the majority of the CRH collection has been digitized and is available online.[13] This is not to say, however, that the CRH collection represents an easy task for historians interested in early and silent cinema, on the one hand, and film historiography, on the other. First, this collection consists of 116 pdf files, each of which contains from one to several dozens of handwritten and/or typewritten pages with different levels of legibility and readability. All these files are also riddled with typos and misspellings, meaning that the names of several filmmakers remain indecipherable. When the filmmaker's name is misspelled but known, I maintain the misspelling and indicate the correct or common spelling between brackets in citations. When typos and misspellings appear to be simple mistakes due to typing, I correct them without comments.

Second, each file often includes several versions of the same interview transcript, which Musidora, Langlois, or someone else corrected, edited, and annotated in the text or in the margins. Because these transcripts were never published, it is difficult to establish which version (if any) constitutes the definitive one. As much as space allows, I indicate in this chapter which version I cite and whether significant edits were made to the version in question. Moreover, handwritten additions to the typed transcripts appear between asterisks (*). My intention is not to confuse the reader but to account for the palimpsestic nature and collaborative mode of production that characterize so many of these interview transcripts.

Third, the collection of the CRH is incomplete, since at least one interview transcript and all the audiotape (and perhaps even film) recordings appear to be missing (as of 2025). It remains unclear what happened to these valuable materials, which the CRH would have assembled with care and diligence. I suspect that they might have been lost during the many moves of the CF to various locations in Paris or during their transfer back and forth to Georges Sadoul, who, according to Bernard Bastide, "took care of adding to his personal archives the original transcripts for all the meetings organized between January 8 and July 29,

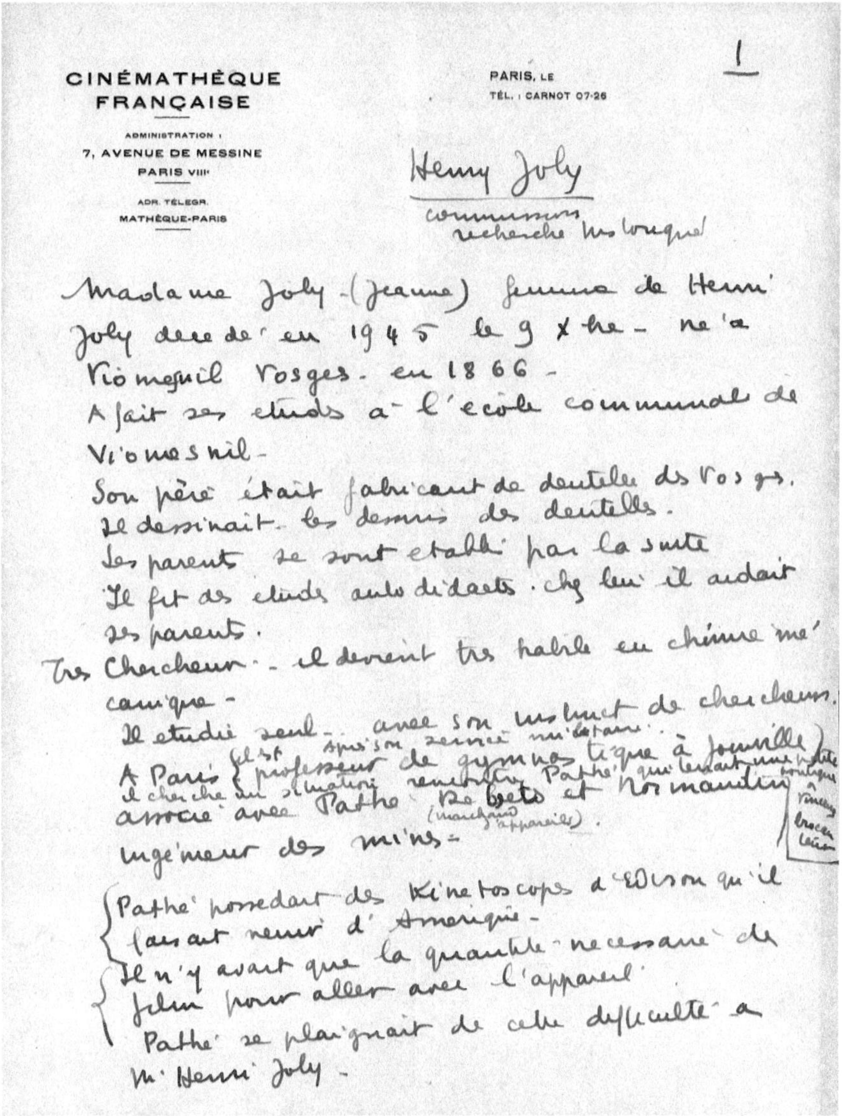
CINÉMATHÈQUE
FRANÇAISE

ADMINISTRATION :
7, AVENUE DE MESSINE
PARIS VIIIe

ADR. TÉLÉGR.
MATHÈQUE-PARIS

PARIS, LE
TÉL. : CARNOT 07-26

1

Henry Joly

communications
recherche historique

Madame Joly - (Jeanne) femme de Henri Joly décédé en 1945 le 9 Xbre - né à Viomenil Vosges - en 1866 -
A fait ses études à l'école communale de Viomesnil -
Son père était fabricant de dentelles des Vosges.
Il dessinait les dessins des dentelles.
Ses parents se sont établi par la suite
Il fit des études autodidacts. Chez lui il aidait ses parents.
Très chercheur - il devient très habile en chimie mécanique -
Il étudie seul - avec son instinct de chercheur.
A Paris { il est professeur de gymnastique à Joinville après son service militaire. il cherche une situation rencontre Pathé qui tenait une petite boutique à Vincennes brocanteur
associé avec Pathé Robets et Normandin (marchand d'appareils).
ingénieur des mines -
{ Pathé possédait des Kinetoscopes d'Edison qu'il faisait venir d'Amérique -
{ Il n'y avait que la quantité nécessaire de film pour aller avec l'appareil.
Pathé se plaignait de cette difficulté à M. Henri Joly -

Figure 9. Handwritten note about the inventor Henri Joly dictated to Musidora by Joly's widow, Jeanne, date unknown. *Source:* CRH82-B4 © DR, Collection La Cinémathèque française.

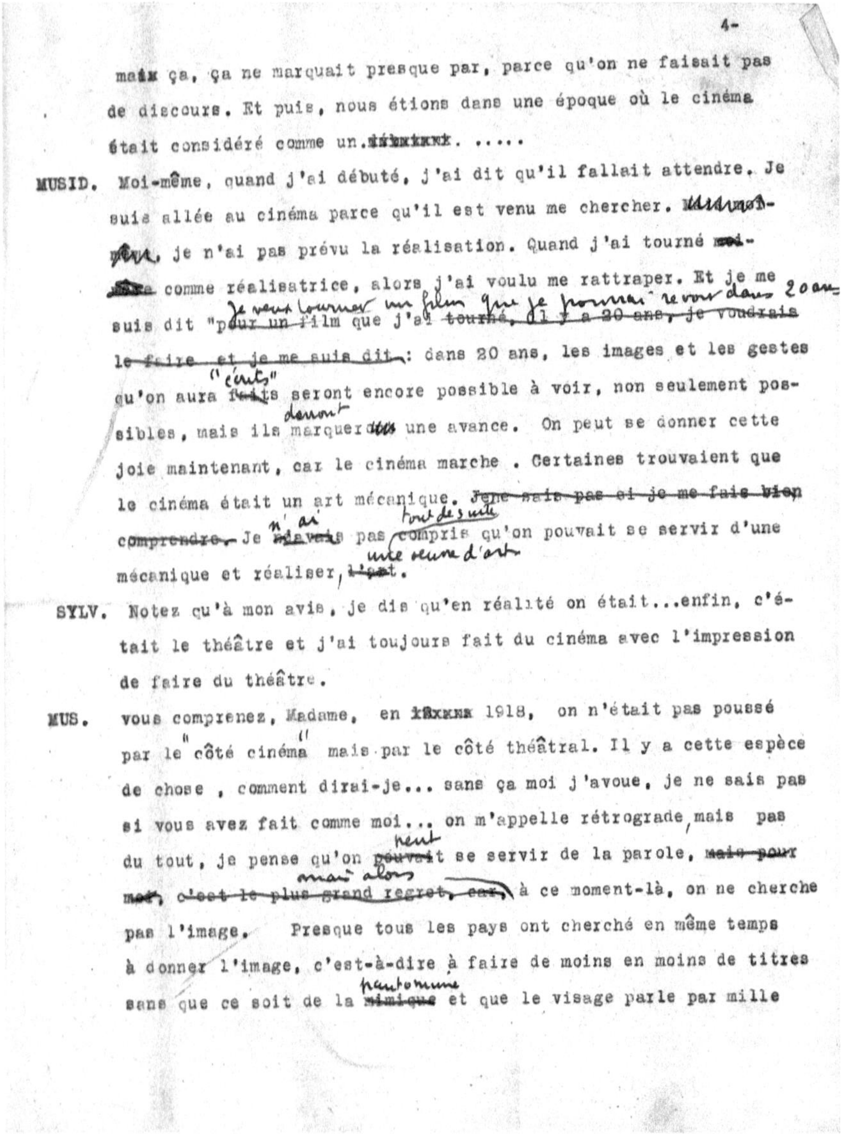

mais ça, ça ne marquait presque pas, parce qu'on ne faisait pas
de discours. Et puis, nous étions dans une époque où le cinéma
était considéré comme un.xxxxxxx. .....

MUSID. Moi-même, quand j'ai débuté, j'ai dit qu'il fallait attendre. Je
suis allée au cinéma parce qu'il est venu me chercher. xxxxxx
xxxx, je n'ai pas prévu la réalisation. Quand j'ai tourné xxx
xxxx comme réalisatrice, alors, j'ai voulu me rattraper. Et je me
suis dit "pour un film que j'ai tourné, il y a 20 ans, je voudrais
le faire et je me suis dit : dans 20 ans, les images et les gestes
qu'on aura faits seront encore possible à voir, non seulement pos-
sibles, mais ils marquerons une avance. On peut se donner cette
joie maintenant, car le cinéma marche. Certaines trouvaient que
le cinéma était un art mécanique. Je ne sais pas si je me fais bien
comprendre. Je n'avais pas compris qu'on pouvait se servir d'une
mécanique et réaliser, l'art.

SYLV. Notez qu'à mon avis, je dis qu'en réalité on était...enfin, c'é-
tait le théâtre et j'ai toujours fait du cinéma avec l'impression
de faire du théâtre.

MUS. Vous comprenez, Madame, en 1xxxxx 1918, on n'était pas poussé
par le côté cinéma mais par le côté théâtral. Il y a cette espèce
de chose , comment dirai-je... sans ça moi j'avoue, je ne sais pas
si vous avez fait comme moi... on m'appelle rétrograde, mais pas
du tout, je pense qu'on pouvait se servir de la parole, mais pour
moi, c'est le plus grand regret, car à ce moment-là, on ne cherche
pas l'image. Presque tous les pays ont cherché en même temps
à donner l'image, c'est-à-dire à faire de moins en moins de titres
sans que ce soit de la mimique et que le visage parle par mille

Figure 10. Typewritten transcript, most likely corrected by Musidora after her meeting with the actress Renée Sylvaire, February 1946. *Source:* CRH29-B1 © DR, Collection La Cinémathèque française.

1944, undoubtedly with the intention of having the exclusive use of the information thus assembled."[14]

Finally, the CRH collection is so rich in stories and generative of so many historiographical questions that no single book chapter could address them all. My focus on the women who contributed to the CRH necessarily excludes many other valuable lines of inquiry. Yet I hope to illuminate the goals, methods, and practices of the CRH and, more importantly, to reveal these women as important witnesses at the CF and beyond.

MEMORY AND/OR HISTORICAL TRUTH: THE CRH AS ORAL HISTORY

Although the CRH never described itself in those terms, it was, to my knowledge, the first oral history project dedicated to cinema in France.[15] To be sure, French film historians in the 1920s and 1930s had often relied on published memoirs and personal interviews with early filmmakers and other film professionals, including Léon Gaumont, Charles Pathé, Emile Cohl, and Georges Méliès.[16] Yet there had been no organized effort to collect oral testimonies from so-called French film pioneers or from their living relatives when these pioneers had already passed. In fact, by the time the CRH scheduled its first interviews in the mid-1940s, oral history was still several decades away from being recognized as a serious discipline in France. Considering the CRH as an oral history project is crucial, however. Not only does this approach illuminate the historiographical merits of the CRH, but it also provides us with a vocabulary to make sense of women's role as witnesses in this context.

Today, the Oral History Association defines "oral history" as "both the interview process and the products that result from a recorded interview (whether audio, video, or other formats)."[17] Furthermore, "the value of oral history lies largely in the way it helps to place people's experiences within a larger social and historical context. The interview becomes a record useful for documenting past events, individual or collective experiences, and understanding the ways that history is constructed. Because it relies on memory, oral history captures recollections about the past filtered through the lens of a changing personal and social context."[18] Although the standards for oral history projects have varied over the years and between institutions, representative examples include, among thousands of others, *Born in Slavery: Slavery Narratives from the Federal Writers' Project, 1936 to 1938*, and the John F. Kennedy (JFK) Oral History Collection (1964), both of which are accessible online. According to the Library of Congress, *Born in Slavery* contains "more than 2,300 first-person accounts of slavery and 500 black-and-white photographs of former slaves.... At the conclusion of the Slave Narrative project, a set of edited transcripts was assembled and microfilmed in 1941 as the seventeen-volume *Slave Narratives: A Folk History of Slavery in the United States from Interviews with Former Slaves*."[19] These microfilms, which constitute the irreplaceable record of US slavery from the perspectives of slaves, were digitized and made available on the website of the Library of Congress in 2000 and 2001.[20] Likewise, the John F. Kennedy Presidential Library initiated the JFK Oral History Collection as a way to document an important time in US history by way of interviews with relevant witnesses. The Presidential Library was especially interested in "people whose lives or work intersected with John F. Kennedy, Robert F. Kennedy, and/or the major events and issues of their times."[21] Starting one year after Kennedy's assassination, in 1964, it conducted about thirteen hundred interviews, whose digitized transcripts are now viewable on site.[22]

Yet acceptance of memory or recollection as a valid source for historical research was not always a given, especially within the narrow confines of academia. Florence Descamps demonstrates that in France, historians' fraught relationship with oral sources dates back to at least the seventeenth and eighteenth centuries, when history became limited to state politics, official documents, facts, and events, "to the detriment of discourses, beliefs, legends, and myths."[23] Starting around 1880, oral sources again posed a problem for French academics looking to establish history as a science rooted in empirical evidence, mainly because oral sources were considered inaccurate, distorted, unverifiable, and so on. Later, when a younger generation of academics formed the Annales School, new fields of study emerged that called for new sources, including visual documents, topographic maps, and oral sources. But for Descamps, it was not until the 1970s and 1980s that oral history was fully accepted by French historians, who then adapted the methods and guidelines coming from Columbia University in New York. Indeed, oral history as a discipline with its own set of practical and ethical rules was born in the United States, where the department of sociology at the University of Chicago took a special interest in oral sources as early as 1915. In the 1940s and 1950s, the new Oral History Research Office at Columbia University (now the Columbia Center for Oral History Research) recorded interviews with US political, economic, and cultural elites, which were then transcribed, certified, and made accessible to the public only after the people interviewed had passed. In Descamps's words, "the recording is but one step in the process whereby documents are produced and oral sources are transformed into written archives," which still describes the work of oral historians today.[24]

What this brief overview helps us understand is that oral history raises concerns not only about the *use* of oral sources for historical research, but also about the *production* of sources by oral historians. As Ronald J. Grele explains, oral history constitutes an archival practice with a shifting understanding of sources, first as historical data and then as historical narrative.[25] Grele writes that, until the 1970s, interviews were "transparent in their meaning and could be tested for their accuracy, verifiability, and representativeness by the historian, whose role was unquestioned and whose cultural position in a world of production was invisible. . . . The goal was the production of information, which could be weighed against the traditional methods of inquiry for its reliability and verifiability."[26] Following the turn to cultural studies, however, history changed from "something to be discovered" ("what happened," in Trouillot's terms) to something "constructed [that] had to be comprehended for it to be understood and analyzed" ("that which is said to have happened").[27] Oral historians thus became less concerned with collecting data than with interpreting the narratives they heard from witnesses or "narrators." This shift prompted Michael Frisch to coin the phrase "shared authority" to describe "the creative role of the interviewee as well as the interviewer and to make the political point for the necessity of the sharing of interpretative power in the process."[28] Simply put, oral history now conceived of history and memory together, as the collaborative reconstruction of the past in the present.

Once again, I have found no evidence that the CRH was conceived of, and publicly perceived as, an oral history project. The unpolished state of the CRH collection would even suggest that the CRH failed to publish its findings in a way that would have benefited the public and researchers alike. Yet the standards of the CRH compare well with the standards of more recent oral history projects like the ones cited earlier. Indeed, the CRH proceeded in a similar way, with Musidora and other CRH members making lists of living film pioneers to contact; then conducting either one-on-one interviews or group interviews at these pioneers' homes, Colson-Malleville's apartment, and the CF; and finally, producing typed transcripts for the film library of the CF. Although nothing points to whether the CRH went into these interviews with a list of predetermined questions, as oral historians would do today, these typed transcripts suggest that film pioneers were asked similar questions about their early stage careers (if relevant), their start in cinema, their work methods, and so on.

Furthermore, documents from the CRH collection betray the suspicion of the CRH toward interviews as historical sources, which also characterized oral history before the 1970s.[29] In an early report from

1943, for example, the CRH indicated: "It is essential that some *serious* historical research be done before all the interviews, and that a filmography and a short bibliography be established. One of the people in charge of the interviews will read the texts from the bibliography beforehand, and the interview will be conducted based on these historical documents."[30] For the period before 1914, however, so little information remained that no filmography or bibliography existed, according to the CRH. The CRH therefore had to proceed with the interviews "without having many illusions about the real value of a material collected without any prior historical research." It is unclear whether this comment referred to the interviewer being unprepared to ask the right questions, to the interviewee whose memories could not be verified, or to both. In any case, the CRH made a clear distinction between "historical documents" and the testimonies of the film pioneers supposed to complement—and certainly not replace—these documents. Although the work of the CRH after interviews were done remains a mystery for the most part, we know that Musidora, Langlois, and others often corrected interview transcripts, perhaps based on the information they had found elsewhere, either in their own memories when it came to names, or in historical documents for other things.

My approach is closely aligned with more recent scholarship about oral history. In what follows, I understand recollection as a historiographical practice that consists of the collaborative reconstruction of the past in the present and based on experience filtered through memory and nostalgia. This chapter also considers the CRH interviews as narratives, its interviewers as oral historians, and its interviewees as narrators with valuable stories to tell. Frisch's concept of shared authority is particularly apt, in my view, to describe the collaborative historiographical work done by interviewers and interviewees, or oral historians and narrators, together. It is through this lens that the women of the CRH emerge as witnesses in this chapter.

MUSIDORA ET ALIA: THE WOMEN OF THE CRH

Filmmakers, critics, and historians have sometimes acknowledged that several women—Suzanne Borel, Yvonne Dornès, Germaine Dulac, Lotte Eisner, Marie Epstein, and Mary Meerson—played a significant part in the creation of the CF in 1936 and in its good operations later on. But close to nothing has been said about the many women employed by the CF as secretaries, for example, and about those who actively participated in the CRH from the 1940s until the 1960s. All these women fall into three categories, detailed later: witness interviewers (Musidora, Francis, and Epstein), narrators, and stenographer typists. As far as I know, they (unlike Eisner, whose first book on Weimar cinema, *L'Ecran démoniaque*, was released in France in 1955) never actually wrote anything that would have earned them the title of film historians. Yet at the CRH they made significant contributions to the production of film historical knowledge by arranging, conducting, and archiving numerous interviews with early filmmakers and movie workers (witness interviewers), telling their own stories during interviews (narrators), and taking notes in shorthand and then transcribing interviews (stenographer typists).

I use "witness interviewers" with the intention of emphasizing the double status of Musidora, Epstein, and Francis as oral historians *and* narrators. But the phrase can be misleading if left unexplained. Although these three women were probably chosen to interview early filmmakers because they were themselves insiders of the early French film industry, their own personal recollections barely made it into the interview transcripts of the CRH. By and large, Musidora and Francis are remembered for their screen acting careers, and Epstein for being director Jean Epstein's younger sister and sometime collaborator. Yet feminist historians have shown in recent years that all three of these women also participated in the French film industry and film culture in other ways: Musidora as director, screenwriter, and producer;

Epstein as director and screenwriter; and Francis as film critic. That the interview transcripts of the CRH bear little to no evidence of these women's prolific careers demonstrates the limited reach of the witness interviewer, whose labor was nonetheless pivotal to the CRH.

Because she arranged, conducted, and archived most of the CRH interviews between 1944 and 1952, Musidora was, without a doubt, the most important of all the witness interviewers involved in the CRH. Based on Annette Förster's extensive research into Musidora's life and multifaceted career, Musidora (née Jeanne Roques, 1889–1957) was born to Jacques Roques, a composer for the popular stage and music teacher, and Marie Porchez, a feminist activist and professional painter, who "raised [her] in an artistic, semi-intellectual, leftist and feminist milieu common for Paris in the *Belle Epoque*."[31] After going to art school, Musidora made her stage debut in 1910 and later appeared in numerous popular plays and music hall revues that often showcased her talent as a comic actress and singer. As Förster explains, at least one of these stage shows included an exclusive Pathé film, *La Ville de Madame Tango* (1914), which suggests that Musidora was already featured in at least one film, and possibly more, at the beginning of her stage career.[32] At the same time, Musidora was a skilled caricaturist for *Comoedia* and a somewhat popular writer whose novellas had been published in *Fantasio* since 1913.[33]

However, Musidora's greatest success came after she was hired by the Gaumont film company, where she acted in films mostly directed by Louis Feuillade, between 1914 and 1917. These included patriotic films (some written by Nora Jonuxi), comic shorts, and most famously, two crime serials, *Les Vampires* (1915–16) and *Judex* (1917), which sealed Musidora's star image as a femme fatale for many years to come. After leaving Gaumont, Musidora then appeared in three dramatic films directed and produced by André Hugon and three films based on her friend Colette's work, mainly *Minne* (possibly never made or unfinished), *La Vagabonde* (Eugenio Perego, 1917), and *La Flamme cachée* (Roger Lion [and

Musidora?], 1918), for which Colette wrote an original scenario as a favor to Musidora.[34] Finally, between 1919 and 1924, Musidora acted in, produced, wrote (or adapted), and directed (or co-directed) at least four films under her own production company, Les Films Musidora: *Vicenta* (Musidora, 1919); *Pour Don Carlos* (Musidora and Jacques Lasseyne, 1921), based on the novel by Pierre Benoit; *Soleil et ombre* (Musidora and Lasseyne, 1922), a so-called Spanish film based on Maria Star's novella *L'Espagnole* and shot on location; and *La Terre des taureaux* (Musidora, 1924), also shot on location.[35] After 1924, Musidora acted in only one other film, *La Magique image*, which she herself directed and produced in 1950. When *La Magique image* was released, however, there was apparently no report in the press.[36]

Yet Musidora's character Irma Vep from *Les vampires* left such an indelible mark upon French audiences, filmmakers, critics, and intellectuals that Musidora the actress was never completely forgotten. Förster explains that Irma Vep was kept alive by Musidora herself, when Musidora evoked Irma Vep in her writings or when she performed on the music-hall stage wearing Irma Vep's signature black silk body suit, for example.[37] It is also well documented that Louis Aragon, André Breton, and other French surrealists of the 1920s were fascinated by Irma Vep, whom they often referred to in their novels, poems, and plays.[38] According to Förster, "this detour from cinema in the afterlife of Irma Vep paved the way for film historians such as René Jeanne and Charles Ford and the former Surrealist Georges Sadoul to include Irma Vep in the film historic standard works they published at the end of the 1940s."[39] Furthermore, in the 1930s and 1940s Musidora was frequently mentioned in the press for her stage appearances (e.g., in the comedies she wrote, *L'As des as*, *L'Heure de la mort*, and *La Vie sentimentale de George Sand*) and for her various publications, including her novel *Paroxysmes: De l'amour à la mort* (1935).

Probably because she remained good friends with many personalities from the silent film era (and from contemporary cinema), Musidora

Figure 11. Publicity photograph of Musidora in *La Vagabonde* (Eugenio Perego, 1917), adapted from Colette's 1910 novel. *Source:* © Neurdein/Roger-Viollet.

was designated by Langlois to organize the interviews by the CRH starting around 1944. In a report to the board of the CF in 1948, Musidora received praise for her dedication, which had already allowed the CRH to compile a large number of interview transcripts with early filmmakers.[40] The report read: "Thanks to her, from 1946 to 1947, more than 50 typed transcripts and more than 60 phonographic recordings were established, more than 100 people were invited to enrich our work."[41] Although these figures are impossible to verify given that the CRH collection of the CF is incomplete today, this public acknowledgment of Musidora's hard labor is significant mainly because it is unusual. In secondary sources too, the extent of Musidora's contribution to the CRH is rarely emphasized, even though the CRH collection contains visible material proof of that contribution. Musidora's unmistakable handwriting is, indeed, everywhere on the documents from the CRH collection, on correspondences with early filmmakers, on folding covers, in the margins or between the lines of typed transcripts, and on biographies and filmographies established before and after the interviews. Based on these documents, Musidora was responsible for all practical aspects of the CRH interviews. She wrote many of the letters inviting film pioneers to participate in the CRH interviews, and to which they often replied out of friendship for her.[42] She reached out to stenographer typists, secured locations, and communicated the date, time, and place of meeting to the pioneers. And after the interviews were over, she was apparently charged with collecting, reviewing, and revising transcripts, which she might have sent to Langlois for final approval before filing.

During the CRH interviews, not only did Musidora relay Langlois's queries when his job kept him elsewhere, but she also asked her own questions and volunteered comments and personal memories.[43] Take, for instance, the interview Musidora conducted with the actress Renée Sylvaire in February 1946.[44] In the middle of their conversation, whose transcript is admittedly difficult to read due to its many handwritten

Figure 12. Folding cover for the CRH meeting with Paul Méliès, July 22, 1944. *Source:* CRH16-B1 © DR, Collection La Cinémathèque française.

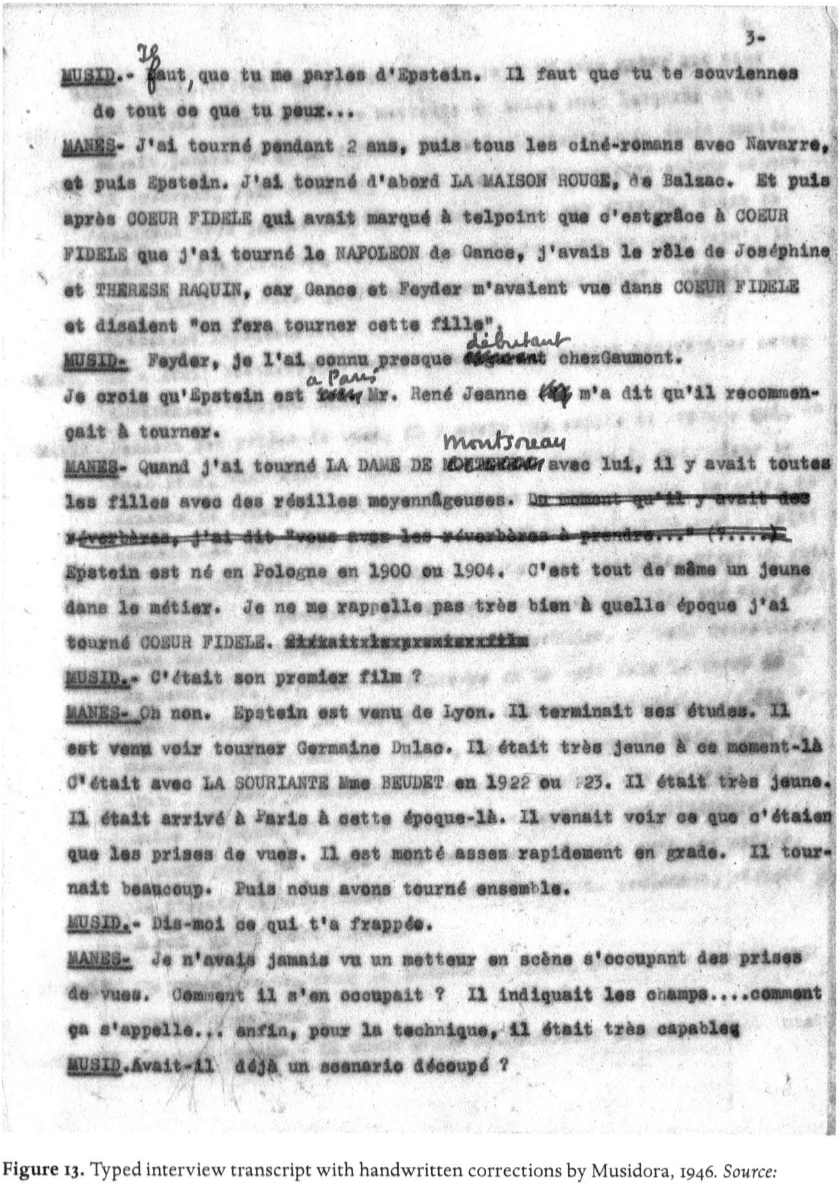

MUSID.- Faut que tu me parles d'Epstein. Il faut que tu te souviennes de tout ce que tu peux...

MANES- J'ai tourné pendant 2 ans, puis tous les ciné-romans avec Navarre, et puis Epstein. J'ai tourné d'abord LA MAISON ROUGE, de Balzac. Et puis après COEUR FIDELE qui avait marqué à telpoint que c'est grâce à COEUR FIDELE que j'ai tourné le NAPOLEON de Gance, j'avais le rôle de Joséphine et THERESE RAQUIN, car Gance et Feyder m'avaient vue dans COEUR FIDELE et disaient "on fera tourner cette fille".

MUSID- Feyder, je l'ai connu presque débutant chez Gaumont. Je crois qu'Epstein est à Paris Mr. René Jeanne m'a dit qu'il recommençait à tourner.

MANES- Quand j'ai tourné LA DAME DE Montsoreau avec lui, il y avait toutes les filles avec des résilles moyennâgeuses. ~~Un moment qu'il y avait des réverbères, j'ai dit "vous avez les réverbères à prendre..." (?...)~~
Epstein est né en Pologne en 1900 ou 1904. C'est tout de même un jeune dans le métier. Je ne me rappelle pas très bien à quelle époque j'ai tourné COEUR FIDELE. ~~xxxxxxxxxxxxxxxxfilm~~

MUSID.- C'était son premier film ?

MANES- Oh non. Epstein est venu de Lyon. Il terminait ses études. Il est venu voir tourner Germaine Dulac. Il était très jeune à ce moment-là C'était avec LA SOURIANTE Mme BEUDET en 1922 ou 23. Il était très jeune. Il était arrivé à Paris à cette époque-là. Il venait voir ce que c'étaien que les prises de vues. Il est monté assez rapidement en grade. Il tournait beaucoup. Puis nous avons tourné ensemble.

MUSID.- Dis-moi ce qui t'a frappée.

MANES- Je n'avais jamais vu un metteur en scène s'occupant des prises de vues. Comment il s'en occupait ? Il indiquait les champs....comment ça s'appelle... enfin, pour la technique, il était très capable

MUSID.Avait-il déjà un scenario découpé ?

Figure 13. Typed interview transcript with handwritten corrections by Musidora, 1946. *Source:* CRH46-B2 © DR, Collection La Cinémathèque française.

corrections, Musidora mentioned that she was a "director" (*réalisatrice*) who wished to make a film that would pass the test of time. When she said, "in 20 years, the images and gestures we would have written should not only survive, but they should also represent an advance [in cinema]," Musidora was expressing her concern with both contemporary sound cinema and the preservation of silent films while suggesting that artistic motives had driven her as a director.[45] The following exchange between Musidora and Sylvaire provides us with further insight into Musidora's filmmaking career:

> MUS[IDORA]: I wanted to learn how to edit my own films, my film *Soleil et ombre*.
> SYLV[AIRE]: Why didn't you direct a film?
> MUS[IDORA]: *I did.* I sacrificed everything I could from the commercial point of view to make a film. . . . When it was accepted by distributors, here's what happened: my *reportedly* very beautiful film was sold along with rubbish films. I made the film, no copyrights. *They said the more copies we printed, the more success I received, and the more money I lost.* On the contrary, I think this is an art.[46]

In a later interview on March 13, 1948, Musidora once again discussed *Soleil et ombre*, this time in the context of a conversation about production methods in the 1910s and 1920s.[47] After the camera operator Stucker explained that his team at Pathé never did any "tests," Musidora and Stucker engaged in the following exchange:

> MME MUSIDORA: I myself shot [a film] in 1922, in Spain, a film [titled] 'Soleil et ombre', and we did some tests. We would watch them on the screen to see if the lighting worked. At that time, we were already looking for artistic effects. Whereas I remember that, at Gaumont, we never did any [artistic effects] and I was saying we should do some.
> M. STUCKER: We didn't even do tests with the actors [at Pathé], the actors had monthly contracts.

MME MUSIDORA: I'm not talking about tests with the actors, but tests for the lighting. I remember having seen, one time, a beautiful Spanish house, exactly what we wanted. We asked the owner if we could paint it, to make it up, *too*.[48]

Musidora's recollection was, unfortunately, cut short by Langlois, who resumed questioning Stucker about the films he had worked on for Pathé.

As Francis Lacassin claims, Musidora met Langlois for the first time when she was a guest of the CRH during the meeting dedicated to Louis Feuillade, on January 29, 1944.[49] The extant record for that meeting consists not of a complete typed transcript but of a one-page handwritten report on Feuillade that gives no indication about Musidora's own career.[50] Musidora was never again an official guest and narrator of the CRH, and ultimately, we learn very little about her own accomplishments from reading the CRH interviews. Yet the two interviews mentioned here might be the reason Förster writes that "Musidora's research at the Cinémathèque française, from which these film historians [Jeanne, Ford, and Sadoul] obtained much information on the silent era, drew their attention to Musidora's career as a film producer and a director in the silent cinema."[51] As evidence of this, Förster cites subsequent publications by Henri Fescourt, Francis Lacassin, and Patrick Cazals, all of which included discussions of Musidora's acting *and* directing career.[52] But while Fescourt, Lacassin, and Cazals referenced the two CRH interviews during which Musidora talked about *Soleil et ombre*, they relied primarily on other sources, including their own memories and their personal correspondence with Musidora, which certainly points to the inadequacy of the CRH interviews when it came to Musidora.

Likewise, the CRH interviews tell us very little about Marie Epstein (née Marie-Antoine Epstein, 1899–1995), officially employed by the CF from 1953 through 1977, and Eve Francis (née Eva François, 1886–1980), whose contributions to the CRH as witness interviewers were less significant than Musidora's but nonetheless were crucial for the recollection of French film history. In *To Desire Differently: Feminism and the French Cinema* (1990), Sandy Flitterman-Lewis gives a fascinating account of Epstein's career as a screenwriter (*L'Affiche*, 1925, and *Six et demionze*, 1927, both directed by Jean Epstein for Les Films Albatros and Les Films Jean Epstein, respectively) and as the co-director of at least eight sound films with Jean Benoit-Lévy.[53] But although Epstein met with two pioneers—director Maurice Tourneur and set designer and producer Francis Jourdain—in 1956, she said nothing about her own films during these interviews.[54] Furthermore, during Musidora's interviews with Jean Epstein, Marie was only mentioned briefly, one time in relation to Benoit-Lévy and another in relation to Jean Epstein himself. In 1946, for example, Musidora asked Jean Epstein if he had made any films with Benoit-Lévy, which prompted the following exchange:

> JEAN EPSTEIN: No, it was a relative of mine, my sister, who collaborated with Benoit-Lévy. She was in charge of the artistic side of things, and he of the administrative side.
> MUS[IDORA]: Is your sister still making films?
> JEAN EPSTEIN: She's like me. During the Occupation we were in hiding. We worked for the French Red Cross. She still works for the French Red Cross. I do, too, actually. I'm at the Service of the Intellectuals of the French Red Cross.[55]

During his second interview with Musidora on March 18, 1950, Jean Epstein likewise omitted or forgot to mention his sister's name, even though he credited her for writing the script of *L'Affiche*. Jean Epstein explained that "after having been fired from CINE ROMANS, I wanted to keep wasting film. My sister had written a script that she offered to ALBATROS, which had accepted it, and even bought it. It was the script for *L'Affiche*. As I went with my sister to discuss copyrights at ALBATROS, [Alexandre] Kamenka said, after all, could you direct this film?"[56]

WITNESSES 89

Unfortunately for Marie, Langlois steered the rest of the conversation away from her screenwriting to Jean Epstein's career and conception of cinema. She only reappeared in the CRH as a witness interviewer in 1956, and her career as a filmmaker was never mentioned again.

Compared to Marie Epstein, who, like Musidora, was never properly interviewed by the CRH, Eve Francis was twice a guest of Musidora before collecting the last testimonies of the CRH from actors Roger Karl, Arlette Marchal, and Emmy Lynn in 1966. On May 7, 1945, and April 5, 1952, Francis was invited to discuss her acting career and her late ex-husband Louis Delluc's involvement in the ciné-club movement of the 1920s.[57] With camera operator Alphonse Gibory, costume designer and director Jacques Manuel, and director Robert Boudrioz in 1945, Francis was asked about Delluc's films, particularly how they were made in a "familial" atmosphere that was nevertheless conducive to innovation. Auriol showed a particular interest in *La Fête espagnole* (1920), directed by Germaine Dulac from a scenario by Delluc, in which Francis (supposedly) wore "the first dress" specially designed for a movie star.[58] Francis offered a few more details about this dress and about the collaboration between Dulac and Delluc, followed by some explanations on Marcel L'Herbier's *El Dorado* (1921) and Dulac's *Ames de fous* (1918), in this order. Like Auriol, Langlois seemed especially curious about the production of these films—their crews of assistants and set designers, their lighting, make-up, and costumes, for example—all with the purpose of finding out more about silent filmmaking ahead of Langlois's exhibition "Comment on fait un film" (How films are made).

Similarly, in 1952, when Francis was invited back to the CRH, the bulk of the conversation between Musidora, Francis, Victor Perrot, Léon Moussinac, and Abel Gance concerned ciné-clubs in the 1920s, in particular those of Delluc and Ricciotto Canudo and the films they screened.[59] Gaffary later remarked that compared to Gance, for example, Francis "couldn't remember a lot of things, last time, she didn't speak for very long."[60] Yet she was still never asked about her own film criticism, which she had often published under the pen name "La Femme de nulle part" (The Woman from Nowhere) since at least 1918.[61] Paula Amad also argues that in addition to having been "the first person to use the term 'avant-garde' in relation to cinema" in 1918, Francis played a major part in the emergence of French cinephilia.[62] In her memoirs, *Les Temps héroïques* (1949), Francis offered, according to Amad, an "intimate chronicle of cinephilia," one that reveals for us today the "ambivalent engendering of one of modernism's allegedly most masculine modes of loving: cinephilia."[63]

Importantly, after her screen acting career declined, Eve Francis was an assistant director on a number of sound films by Marcel L'Herbier, including his 1937 remake of *The Cheat*, and she also presented at several conferences, where she discussed Delluc's films as well as film history more broadly.[64] Although more research must be done about this later time in Francis's life, what we already know suggests that Francis was not only the keeper of Delluc's memory, but also a filmmaker in her own right, none of which was recorded in her CRH interviews. As with Musidora and Epstein, this breach in the CRH collection was also a missed opportunity for women's film history, one that I return to at the end of this chapter.

In addition to witness interviewers, women served as narrators for the CRH. Borrowed from oral history, the term "narrator" suggests that historical truth is constructed, not accessed, and that the job of oral historians is less to fact-check interviews than to understand their context, form, style, tone, intentions, and so on. When it comes to people and communities who have been traditionally marginalized, erased, and silenced throughout history, and then again within the historical master narrative, this historiographical approach is not only valuable but essential to recollection. Although Alice Guy Blaché was, to my knowledge, never invited to participate in the CRH, the many other public interviews she gave in the 1950s and 1960s are good examples of why oral history's understanding of narrators is particularly helpful when it comes to women and silent film. In these interviews, Guy Blaché claimed that she was not only the first woman filmmaker, but also the first filmmaker to have made a fiction film, *La Fée aux choux* (1896), before Méliès. As the next chapter addresses, historians have wrestled with this statement and sometimes even downright rejected it, mainly because little evidence remains that would prove Guy Blaché right or wrong. We are stuck in a game, in other words, in which Guy Blaché said one thing, and historians said another, either of which could be true or false. But considering Guy Blaché as the narrator of her own personal history might be our way out. By admitting that Guy Blaché's testimony is neither true or false, but that it is a narrative she constructed *with* witness interviewers after the fact, we not only change the terms of the conversation; we also revitalize the topic by way of a multiplicity of voices and historical sources once considered inadequate. Importantly, my claim here is not that "alternative facts" should be tolerated, but that the discursive functions of history—who says what and why—must be interrogated in greater depth.

Out of the 150 narrators of the CRH whose interview transcripts I have read, at least 35 are women. These women include both women pioneers and living relatives of deceased (male and female) pioneers whose names rarely appear in full. In the following list, occupations and personal relationships with pioneers are indicated in parentheses, and full names, when available, appear in brackets.

> Marie-Anne Colson-Malleville (director, screenwriter, set designer, movie theater manager, Germaine Dulac's partner)
>
> Mme Monca [Blanche Monca, née Poupart] (Georges Monca's widow)
>
> Mme Liézer [Janine Liézer] (actor)
>
> Renée Carl (actor, director)
>
> Alice Tissot (actor)
>
> Yvette Andréyor (actor)

Josette Andriot's niece [name unknown]

Mme Tourneur [Louise Lagrange] (actor, Maurice Tourneur's wife)

Janine Bouissounouse (critic)[65]

Nicole Védrès (writer, director)

Mme M. Carré (Michel Carré's wife)

Mme Bardinon (somebody's granddaughter)

Mme Méliès [Jehanne d'Alcy, also known as Fanny Manieux] (actor, head of costume atelier, Georges Méliès's widow)

Mme Prince [Gabrielle Debrives] (actor, Charles Prince's widow)

Mrs. X [name unknown] (actor, Charles Prince's colleague)

Melle Escoffier [Lotte Eisner] (critic, historian, archivist)[66]

Mme Champreux [Isabelle Champreux, née Feuillade] (Louis Feuillade's daughter)

Sandra Milowanoff (actor)

Mademoiselle Bora (Lumière factory worker)

Madame Pupier (Lumière factory worker)

Djemil Anik (dancer, actor)

Nora Jonuxi (playwright, screenwriter, critic)[67]

Mme Marken [Jane Marken] (actor)

Gina Manès (actor)

Madame Pathé [Antoinette Pathé, née Poueydebat] (Charles Pathé's wife)

Mme Sylvaire [Renée Sylvaire] (actor)

Gabrielle Robinne (actor)

Jeanne Marie-Laurent (actor)

Mme Meerson [Mary Meerson] (CF administrator, Lazare Meerson's widow)

Mme Bourgeois [Bernadette "Nadette" Bourgeois?] (actor, editor?, Gérard Bourgeois's widow)

Mme Asselin (Georges Asselin's widow)

Melle Suzanne [Suzanne Bon] (script girl)

Jeanne Joly [née Delalonde] (Henri Joly's widow)

Arlette Marchal (actor)

Emmy Lynn (actor)

Not all narrators listed here contributed to the CRH equally. Whereas some of the women present during the CRH interviews came along with their usually older husbands, as was the case for Louise Tourneur, Mme M. Carré, and Antoinette Pathé, others, like Blanche Monca and Bernadette Bourgeois, stood in for their deceased husbands in an effort to guarantee their place in film history. On December 16, 1950, for example, Musidora and Sadoul addressed questions about the late director and screenwriter Gérard Bourgeois to his wife Bernadette, who was able to discuss his early stage career, his start with Jean Durand at the Lux film studios, his subsequent years at Pathé, and his work methods, among other things, as well as identify some of the production photographs brought by Sadoul.[68] However, when Musidora and Sadoul met with Blanche Monca a few days earlier, on December 2, 1950, Blanche could not speak to anything her late husband and director Georges Monca had done before they met in 1915.[69] With other family members, testimonies were likewise hit or miss. Louis Feuillade's daughter, Isabelle Champreux, had been "very little involved in cinema," but she explained that she still "lived in the film world because [her] father entertained a lot," and that she "knew all the artists who worked for him."[70] Yet during the two meetings she attended in 1945 and 1948, she provided very little information, only that her husband Maurice Champreux had finished the feature drama *Le Stigmate* (1925) for Feuillade after he died during filming.

On the other hand, Marie-Anne Colson-Maleville, who attended at least sixteen meetings of the CRH between 1943 and 1952, was incredibly valuable in filling the gaps in the life and career of Germaine Dulac, her longtime collaborator and partner. (Although Colson-Malleville's love relationship with Dulac was never discussed explicitly, it seems to have been clear to everyone that Colson-Malleville was invited by the CRH as Dulac's sole beneficiary.) During the meeting entirely dedicated to Dulac on July 6, 1946, especially, Colson-Malleville discussed how Dulac became interested in making films after her visit to Stacia Napierkowska on a set in Italy; how she herself met Dulac in Paris in the early 1920s; and how she and Dulac collaborated "in the shadows," for Dulac liked to be the only woman in charge.[71] Like some of the other (male and female) narrators of the CRH, Colson-Malleville also divulged personal information about Dulac, including her health issues, her poor relationship with Eve Francis, and the last moments before her death. (In a handwritten note, Musidora complains that the stenographer failed to record this last bit.)

Yet in typical fashion for the CRH, the interview with Colson-Malleville deals only tangentially with her own career as a director, screenwriter, set designer, and theater manager. When Musidora asked Colson-Malleville how she made Dulac's acquaintance, for example, Colson-Malleville answered that she had come to Paris with the intention of making educational films, but that she ended up managing several of the movie theaters owned by Edmond Benoit-Lévy. Eve Francis then recommended that Dulac show her film, *La Mort du soleil* (1922), to Colson-Malleville, who found Dulac "excessively attractive" when they first met. Their collaboration started soon after that, although Musidora seemed far more interested in what Colson-Malleville had to say about Dulac alone. In countless other interviews, including those with Musidora, Epstein, and Francis discussed earlier, readers of the CRH are likely to get the same impression: that women narrators with a film career of their own were invited by the CRH not for their active contributions to the early French film industry, but for their status as witnesses to the achievements of others during those years.

Two exceptions come to mind that might nuance our understanding of the CRH when it comes to its level of interest in women's contributions to film history. In addition to "Madame Pupier," a Lumière factory worker interviewed in early 1946, the other exceptional narrator of the CRH would be the journalist, playwright, and screenwriter Nora Jonuxi, whom Musidora had met at the Gaumont studios early in her screen acting career. Notably, on the folding cover of the interview transcript from 1946, Musidora wrote under Jonuxi's name "first screenwriter" (*premier scénariste de cinéma spécialisé*), which Musidora returned to several times during the interview. "We must emphasize," said Musidora, "that Nora Jonuxi was the first woman who did shooting scripts [*découpages*] because even [Louis] Feuillade didn't have a shooting script. It was in 1914."[72] Then, later in the conversation, Musidora repeated: "But Nora Jonuxi deserves to be recognized as the first author [*auteur*] of that period," showing both her admiration for Jonuxi and her interest in the professionalization of screenwriting during the silent era.[73]

In the example of Nora Jonuxi's interview, one of the key issues for the CRH was to determine when silent filmmakers began to rely on (more or less) detailed scripts by professional screenwriters, as opposed to drafting short synopses and treatments themselves. Jonuxi explains that, before she was hired by Gaumont director Gaston Ravel, for whom she wrote *Le Grand Souffle* around 1915, she had already sold a few scripts to Eclair by way of intermediaries, which Alain Carou tells us was then common practice for young writers without direct access to film studios.[74] Furthermore, when prompted by Musidora, Jonuxi described her writing process as follows: "First I wrote a summary for the director and then the dialogue—because you had to talk even if films were silent. And the screenwriter did everything. So, I wrote the scene and described the movement, the set, the thoughts, the dialogue. And when you had a [truly] silent scene, you had to describe the thoughts. In sum, it was a shooting script [*découpage*]."[75] But even as Jonuxi became a regular screenwriter for Gaumont and later for Pathé, where she wrote several films in the Rigadin series, her name was never mentioned.[76] "At that time," Jonuxi explained to Musidora, "screenwriters were neglected. They didn't exist. . . . We received no credit, really. Our name never appeared anywhere. It's like we didn't exist. Actually, at the beginning, they didn't even include the artists' names."[77]

Not only does Jonuxi's testimony inform us about practices for crediting in the French silent film industry, but it also gets to the crux of why Jonuxi's interview was so valuable for the recollection of her film career as well as the careers of women in film. For one thing, because most primary and secondary sources I consulted describe Jonuxi as a playwright, not a screenwriter, her interview fulfills the mission of the CRH to reconstruct what has been missing from written histories so far. In extant newspapers, for example, I have found only one instance in the early 1920s in which Jonuxi was mentioned in relation to cinema.[78] (On January 23, 1923, *L'Oeuvre* reported that Jonuxi, like Marie Epstein that same year, won a script competition after she had written "several scripts" that had already been filmed.)[79] For another thing, in speaking about the little recognition she received, Jonuxi unknowingly revealed the limits of writing film history based on extant films alone. As Langlois made clear, however, extant films were usually the starting point for the CF's historiographical and archival projects, which might explain why uncredited men and women rarely participated in the CRH. That Musidora had been the driving force behind the interview with Jonuxi was certainly no coincidence.

Like women interviewers and narrators, stenographer typists were key to the CRH. Including stenographer typists (or steno-typists) among the women of the CRH might seem a bit forced at first sight. Compared to witness interviewers and narrators, who, this chapter argues, shared authority in producing film historical knowledge, steno-typists were tasked with taking notes in shorthand and translating these notes into interview transcripts later on. It would be easy, then, to discount the steno-typists' work as being purely practical as well as trivial and unimportant. Yet as the literal writers of an archival collection specifically designed to record a history (almost) never told before, steno-typists were perhaps the most valuable contributors to the CRH. During the very first meeting of the CRH on November 20, 1943, the general secretary Georges Denola asked that a typed transcript be appended to subsequent meeting reports, "in order to save the most complete details regarding the work of the Commission."[80] Indeed, without the transcripts produced by the steno-typists, the work of the CRH would have been sketchy at best and bootless at worst.

Today these typed transcripts are the only extant records of the CRH interviews, as well as valuable documents of the kind of feminized labor performed at and for the CRH and the CF. Indeed, in addition to being women, the steno-typists of the CRH were doing a job that had been considered "woman's work" since the late nineteenth century. Delphine Gardey reminds us that private business offices used to be exclusively male spaces of the likes depicted by Balzac in *Les Employés* (*The Bureaucrats*, 1838) and Herman Melville in *Bartleby* (1889). Then, starting around 1890, these offices began to hire more women in clerical positions, as secretaries and steno-typists especially. (A good example is the typist in D. W. Griffith's *The Lonedale Operator* [1911], whom Tom Gunning hypothesizes might have been played by actress and future screenwriter and director Jeanie Macpherson.)[81] That these women were paid lower wages and considered more servile than men certainly played a role in the so-called feminization of office labor. As Gardey also explains, the first typewriter manufactured by Remington in the United States was imported to France in 1883, a few years after the job of steno-typist had already become closely associated with American female office workers. Gardey writes that "the technical characteristics of this object [the typewriter], its look resembling that of the sewing machine, and then its keyboard associated with that of the piano are constructed as 'feminine.'"[82] These associations between stenography and domestic activities like sewing and playing the piano meant two things: not only were young women considered "natural" fits for stenography, but stenography also came to be regarded as an appropriate position for young women living in large American cities. Yet in France it was not until the turn of the twentieth century that companies started to give this job to educated young women almost exclusively. Then, during and after World War I, many women with a more modest background were frequently employed as steno-typists, pushing forward this trend of feminization in France.

To use a well-known example, we might turn to the first woman filmmaker, Alice Guy Blaché, who wrote in her memoirs that she learned typing and stenography as a way to support her family after her father's death in the late 1880s or early 1890s.[83] This was, in Guy Blaché's words, "a science quite new in those days. The course director was an excellent legal stenographer for the Chamber of Deputies, where he sometimes led me, as well as at the Sorbonne. Having remarked on my rather rapid progress, he decided to give me private lessons. Very soon he judged me ready to take a secretarial post in a little factory in the Marais neighborhood of Paris."[84] Guy Blaché described the very masculine environment of that "little factory," where she sat at a desk in the "great room" with the foreman and several accountants.[85] "I stayed alone among a dozen men," Guy Blaché recalled, before telling the story of a male employee harassing her at their workplace. As Gardey helps us understand, this was, in fact, a fairly typical path for an educated bourgeois young woman whose family had fallen on hard times.[86]

What was unique to Guy Blaché, however, was her relatively quick ascension from secretary to the higher ranks—director and head of film production—at the Gaumont studios between 1895 and 1907. To be sure, secretary was a position of trust, which explains why it was generally assigned to men at the time. But as the Gaumont studios developed its film production, creative roles like director certainly offered more power. Erin Hill suggests in *Never Done* that, in the "informal work system" of "early film production (1890–1909)," "a few women infiltrated such male-dominated fields as cinematography, location scouting, publicity, and even studio management. Many others who emerged as figures of creative or managerial importance in the early film industry similarly ascended from the lower ranks of film companies to roles as writers, directors, producers, and production company owners."[87] Hill cites, for example, Jeanie Macpherson, who was Cecil B. DeMille's stenographer before becoming his screenwriting collaborator, and Dorothy Arzner, who started her film career as a typist for DeMille's brother, William, himself a screenwriter and director.[88] Although Hill mentions Guy Blaché at Gaumont, opportunities for female clerks might have been more limited in early French cinema than they were in Hollywood later on.[89] Based on extant information, Guy Blaché was likely the only secretary to become a filmmaker in France in those years.

In any case, the main skills of a secretary—stenography and typing—remained "woman's work" well into the second half of the twentieth century, in both France and the United States. When it comes to the CRH, foregrounding stenography and typing as feminized labor helps contextualize some of the women's involvement in the CRH from the 1940s to the 1960s. It also raises questions about, for example, the steno-typists' social identities, their wages, and their relationship to the witness interviewers and narrators of the CRH. Although I have found no information regarding these women outside the CRH collection, a few traces remain in that collection that give us some indications about some of these steno-typists and their work: on the transcript for the meeting with Michel Carré, which took place on February 12, 1945, at Carré's home in the 17th arrondissement in Paris, the steno-typist's name—"Melle Roussel"—appears typewritten on the last page.[90] On the transcript for the meeting with Georges Méliès's widow, "Mme Méliès" or Jehanne d'Alcy, on February 17, 1945, a stamp appears at the bottom of the first page, indicating that the steno-typist was Anne Leyraud.[91] Another stamp with the name "F. Rupalley" is visible on the transcript for the meeting of April 26, 1952, about the first French ciné-clubs.[92] On September 16, 1956, the stenographer present at Marie Epstein's visit to Maurice Tourneur was "Mme Anglade," whom Epstein had first contacted on the phone.[93] Epstein had also sent a brief letter to Anglade confirming that she was expecting her on September 16 at Tourneur's apartment in the 16th arrondissement. These examples are evidence that the steno-typists were (probably) all women, that the person organizing the interview was also in charge of hiring a steno-typist and of arranging that she come at the right time and place, and that each steno-typist worked for herself and provided her services to the CRH only once or occasionally. (Most steno-typists were probably not full-time employees of the CF, in other words.) It is possible too that the CRH placed advertisements in Harlé's film magazine *La Cinématographie française*, which often published notices from film companies seeking steno-typists and from steno-typists seeking work in the film industry. Although these ads would suggest that steno-typists with professional experience in the film industry considered that they specialized in that field, not enough information exists to determine whether this was the case for the steno-typists of the CRH. On the contrary, the misspellings contained in the interview transcripts could be proof that these steno-typists knew very little about film, let alone film history.

Elsewhere in the CRH collection, other examples hint at some of the difficulties encountered with narrators concerned with their image and legacy, as well as the steno-typist's uneasy position as an intermediary between witness interviewers and narrators and their future readership. During the meeting with actress Gina Manès in 1946, for example, Manès addressed the stenographer directly, asking her not to write down her crude words.[94] Musidora, on the other hand, wanted these words to be transcribed so as to capture the tone of the conversation. ("Oh yes, that will be very nice, very amusing, very lively.") Indeed,

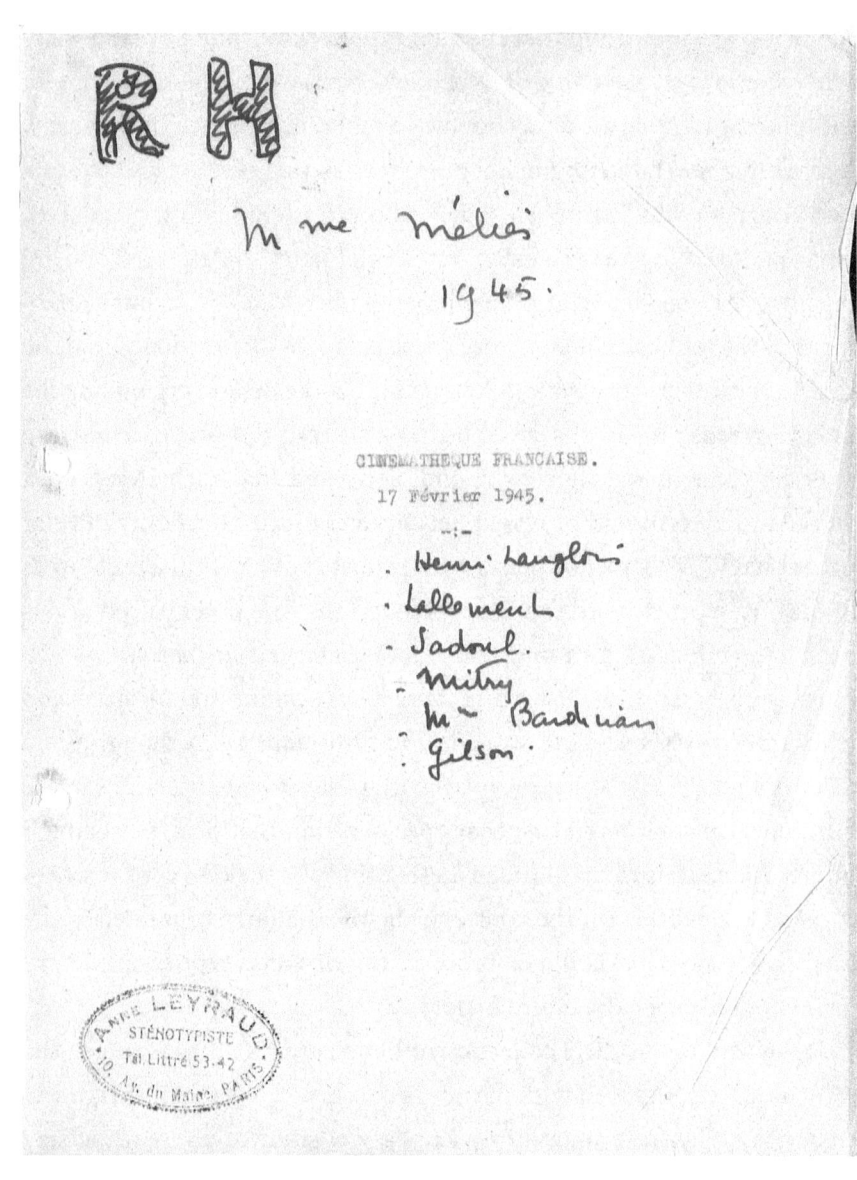

Figure 14. Cover sheet for the interview with Mme Méliès (Jehanne d'Alcy), with Anne Leyraud's stamp at the bottom left, February 17, 1945. *Source:* CRH20-B1 © DR, Collection La Cinémathèque française.

one of the reports from the CRH to the CF indicated that the interviews should transcribe "the speech, tone, and character of each [participant], so as to reveal not only documents but also the very faces of the pioneers, whose contradictory testimonies make them all the livelier."[95] On the transcript from July 6, 1946, Musidora also added a handwritten note that expressed her disappointment in the stenographer, who "didn't think she had to write down what Mme Malleville said about the last moments before Germaine Dulac's death."[96] That same year, Musidora further noted that a stenographer had made a mistake in identifying the speakers.[97] Musidora later wrote that the transcript for the meeting of November 24, 1951, was "poorly typed, filled with mistakes."[98] Another time, during Musidora's meeting with Jean Epstein, Epstein asked the stenographer not to record what he was saying about Langlois, whom he accused of not always keeping his promises.[99] (The stenographer seems to have done so anyway.)

By and large, however, steno-typists are rarely mentioned in the CRH collection, which certainly suggests that their contributions were thought of as accessory to the task at hand. Yet these women's labor, especially their typing skills, were crucial to the CRH as a historiographical project designed to record the testimonies of early filmmakers. Simply put, steno-typists were not only doing the *actual* (mechanical) writing in the CRH's writing of film history; they also shaped the interviews of the CRH by being in the room with the witness interviewers and narrators, (supposedly) recording every word they said for posterity.

CONCLUSION: THE CRH AS WOMEN'S FILM HISTORY

As witnesses, and sometimes as filmmakers and movie workers in their own right, women played an important yet unrecognized part in the CRH from the 1940s through the 1960s. Their collective and collaborative labor also made possible the production of film historical knowledge on a global scale and for many years. Although the CRH remained somewhat unfinished, its impact has been significant, at the CF and beyond. To begin with, the CRH formed the basis for Langlois's exhibits and the Musée du Cinéma at the CF, and arguably, for many of the CF's subsequent exhibits to this day. The overall mission of the CRH to not only collect archival materials but also foster collaboration between film archives and historians also quickly found global resonance in the FIAF's activities, for example, the Bureau of Historical Research into the Cinema (known as the BIRHC; Bureau International de la Recherche Historique Cinématographique; 1952–1960), cofounded by Langlois and Sadoul, and directly inspired by the CRH; and several FIAF Symposia, including the one titled "Cinema: 1900–1906," which initiated New Film History in Brighton in 1978. Since the late 1960s, when the CRH apparently stopped, its interviews have also become well-known among especially French film historians. Bernard Bastide explains that the CRH interviews have been used "sparingly" by the first French film historians, including Sadoul (himself involved in the CRH), Francis Lacassin, and Jacques Richard.[100] With the caveat that the CRH interviews are often unreliable and incomplete, Bastide argues that they still contain valuable information for anyone interested in French cinema's economic, technological, and cultural history.

Importantly, the women of the CRH also bring to the fore today how French film archives like the CF contributed to erasing, or at the very least marginalizing, women's film history in a complicated and often paradoxical manner. Built upon women's work, the CRH was nevertheless imbued with patriarchal impulses, from everyday misogyny to male-centered cinephilia. Yet these impulses function in complex ways. On the one hand, the CRH was less interested in uncredited and anonymous workers, which women often were, than in mostly male directors, screenwriters, and set designers, whose names were still somewhat recognizable among historians and cinephiles. Some women were even the targets of misogyny, such as when Berthe Dagmar and Valentine

Perret were mocked for their strong characters, and when "Mme Corbeau," the head of Pathé's studios in the 1920s, was described as a former prostitute with no knowledge of film production.[101]

On the other hand, important information about women's contributions to cinema may still be gleaned from the CRH interviews, especially regarding the jobs these women occupied and the lack of recognition they received. In addition to the witnesses of the CRH, there were at least thirty-six women film pioneers mentioned but not present during the CRH interviews. While some of these women—Josette Andriot, Berthe Dagmar, Sarah Duhamel, Alice Guy Blaché, Julienne Mathieu, Sonika Bo, Germaine Dulac, Irène Hillel-Erlanger, Catherine Hessling, Marie-Louise Iribe, and Stacia Napierkowska—are fairly to very well-known among film historians, others, like "Mme Corbeau" (Pathé worker), "Mme Lafond" (movie theater director), "Mme Burel" (editor), and "Mme Pupier" (Lumière worker), remain "unhistoricized," meaning that little to no historical work has been written about their involvement in the cinema.[102]

But while the CRH constitutes a missed opportunity for women's film history, whereby early women filmmakers and movie workers could have been given far more attention, it also attests to the powerful feminist possibilities of women's engagement in, with, and against the film archive. Brief moments initiated by Musidora indeed stand out that put pressure on the patriarchal impulses of the CRH and of French film archives more broadly. Musidora not only expressed her interest in women's contributions to film history, as well as her desire for these women to be recognized as workers, artists, writers, authors, and directors; she also began to do the work necessary for the recovery of French women filmmakers and movie workers. For example, during Musidora's visit to the Lumière factories in Lyons, where she discovered the existence of a worker named "Mme Pupier," Musidora said something seemingly innocent but in fact quite radical in the context of (French) film history. "What's amusing," according to Musidora, "is that we might say she [Mme Pupier] was both a worker and an artist," which certainly attests to Musidora's awareness of Pupier's contributions to cinema.[103] During her meeting with Nora Jonuxi in 1946, Musidora also described her as the "first film writer," "the first woman to do her own *découpages*," and one of "the first [film] authors [*auteurs*] from that time," thereby advocating for Jonuxi to be recognized as such.[104] Finally, on July 6, 1946, Musidora told Marie-Anne Colson-Malleville that she would love to organize a gala dedicated to Germaine Dulac, to which Colson-Malleville answered, "Langlois never did anything for her."[105] Although Colson-Malleville's statement might be exaggerated, it reads to me as a powerful challenge to the masculinist biases of French cinephilia that Musidora, through her work at the CRH, also began to test.

TROISIEME ENTR'ACTE

RECOVERY

IN ADDITION TO "collection" and "recollection," the main historiographical practice that Lotte Eisner engaged in was "recovery," specifically understood as the production of a counter-narrative through new archival findings. Because German expressionist films like *The Cabinet of Dr. Caligari* (Robert Wiene, 1920), *Destiny* (Fritz Lang, 1921), and *Nosferatu* (F. W. Murnau, 1922), have become canonical in Western cinema, it is somewhat difficult for us to consider Eisner's work as truly novel. Yet these films, if already widely known in France by the 1950s, remained understudied and even misunderstood among film historians, critics, and general audiences. With her work for the CF and her writings, Eisner did more than just add to cinema's history; she corrected false impressions with evidence and passion, both of which inform recovery as film historiographical practice.

One common false impression was about *Caligari*, which the French long considered the first and most important

German expressionist film. Retrospectively, it is clear that the film's initial screening, organized as a private event by Louis Delluc in Paris on November 14, 1921, represented a major event with enduring impact on French film historiography. Not only did the film offer a new artistic approach to mise-en-scène, but it was also the first official release from Germany in France since the beginning of World War I. Its critical success allowed for many more German films, including Lang's *Destiny* and Murnau's *Nosferatu*, to receive French distribution afterward. As such, *Caligari* transformed how various audiences so far perceived pre- and early Weimar cinema as mostly propaganda. It also came to dominate most critical and historical discourses about Weimar cinema in France from the 1920s through the 1950s.[1]

Yet in her published work, Eisner made it clear that perceptions had been mostly skewed against Germany's cinema, and that Germany's cinema deserved renewed archival and critical attention. The cornerstone of Eisner's counter-narrative was, in fact, *Caligari*, precisely because of its significance for contemporary French film historians and critics. For example, *The Haunted Screen*, initially published as *L'Ecran démoniaque* in France in 1952, begins its second chapter with a brief and somewhat negative description of *Caligari*, which Eisner found lacking in stylistic unity.[2] (She likely had access to the print of *Caligari* from the CF that Langlois had shown at the inaugural screening of his ciné-club in Paris on March 23, 1937.) At the beginning of chapter three on the "influence of Max Reinhardt," Eisner also wrote that "this film [*Caligari*], contrary to what many people seem to think, was hardly the first film of value to be made in Germany."[3] Without missing a beat, she then moved on to talk about *The Student of Prague* (Stellan Rye, 1913), *The House Without a Door* (Stellan Rye, 1914), *Homunculus* (Otto Rippert, 1916), and *The Pied Piper of Hamelin* (Paul Wegener, 1918), as precursors of the "chiaroscuro effects, so often thought Expressionist."[4] But the rest of the book remains filled with references to *Caligari*, which then functions as a (low) standard for other (better) German expressionist films like *Destiny* and *Nosferatu*. For Eisner, *Caligari* was not a masterpiece, as the French thought, but the mediocre product of a "second-rate" director and a poor example of Weimar cinema.[5]

The stakes of Eisner's recovery work might seem unimportant outside film history. Yet they were urgent for Eisner after World War II and the fall of Nazi Germany. As a Jewish émigré from Berlin whose mother had been killed in the Theresienstadt ghetto of German-occupied Czechoslovakia, Eisner had a complicated relationship with her native country. Although she never returned to live in Germany, she kept at least some ties by taking several work trips, maintaining friendships with older friends, forging new friendships with young emerging filmmakers like Werner Herzog and Wim Wenders, and preserving Weimar cinema in France. In her case, and in the case of many other women involved in the production of film historical knowledge, recovery was all the more serious that it was painfully personal.

3

ACTIVISTS

ONE DAY IN 1973 OR 1974, a young American named Dana Sardet visited the CF with the intention of researching women's film history.[1] She had moved to Paris from the United States with her French husband some months before and was a member of the newly formed feminist film collective "Musidora" (1973–77), whose name paid homage to the actress, director, screenwriter, and film critic Jeanne Roques, also known as Musidora.[2] By the time Sardet went to the CF, other film archives such as the Cinémathèque de Toulouse (1964–) and the Archives françaises du film (1969–) had developed that effectively decentralized film preservation in France. Yet the CF remained well-established (if quite controversial because of Langlois's chaotic style of governance) and a natural first stop for anyone interested in the cinema's historical past. Thanks to Mary Meerson, who assisted her, Sardet consulted card catalogs and other materials that gave her just enough information to compile a list of mostly French names and some short and feature films directed by women since the 1890s. She and the other members of "Musidora" already knew about Alice Guy Blaché from Francis Lacassin's book *Pour une contre-histoire du cinéma* (1972). But they came to realize—through their perusal of the CF's collections—that many more women, now forgotten and difficult to research, had been making films in France for several decades.[3]

As Sardet's trip to the CF begins to suggest, and as this chapter further demonstrates, the "Musidora" collective became key to the development of women's film history in France in the 1970s. Founded by a group of white (mostly French) women-identified intellectuals and film professionals—Nicole-Lise Bernheim, Claire Clouzot, Françoise Flamant, Dana Sardet, Claudine Serre, and Danie Dubos—in Paris in October 1973, the "Musidora" collective was a product of the women's liberation movement, whose major fighting points in France included not only equality in the workplace and at home, free and accessible abortion, and the end of violence against women, but also better representation, both onscreen and behind the scenes, in popular culture, film, and media.[4] In a similar spirit, "Musidora" aimed to give women greater access to production equipment and to organize workshops at which women could discuss their ongoing projects and the work of other women film- and videomakers. "Musidora" also quickly emerged as a major force whose activities were precursors to women's film history in France. Whereas Charles Ford, Françoise Audé, Emile Breton, and Paule Lejeune had already written about French women directors from past eras, Geneviève Sellier maintains that, until the 1990s, the French tradition of cinephilia, which emphasized auteurism and aesthetic formalism, still represented an obstacle to the study of women both in front of and behind the camera. At a time when few historians ever traveled to French film archives with the intention of researching women's film history, Sardet's trip to the CF stood out as a significant step forward, which this chapter revisits.

To my knowledge, most archival materials related to the "Musidora" collective remain privately owned and fairly difficult to access. This chapter relies instead on "Musidora"'s published writings, as well as Bernheim's short film, *Qui est Alice Guy?* (1976), all of which lay bare a deep engagement with the film archive as instrument of both patriarchal power and feminist empowerment. On the one hand, the "Musidora" collective often questioned the biases of French film archives against women, primarily Guy Blaché, who they thought had been largely forgotten as a result of historians and archivists' general indifference toward her. On the other hand, the "Musidora" collective made publicly available extant films and other archival documents at the women's film festival they organized in Paris in April 1974 and through the publication of Guy Blaché's memoirs between 1974 and 1976. My interest lies in particular in how the members of the "Musidora" collective, who often represented Guy Blaché *in their image*, as a strong independent woman struggling to be recognized as a filmmaker in France, used the film archive to transform Guy Blaché into a feminist figure of (French) film history. To be clear, I do not consider whether Guy Blaché *was* a feminist during her lifetime, but rather how Guy Blaché *was constructed as* a feminist figure retrospectively and, most importantly, speculatively. Speculation here designates, in Allyson Nadia Field's words, "not only a response to archival absences but a generative method for creative engagements" within film historiography.[5] As feminist film activists, the "Musidora" collective indeed contributed to the emergence of women's film history outside the narrow confines of academia and other established film cultures (the CF, the *Cahiers du cinéma*, etc.), but they also demonstrated the feminist creative possibilities of the archive when it comes to women's film history.

"I WANT TO BE A DIRECTOR!":
THE "MUSIDORA" COLLECTIVE IN CONTEXT

During an interview with the *Revue des deux mondes* published on February 15, 1961, Jacqueline Audry explained that becoming a director had been incredibly difficult.[6] "In my candor," she recollected, "I didn't think that this was a job reserved for men only and jealously guarded. I hit that great wall only when I heard people on a set where I was production secretary laughing at my saying 'I want to be a director!' All the men around me laughed loudly, endlessly, mockingly, and I'm still mortified to this day."[7] Audry, who later worked as a script girl and the assistant director to Max Ophüls (*Le Roman de Werther* [*The Novel of Werther*], 1938), G. W. Pabst (*L'Esclave blanche* [*Pasha's Wives*], 1939; *Jeunes filles en détresse* [*Young Girls in Trouble*], 1939), and others for ten years, finally directed her first short film, *Les Chevaux du Vercors* in 1943, and then her first feature film, *Les Malheurs de Sophie* in 1946. But finding a producer who would invest in her next films remained a challenge throughout her career, even though some of those films were considered commercial successes in France. When asked about the Nouvelle Vague (New Wave), Audry also expressed her disappointment with the roles offered to actresses in their films—"it's a little bit like 'be pretty and shut up'"—and the lack of women directors among them.[8] As she said with great humor, "Even in their films, girls have no character: they must think it's safer [that way]!"[9]

By the early 1970s, Audry had all but disappeared from the French film industry, partly as a result of the growing success of the male filmmakers of the Nouvelle Vague in France.[10] Yet she found a resounding echo in the French feminist film collective "Musidora," whose members expressed similar ideas about the representation of women on screen and women's access to the French film industry.[11] From the beginning, these French feminists of "Musidora"—like their counterparts in Great

Britain and the United States—had a complex relationship with cinema, which they wished to appropriate and revolutionize at the same time. They also held somewhat contradictory positions regarding the "absence" of women in cinema, where women were both generally excluded and crucially important. This was perhaps best exemplified by the women's film festival organized by "Musidora" in April 1974, which also prompted the publication of a special dossier titled "Les femmes et le cinéma" (Women and cinema) and edited by "Musidora" for the *Revue du cinéma: Image et son* around the same time.[12] In that publication, members of "Musidora" did not merely repeat some of Audry's complaints; they also produced new feminist film discourses outside established film cultures, whose misogynistic practices they openly and repeatedly criticized throughout the 1970s.

Like many French women at the time, the feminist cinephiles and filmmakers grouped together to form "Musidora" were either directly involved with or closely following the women's liberation movement, which believed that women's labor and accomplishments, their struggles and experiences, should more often be socially acknowledged. Christine Delphy tells us that in France, at least three groups of feminist women (and sometimes men) assembled to discuss discrimination against women as early as 1967 and 1968, right before and around the same time as the events of May 1968 unfolded.[13] But the women's liberation movement was truly born when nine women (including Delphy) from the Mouvement de Libération des Femmes (MLF; Women's Liberation Movement) laid flowers on the tomb of the Unknown Soldier under the Arc de Triomphe in Paris on August 26, 1970.[14] That very same day, across the United States, the Women's Strike for Equality spearheaded by Betty Friedan and sponsored by the National Organization for Women (NOW) rallied thousands of women who celebrated the fiftieth anniversary of the Nineteenth Amendment while demanding "free abortion on demand," "equal opportunities in jobs and education," and "free 24-hour childcare centers."[15] In solidarity with their American sisters, the nine women at the Arc de Triomphe flaunted banners with a similar message about "woman power" and liberation. On one of these banners, the slogan "Il y a plus inconnu que le soldat inconnu: sa femme" ("There's someone who's more unknown than the unknown soldier: his wife") made it clear not only that these flowers were intended for the soldier's wife, but that women's visibility and recognition were also central concerns of the women's liberation movement from the very beginning.[16] As testimonies from women who participated in the movement in France suggest, the movement changed women's private and professional lives by enabling them to express themselves, giving them a voice in the public sphere, and pushing women's rights—especially free and accessible abortion and contraception—to the forefront of public debate.

For reasons having to do with their mass appeal and cultural status within French and global Western culture, visual media, particularly films and videos, were often utilized as educational tools, "agitprop," and conversation starters during the meetings of the women's movement.[17] As Françoise Picq explains, for example, the Mouvement pour la liberté de l'avortement et de la contraception (MLAC; Movement for Free Abortion and Contraception), whose membership often overlapped with the MLF, organized clandestine screenings of Charles Belmont and Marielle Issartel's documentary *Histoires d'A* (1973), which showed an illegal abortion being performed in France following the method introduced by the American psychologist and abortion activist Harvey Karman.[18] New video works by women and about women's experiences with rape, sexual harassment, domestic violence, and workplace discrimination, among others, were also shown regularly at feminist group meetings in France. Indeed, according to Hélène Fleckinger, video gave women the opportunity to participate in the emerging "militant cinema" that had largely excluded them so far.[19] Similar to "early cinema" (*cinéma des premiers temps*), in which the lack of a standardized system and strict hierarchy meant that women had relatively better access to filmmaking, "early video" (*vidéo des premiers temps*), in

Fleckinger's terms, made it easier for women and feminists in particular to claim this new medium as their own. Fleckinger writes that, in France in the late 1960s and early 1970s, "feminist militants who [took] over video advocate[d] for a political approach that relie[d] on self-representation, thus responding to the principle of self-emancipation advocated for by the MLF."[20]

At the same time, commercial cinema, which in Europe included art cinema, came under strict scrutiny for its representation of women and girls on screen, for women's limited access to certain jobs, and for women's lack of support and recognition in film industries around the world.[21] In an interview published in the *Saturday Review* of August 2, 1972, for example, French filmmaker Agnès Varda complained that "the image of women is crucial, and in the media of movies that image is always switching between the nun and the whore, the mama and the bitch."[22] Likewise, in 1973 US film critic Molly Haskell published *From Reverence to Rape: The Treatment of Women in the Movies*, in which she offered one of the first extensive feminist critiques of Hollywood representation based on such new evaluation criteria as gender roles and screen time. Specifically, Haskell lamented how Hollywood cinema portrayed women as either sexual objects—"whores"—"incapable of an intelligent thought or a lapse of sexual appetite," or wives and mothers—"virgins"—"equally incapable of a base instinct or the hint of sexual appetite."[23] This was not to say, however, that such actresses as Marilyn Monroe and Elizabeth Taylor, or Audrey Hepburn and Grace Kelly, held no significant power in Hollywood, or that their performances deserved no praise whatsoever. Haskell argued instead that Hollywood movies were generally shaped by a male director's point of view, because "directing—giving orders, mastering not only people but machinery—is a typically masculine, even militaristic, activity."[24]

To a certain extent, directing had been considered men's work in the United States and many other national film industries since the silent era. Brigitte Rollet also explains that, in France for example, the film industry had long been divided along strict gender lines, with creative and technical jobs generally reserved for men, and costumes, make-up, and script supervision generally considered more suitable jobs for women.[25] Haskell suggested that auteurism reinforced the idea that directing was synonymous with creative power, authority, and masculinity. Auteurism, which was popularized from the *Cahiers du cinéma* and the Nouvelle Vague by Andrew Sarris of *The Village Voice* in the early 1960s, posited that "the director [was] the ultimate authority and the sole arbiter of a film's meaning . . . [and] that the director should have a strong personality and that he should be able to project his convictions."[26] As Sarris's book *The American Cinema* (1968) later demonstrated, auteurism provided mostly male critics with the opportunity to "reappraise" many famous male directors (Howard Hawks, Josef von Sternberg, Orson Welles, etc.) whose Hollywood films had sometimes been undervalued as factory products with very little personality and style. By comparison, Ida Lupino and many other women filmmakers, like "Jacqueline Audrey [sic], Shirley Clarke, Mrs. Sidney Drew [née Lucille McVey], Lillian Ducey, Julia Crawford Ivers, Joan Littlewood, Frances Marion, Vera McCord, Frances Nordstrom, Mrs. Wallace Reid [née Dorothy Davenport], Lois Weber and Margery Wilson," were categorized as "oddities" that belonged to what Sarris famously called the "ladies' auxiliary."[27] As the feminists of the women's movement were quick to point out, "the auteur theory . . . ha[d] evolved into a male and masculine theory on all levels," which had disastrous consequences for generations of women filmmakers.[28] Whereas the contributions of so-called women film pioneers were seldom acknowledged, women directors' chances of success within the film industry after the Second World War paled in comparison with those of male directors, whom (mostly male) critics were more inclined to celebrate as *auteurs* regardless of—and sometimes because of—the chauvinistic tendencies of both the stories and the aesthetic in their films.

Still, "women's cinema," as films directed by women came to be known in the 1970s, seemed to be the solution to cinema's misogyny problem. Like the first women's film festivals that took place in the United States, Canada, and Great Britain at the time, the women's film festival organized by "Musidora" in Paris from April 3 to 11, 1974, meant to address the issues outlined here by showing works by women film- and videomakers that had been forgotten, ignored, or dismissed before, or that had received limited releases.[29] Françoise Flamant stated that, with the Musidora Festival,

> We ["Musidora"] want to break the silence around women's films, bring women filmmakers out of their isolation, [and] show women that cinema is within their reach, for more and more women are now making films. We want to pay homage to the [women] pioneers [*pionnières*], to the women who carried on in an exclusively male environment (like Jacqueline Audry), to the women who succeed in expressing themselves today.[30]

Amid a total of about 150 titles, the Musidora Festival's program included the recent works of professional women filmmakers like Chantal Akerman, Jacqueline Audry, Liliana Cavani, Vera Chytilová, Shirley Clarke, Marguerite Duras, Nelly Kaplan, Liliane de Kermadec, Agnès Varda, Lina Wertmüller, and Mai Zetterling; experimental, political, and documentary films and videos by Joyce Chopra, Claudia Weill, Joyce Wieland, Carole Roussopoulos, and many others; and older films by such so-called women pioneers as Alice Guy Blaché, Musidora, Germaine Dulac, and Lotte Reiniger, most of which had been featured in other women's film festivals abroad. As Marie-Jo Bonnet explains, Clouzot and Bernheim of the "Musidora" collective had enlisted the help of Mary Meerson at the CF, where, Bonnet claims, Meerson kept copies of films directed and produced by Musidora, Dulac, and Guy Blaché.[31] Moreover, in the spirit of the French women's liberation movement and the international women's movement, several screenings were followed by discussions in which any audience member could express their opinions on the films, while workshops and public debates were scheduled throughout the festival so that women could reflect on gender representation and "oppression" in international film industries.[32]

Major differences set apart the Musidora Festival from better-known women's film festivals in the United States, Canada, and Great Britain, where these festivals functioned as a catalyst for various feminist debates that transformed the critical study of film and media. The New York Festival of Women's Films (June 13–21, 1972), the Women's Event at the Edinburgh International Film Festival (August 21–6, 1972), and Toronto Women & Film (June 8–17, 1973), to name a few, were not only cohesive events for feminists, but also brought about new ideas about gender and sexual difference and cinema's politics and ideology that became the basis for feminist film criticism and theory.[33] According to B. Ruby Rich, two different approaches emerged as a result: the American "sociological" approach, which focused on "legitimizing women's own reactions and making women's contributions visible," and the British "theoretical" approach exemplified by Claire Johnston and Laura Mulvey.[34] Antoine Damiens reminds us that in Great Britain the early writings of Johnston and Mulvey were directly connected to the Women's Event that they curated with Lynda Myles at the Edinburgh Film Festival (EFF) of 1972.[35] According to Damiens, "*Notes on Women's Cinema* [edited by Johnston] capitalized on debates held at the Women's Event, with its structure—combining interviews, articles, and interviews with directors—reflecting Johnston's position as curator for the EFF."[36] Likewise, Mulvey's "Visual Pleasure and Narrative Cinema," which first appeared in *Screen* in 1975, was as much political and practical as theoretical in its critique of cinematic pleasure. Damiens, following Mandy Merck, argues that "Visual Pleasure" was a feminist "manifesto" for a new form of radical filmmaking, one that veered away from the kind of voyeurism and scopophilia, identification and narcissism, and verisimilitude that would traditionally

Figure 15. Poster for the Festival international de films de femmes (International Festival of Women's Films) organized by the "Musidora" collective, April 3–11, 1974, in Paris, with drawing by Claire Bretécher. *Source:* © Claire Bretécher, Collection Les Amis de Musidora.

construct women as sexual objects on screen.[37] Yet the British approach remained much more "theoretical" than the American approach, mainly because "this [British] approach has tried to come to terms with how films mean—and to move beyond regarding the image to analyzing the structure, codes, the general subtext of the works."[38]

But although feminist film theory in Great Britain and the United States was informed by various French theorists in the fields of structuralism, semiotics, linguistics, and psychoanalysis (Luce Irigay, Julia Kristeva, and Jacques Lacan, among others), feminist film theory and criticism were nonexistent in France at the time. Writing for *Screen* in 1987, almost two decades after the inauguration of the women's liberation movement, Ginette Vincendeau advances the idea that "the connection between theoretical debates about gender and feminism and women's filmmaking in France is at best oblique and at worst conflictual, as there is virtually no indigenous feminist film theory or theorizing of gender and sexual difference in relation to the cinema, and precious little awareness of these issues in French film criticism."[39] Indeed, "for French film academics—men or women—feminism and sexual difference are, precisely, not theoretical," but ideological and sociological, which explains why these concepts were mostly absent from theoretical discussions about, for example, spectatorship and voyeurism.[40] According to Vincendeau, other reasons for this "elision" from French film theory include the institutional sexism that forced "women intellectuals on the whole . . . to emulate male models to get recognition" and thus to reject gender and sexual difference as theoretical concepts, as well as the institutional gap that separated academics and mostly male film critics from the new generation of women and feminists interested in women's films.[41] Vincendeau refers more specifically to the women's film festivals organized first by "Musidora" in Paris in 1974 and then by others in Sceaux and Créteil after 1979, which, unlike their international counterparts, had very little influence on film theory and criticism.

Press coverage for the Musidora Festival wasn't apparently very extensive in France, which might indicate that very few journalists and film critics were interested in promoting the event. For example, Colette Godard, a drama critic for *Le Monde*, wrote a short review in which she said nothing about the screenings and focused instead on the limits of the festival's debates among "privileged women."[42] In the United States, however, the Musidora Festival was apparently better received, probably because of the wider reach of the American women's liberation movement. Barbara Halpern Martineau (aka Sara Halprin), who attended the Musidora Festival and reported back to the American magazine *Women and Film*, explained that the festival was disrupted by the death of French President Georges Pompidou on April 2 and a National Day of Mourning on April 6, and that too much traffic made it difficult for participants to go from the Olympic Theater to the Musée d'Art Moderne de Paris, where screenings took place, in time to catch certain films.[43] Still, for her, "It was a crazy 9-day event, with so many films, so many languages, so much energy and argument expanding in April in Paris."[44]

The critical discourses of "Musidora" on cinema also appeared in the film magazine *La Revue du cinéma: Image et son*, which was addressed primarily to *animateurs* of film societies that belonged to the Union Française des Oeuvres Laïques d'Education par l'Image et le Son (UFOLEIS; French Union of Secular Educational Audiovisual Works), and which published film reviews, festival reports, interviews, and theoretical texts.[45] In April 1974 the cover of this magazine consisted not of the usual production still or movie star photograph, but of a high-contrast photograph by Pierre Zucca that showed a group of six women garbed in black, head-to-toe bodysuits. Although these women might have looked intriguing to some readers of this special issue dedicated to "Women and Cinema," others might have recognized in them a resemblance to Musidora's character Irma Vep in Louis Feuillade's *Les Vampires* (1915), which had remained a familiar image engraved in the public consciousness. On this cover, however, Musidora is no longer a femme fatale, nor a figure associated with the mysteries of urban space. Instead, the members of the "Musidora" collective reimagine her as an activist and agitator fighting for women's right to make films. With their bodies fully covered except for their eyes, these feminist "Musidoras" apparently refused to be looked at and called our attention to their gaze instead. Drawing inspiration from film history, the "Musidora" collective was therefore declaring their liberation and affirming the power of "women's gaze" at the same time.

Published upon the occasion of the Musidora Festival, this special issue of *La Revue du cinéma* consisted of a number of articles by members and friends of the "Musidora" collective, including Bernheim, Flamant, Serre, Sardet, Clouzot, Nelly Kaplan, Jeanne Moreau (who would soon write and direct her first film, *Lumière*, in 1976), Mireille Dansereau, and Varda, to name a few. Marcelle Fonfreide indicates in the introduction that, in parallel to the Musidora Festival, women wished to respond to the common assertion that "there are almost no women filmmakers" in the world.[46] Whereas some of these women argued that many women filmmakers had contributed to the cinema since the early days, others complained that not enough women had access to a filmmaking career, while calling for more women to make films informed by their own vision of the world. As a result, two lines of thought run through this special issue: one about access, which repeated common feminist concerns about film production, and the other about structures of screen representation, which anticipated the British "theoretical" approach to feminist film criticism. About access to film production, for example, Kaplan, whose films often explored women's sexual exploitation, wrote that women filmmakers were "allowed" to be "sensitive. Sometimes intelligent. Never brilliant [*géniale*]," while Bernheim listed the many ways men brushed aside, ignored, and attacked women's films in France and elsewhere.[47] Two women named Françoise and Bénédicte discussed the scarce number of women working as image and sound technicians in France, whereas the script girl

Edith Vergne addressed the difficulties encountered by women eager to learn filmmaking at school or during practical trainings.[48]

But the true novelty of the discourses published in this special issue was that they began to address not only gender representation or "woman's image" on screen but also the gender bias of the film apparatus itself. Jeanne Moreau explained that lesser-known actresses were usually forced to accept objectifying screen roles, which is why more women should make films and "show a world through women's gaze [*le regard des femmes*]."[49] Likewise, Viviane Forrester mused about the "women's gaze" (*le regard des femmes*) that the supremacy of "men's gaze" (*le regard des hommes*) had expunged so far. She wrote, "Women's gaze, we don't know what it is. What does it see? How does it cut [*découpe*], invent, decipher the world? I don't know. I know my gaze, a woman's gaze [*le regard d'une femme*], but the world seen by others? I know only men's world."[50] Forrester's reference to *découpage* in French is crucial here, for it suggests that she had in mind the ways in which gender informs what we see on screen beyond the narrative level. This reflection about women's gaze continued in one of the two books published by "Musidora" in 1976, *Paroles . . . elles tournent!* (Speech... they're filming!), which included Forrester's essay together with original essays by Mai Zetterling and others on the same topic.[51] As Aurore Turbiau points out, *Paroles . . . elles tournent!* vacillated between constructivist and essentialist positions that consider gender as a social construct and a fixed essence, respectively.[52] Yet in *La Revue du cinéma* a few years earlier, Forrester had remained vague enough that no clear position emerged, even though she certainly had suggested that women's gaze was shared by women in general. Indeed, for Forrester and the "Musidora" collective more broadly, women's gaze was not a fully formed concept but a proposition for women to pick up a camera and start filming.

Significantly, this issue of *La Revue du cinéma* also included an excerpt from Guy Blaché's memoirs as well as the "first index of French filmmakers" edited by Sardet with Clouzot's help. (This index resulted in part from Sardet's trip to the CF.) Of course, the name that the "Musidora" collective had picked for themselves already indicated their interest in such early women filmmakers as Musidora.[53] What they found particularly appealing about Musidora, whom the French public remembered mostly for her iconic portrayal of Irma Vep, was that she also had a career making her own films, including *Soleil et ombre* (with Jacques Lasseyne, Société des Films Musidora, 1922) and *La Terre des taureaux* (Société des Films Musidora, 1924).[54] But the collective's rehabilitation of women's film history and engagement with the film archive went far beyond this tribute to one forgotten woman filmmaker. It was, indeed, no coincidence that *La Revue du cinéma* combined discussions of gender and sexual difference and cinema in France with Guy Blaché's previously unpublished memoirs and a list of French women filmmakers that included Renée Carl, Marie-Anne Colson-Maleville, Lucie Derain, Dulac, Guy Blaché, Marie-Louise Iribe, Musidora, and others. Although Mulvey and other feminist film theorists in Great Britain and the United States rarely acknowledged that women had been making films for several decades, critical appraisal by "Musidora" of cinema went hand in hand with the historical recovery of women's film history, and with a critique of traditional film historiography and film preservation that anticipated some of the issues raised elsewhere by feminist film historians.

In *La Revue du cinéma*, Flamant expressed the surprise of "Musidora" when they found out that, "at the beginnings of cinema, women and men were able to express themselves," as well as their "deep-seated conviction" that "women's cinema was yet to come."[55] Likewise, in a conversation with Flamant in the early 2000s, Bernheim remembered thinking that "women's absence from cinema [was] revolting," but also learning about early women filmmakers whom historians had failed to acknowledge.[56] Based on their published discourses, the major historical "discovery" by "Musidora" was without any doubt Alice Guy Blaché, whom they referred to by her maiden name Alice Guy, not in the least because she was the first woman filmmaker and possibly the first fiction filmmaker in the world. As Bernheim once explained, Sardet had come into contact with Anthony Slide of the American Film Institute during one of her trips to the United States, and Slide "had given her the autobiography so that the Association Musidora would try and publish it" in France.⁵⁷ This discovery led them to rehabilitate women's film history as a way to establish that women had contributed to the development of cinema, to denounce the absence of women from film history, to counter claims that there were few women filmmakers, and to advocate for women's access to the film industry. Put differently, "Musidora" was instrumental in questioning not only women's current access to filmmaking, but also the absence of women filmmakers from public and academic history, as well as from the film archive.

"IN THE DUSTBIN OF WOMEN'S HISTORY": ALICE GUY AS WOMAN FILM PIONEER

For French feminists in the 1970s, what happened to Guy Blaché—her fall into almost complete anonymity after the 1920s—was an outrage and a sign that women were constantly and systematically reduced to silence and oblivion.⁵⁸ If Guy Blaché had made the first fiction film in the world (as she claimed she did), if she had been the first woman filmmaker in the world (as she truly was), then why wasn't she considered a so-called film pioneer? Why wasn't she remembered at all? Bernheim and Clouzot of the "Musidora" collective said it loud and clear in their prefaces to Guy Blaché's *Autobiographie d'une pionnière du cinéma* (Autobiography of a [woman] film pioneer), which they helped publish in 1976: Guy Blaché was "one more woman [thrown] in the dustbin of women's history," meaning that French film historians and archivists had somewhat deliberately ignored her contributions to early cinema precisely *because* she was a woman.⁵⁹ Whereas Clouzot admitted that very few of Guy Blaché's films and archival materials had been uncovered or remained extant, she and Bernheim found it astonishing that neither French film historians nor the Gaumont company had been interested in publishing Guy Blaché's memoirs since she apparently completed them around 1953.⁶⁰ In these memoirs, Guy Blaché not only provided a clear picture of the early days of the cinematograph but also claimed her place as a so-called film pioneer while demonstrating that a woman filmmaker could thrive in France and the United States.⁶¹ As such, she was without a doubt a source of inspiration for such feminists and filmmakers as Bernheim and Clouzot, who, from the moment they encountered Guy Blaché's memoirs in 1973, did everything they could to rehabilitate, celebrate, and recover her life and career.

Spearheaded by "Musidora," whose efforts were concentrated on publishing Guy Blaché's memoirs for the first time, this recovery project was obsessed by the urge to proclaim "Alice Guy" a "[woman] film pioneer," or *pionnière du cinéma* in French. It was, indeed, no coincidence that "Musidora" and Colette Audry, the editor of the Collection Femme at the publishing house Denoël Gonthier, chose to reinstate Guy Blaché's maiden name and to title her memoirs *Autobiographie d'une pionnière du cinéma* (Autobiography of a [woman] film pioneer).⁶² Similar to "director," which had been associated with male power, "pioneer" (*pionnier*) in French was officially recognized as an exclusively masculine noun that designated a (white) man who "associates himself to a new enterprise, [and] advances a new field," until at least 2011, when the Académie française published the third volume of the ninth edition of its dictionary, which also included the feminine version of this noun (*pionnière*) for the first time.⁶³ The status of "film pioneer" (*pionnier du cinéma*) was thus traditionally assigned to such male industrialists and filmmakers as the Lumière brothers, Léon Gaumont, Charles Pathé, and Georges Méliès, and not to Guy Blaché, whose contributions to early cinema remained a serious bone of contention among French film historians. Only Charles Ford called Alice Guy an "authentic pioneer" (*pionnier authentique*) in his book about women directors,

Femmes cinéastes; ou le triomphe de la volonté, which was also published by Audry in the Collection Femme in 1972.[64] But Ford's use of the masculine noun—*pionnier*—instead of its feminine version—*pionnière*—was a dead giveaway that this status was still the prerogative of (white) men in his eyes.

The main point of historical debate was Guy Blaché's repeated claim that she had made her first (fiction) film, *La Fée aux choux*, before Méliès in 1896, which would make her not only the first *woman* filmmaker but also the first *fiction* filmmaker in the world.[65] In 1971, for example, Francis Lacassin, who had exchanged letters and met with Guy Blaché when she was in her nineties, cast doubt on the historical accuracy of Guy Blaché's claim, first in the French and British magazines *Cinéma 71* and *Sight and Sound*, and then in his book *Pour une contre-histoire du cinéma*. In *Sight and Sound*, Lacassin wrote: "When I spoke to her, Alice Guy claimed that she had started making films before Méliès. It seems unlikely, however, that Gaumont would have envisaged producing fiction films before they started mass-producing their projectors in 1898; or, at the very earliest, their combined camera-projector in 1897."[66] But although Lacassin was skeptical about the date of Guy Baché's first film, he believed Guy Blaché when she explained that she had directed all the Gaumont films until 1905 and when she vehemently denied having made the film *Les Méfaits d'une tête de veau* (1899), which she attributed to Ferdinand Zecca instead. But did Lacassin always have empirical evidence to invalidate and corroborate Guy Blaché's testimonies alternately? Or did he choose to believe her testimonies only when they confirmed already established French film histories? In his book cited previously, Ford demonstrated another historiographical move that posed similar issues. He wrote, "Alice Guy directed her *Fée aux Choux* at the beginning of 1896, a few weeks before Georges Méliès, who is nevertheless rightly considered the true creator of the cinematographic spectacle, first because of his abundant production, and then because of his ingenuity when it came to film techniques."⁶⁷ While Ford also admitted in the next breath that Guy Blaché had employed such film techniques as superimpositions *before* Méliès, and that she had been "crushed by Georges Méliès's famous reputation," Ford, in a different yet comparable manner to Lacassin, ultimately prevented Guy Blaché from really challenging what historians and archivists thought they already knew about French cinema.⁶⁸

This debate about the historical past, historical truth, and empirical evidence was of little interest to the "Musidora" collective, however. As far as I can tell, Bernheim, Clouzot, and Sardet, and perhaps even other members of "Musidora," did only some research into Guy Blaché's career in France and the United States and into her extant films, just two of which—*Matrimony's Speed Limit* (Solax, 1913) and *A House Divided* (Solax, 1913)—could be screened on April 3, 1974, during the Musidora Festival. Although the film archive was admittedly lacking in Guy Blaché's case, these women firmly believed Guy Blaché when she asserted that she had made her first film in 1896, just as they firmly believed the many women at the meetings of the women's movement who recounted their experiences of social inequalities, work discrimination, and sexual assault. And here lies the crux of the matter: to believe all women in the 1970s was to believe Guy Blaché, no matter the archival evidence or lack thereof. "Musidora"'s relationship to the historical subject "Alice Guy" was, in this regard, entirely different from the relationship between established (male) film historians and "Alice Guy." Whereas Alice Guy constituted a historiographical problem to film historians and even archivists who valued objectivity and distanciation, "Musidora" showed interest in Alice Guy precisely because she was, like many of its members, a woman filmmaker whose accomplishments had been questioned or downright rejected for the challenge they posed to gender roles and expectations.

This was, at least, how "Musidora" perceived or rather constructed Alice Guy in the context of the women's liberation movement. For example, Bernheim described Guy Blaché as a "strong woman" and a "fighter"; as the victim of a patriarchal system that forces young women into marriage; and near the end of her life, after her divorce from Herbert Blaché, as a "broken woman, forgotten, who can't fight anymore. Who lets herself be forgotten, who doesn't want to hear about cinema and her oeuvre anymore."[69] Based on the empirical evidence we now have, including Guy Blaché's personal archives, interviews, and extant films, and more easily accessible magazines and newspapers, feminist film historians in the twenty-first century may find Bernheim's version of "Alice Guy" very different from ours and even historically untrue or inaccurate. Yet we must recognize at this point that "Musidora" operated not outside of history but in a different historiographical mode, one that offered counter-narratives, and engaged with archival absences, in the writing of women's film history.

Although the group of feminists, cinephiles, and filmmakers that formed "Musidora" were not professional or academic historians, their curiosity about Alice Guy, combined with their own personal, social, and political ambitions, was a powerful force, one that rattled French film historians, reactivated debates about the French film historical narrative, and called out French film archives for their indifference toward women. This is best exemplified by a conversation between Clouzot, Bernheim, Daniel Toscan du Plantier, Ford, Langlois, Lacassin, Jacques Deslandes, André Zwobada, and the feminist filmmaker Liliane de Kermadec, which was broadcast on the radio on July 2, 1975, right before the publication of Guy Blaché's memoirs.[70] This conversation also included a brief excerpt from a radio interview with Guy Blaché; several excerpts from Guy Blaché's upcoming memoirs read by the French actress, videomaker, and feminist activist Delphine Seyrig; and a short passage from Guy Blaché's short story "Ruse de guerre" (1939), also read by Seyrig.[71] Throughout the conversation, Bernheim and Clouzot asked questions meant to probe into the biases of film historians and archivists against Alice Guy, who, they were convinced, had been forgotten and erased from French film histories because she was a woman. Once again, for Bernheim and Clouzot the interest lay in Alice Guy's status as the first fiction filmmaker in the world, which would then ensure her place among such French film pioneers as the Lumière brothers and Méliès. But the stakes were, in fact, much higher for these feminists, who aimed not only to reinsert Alice Guy within established film historical narratives, but also to address the misogyny at the heart of the historiographical and archival process. As they stated early in the conversation, "We have the impression that, because things are what they are, because history is governed by men, as we all know, Alice Guy was more easily forgotten, regardless of her genius. It was easy to say that she wasn't a genius because she was a woman, that what she did wasn't brilliant."

To reiterate, Ford had already admitted in his book *Femmes cinéastes* that Alice Guy was a pioneer whose first film, *La Fée aux choux*, was possibly the first fiction film made in France in 1896.[72] But the other male participants in this conversation were less confident about Alice Guy's early French career. Deslandes, who never mentioned Alice Guy in his *Histoire comparée du cinéma* (1968), co-written with Jacques Richard, could not believe that Léon Gaumont would have given his secretary the responsibility to make fiction films, even though that secretary was to become a filmmaker whom Deslandes described on the radio as "a very pretty woman, we haven't said it yet, a strong woman, and a remarkable businesswoman." By contrast, Lacassin, whose book *Pour une contre-histoire du cinéma* included a chapter on Alice Guy, agreed with Alice Guy when she said that Gaumont did not consider film production important in the late 1890s, meaning that Gaumont could have allowed his secretary to make the studio's first story films. But Lacassin still questioned the validity of Guy Blaché's claim, especially whether *La Fée aux choux* dated back to 1896 or 1900. Finally, Langlois, whose CF had organized an homage to Guy Blaché in 1957, acknowledged that he did not know whether Alice Guy was the first fiction filmmaker, but he remembered a few anecdotes he had been told about her tendency to play matchmaker at the Gaumont studios.[73] Zwobada, the director of the Gaumont archives, and Toscan du Plantier, Gaumont's newly appointed president, knew very little about Alice Guy and her films, whose preservation, they explained, would require vast funds that Gaumont was apparently unable to secure at the time.

In comparison, Bernheim, Clouzot, and Kermadec expressed their frustration and even anger at film historians and archivists and their solidarity with Alice Guy, whose fate they recognized as their own. For example, Kermadec said near the end of the conversation that she was "distraught" to hear film historians debate Alice Guy's career in those terms. She then continued:

> I remain convinced that the problem is that Alice Guy was a woman. Nobody's denying that these [Alice Guy's] memoirs are sincere. So, isn't it always the same problem with women who do something? We accept that women do something, but they shouldn't push their luck. And I think that's what's happening with Alice Guy. She shouldn't push her luck. If I understood what you said and what she wrote correctly, it seems to me that she had the idea to make story films. . . . It seems to me that it's such an enormous idea—at least for me who loves what cinema has become—it seems to me that it's such an enormous idea that it deserved to be treated better. I haven't seen these films, but what I'm hearing frightens me. I'm hearing that early films are childish. *La Fée aux choux* is childish. Langlois hasn't seen it, because, of course, *La Fée aux choux,* that's not appealing enough. . . . And, on the other hand, she [Alice Guy] looked pretty and elegant on set, but was she really on set? And [I'm hearing] many other things that have nothing to do with this important idea, the idea for story films. Or I didn't understand anything, which is possible. But it seems to me that this idea is enormous, and that's what we should be talking about.

The rest of the conversation between Kermadec, Deslandes, Lacassin, and Zwobada saw Kermadec on one side, and Deslandes, Lacassin, and Zwobada on the other, stick to positions that were not only irreconcilable but also incommensurable. Deslandes, Lacassin, and Zwobada repeated that no evidence had been found that would corroborate Alice Guy's testimonies, and that many early filmmakers besides Alice Guy also were absent from film histories, which was meant to refute Kermadec's accusations of gender bias. But these issues did not really matter to Kermadec, and to Bernheim and Clouzot, who stood firm in their condemnation of historiographical categories like "genius" that made it impossible for such women as Alice Guy to ever be recognized for their ideas. Furthermore, the excerpts from Alice Guy's memoirs read by Seyrig, who embodied and channeled her voice throughout the conversation, closed the historical gap between Alice Guy and French feminists of the 1970s, who all belonged to the same "constellations" of women filmmakers.[74]

That these feminists felt close to Alice Guy was evident, both in the conversation discussed here and in the frontmatter of Guy Blaché's memoirs, in which Bernheim used the first-person pronoun to speak as Alice Guy in her name.[75] According to Bernheim, however, Guy Blaché's films at the Musidora Festival did not particularly stand out among the myriad of other films shown during the festival.[76] Furthermore, the excerpt from the memoirs published in *La Revue du cinéma* went fairly unnoticed, which prompted Bernheim to ask whether "women were even interested in their own history, in their ancestors, when they're lucky enough to have them. How is it possible? Or is the grandmother of cinema so troublesome that we're better off not remembering her? Glory to Méliès, glory to Zecca! But let us please forget Alice Guy. We're better off thinking that: WOMEN ARE NOT CREATORS AND THERE IS NO FEMALE GENIUS."[77] However, this recovery project was not over for Bernheim, who went on to make a short film about Alice Guy titled *Qui est Alice Guy?* (1976). Bernheim had been a writer and the trainee assistant director to Marguerite Duras on the set of *India Song* (1975), and *Qui est Alice Guy?* was the first and only film she ever directed, a passion project about one of the women who gave her "energy and confidence."⁷⁸ As Bernheim explained some years later, "[She] had dreamed of [making] a feature film, but it didn't happen because of a lack of money."⁷⁹ *Qui est Alice Guy?* nonetheless continued the "Musidora" recovery project by engaging with the patriarchal limits and feminist potentials of the film archive in similar ways.

WHO IS ALICE GUY?

Produced by the Institut national de l'audiovisuel (INA) and broadcast as one episode of the French television series *Hiéroglyphes* on January 25, 1976, Nicole-Lise Bernheim's *Qui est Alice Guy?* aimed to educate the public, revise the French film canon, question the writing of film history, and advocate for the recognition of women's accomplishments at the same time.⁸⁰ This ambitious thirteen-minute film consists of archival footage and photographs of Alice Guy Blaché, excerpts from her French (Gaumont) and American (Solax) films, one animated sequence by Monique Renault, and a few other original sequences in which the stage and film actress Hermine Karagheuz alternately plays "Alice Guy" and speaks in her defense.⁸¹ In the spirit of the "Musidora" recovery project, Karagheuz's performance in this film contributes less to the knowledge of Guy Blaché as a *historical* figure than to the reinvention of Guy Blaché as a *feminist* figure for French feminists in the 1970s. Its blend of archival and original materials is also characteristic of the collective's challenge to the masculinist tendencies of both film historiography and film preservation in France and beyond.

Bernheim's central claim in *Qui est Alice Guy?* is that Alice Guy, who insisted that she had made the first fiction film in France around 1896, has been completely forgotten. *Qui est Alice Guy?* begins with Guy Blaché's 1957 television interview with French journalist François Chalais, during which she explains how she came up with the idea to make the first fiction film. "At that time," Guy Blaché says to Chalais, "they were still filming views on the streets, street views, little things, *The Arrival of the Train [at La Ciotat]*, etc. I was the daughter of a bookseller. I loved reading. I had read a lot. I had been in amateur theater. And I thought we could do better. I proposed to Monsieur Gaumont to film some scenes. He said, 'Yes, it is indeed a young woman's affair. You can try. But at the one condition that your correspondences don't suffer from it.'"[82] Bernheim then cuts to Renault's animated sequence, in which a baby emerges from a cabbage (in reference to Alice Guy's *La Fée aux choux*) and turns into a young woman who then metamorphoses into Georges Demenÿ's camera for Gaumont, the chronophotographe. "Méliès, yes; Lumière, yes; Alice Guy . . . who?" read the next two intertitles. "Who is she?" continues Karagheuz in the next medium shot. "She's the old lady we just saw. Nobody knows her. She lived at the beginning of the century. She liked the cinema very much. She made 500 films. She worked for Léon Gaumont in Paris. She was a secretary."

The rest of the film builds a sort of monument to Alice Guy, as the shot of Alice Guy (Karagheuz) standing on a stone pedestal with her name on it already suggests at the beginning. As the viewer watches Guy Blaché speak on television, as they see photographs of her on the sets of her films, still photographs from her films, and excerpts from *La Passion* (aka *La Vie du Christ/Life of Christ*; Gaumont, 1906) and *The Detective's Dog* (Solax, 1912), Alice Guy becomes a historical subject to be reckoned with, a film pioneer whose contributions to early cinema and popular culture more broadly can no longer be ignored. To be sure, Bernheim acknowledges in this film that anyone's understanding of Alice Guy remains fragmentary, since so many of her films, including *La Fée aux choux*, have "disappeared, been lost or stolen." But while ten films are known to have survived out of the five hundred films that, according to Bernheim, Alice Guy probably made between 1895 and the 1920s, Bernheim also suggests that such absences in film archives should not diminish our interest in Alice Guy.[83] So what if we

Figure 16. Alice Guy Blaché with François Chalais, 1957, in *Qui est Alice Guy?*, directed by Nicole-Lise Bernheim. *Source:* © INA 1976.

Figure 17. Animation by Monique Renault in *Qui est Alice Guy?*, directed by Nicole-Lise Bernheim. *Source:* © INA 1976.

cannot see some of her films right now? The archival materials cited previously still document Alice Guy's life and career and at the very least signal her presence and, indeed, her active participation within the French and US film industries at the turn of the century. In other words, for Bernheim—and the "Musidora" collective she co-founded—archival absences were not a valid excuse for ignoring Alice Guy and even erasing her from film histories, but a difficulty Bernheim aimed to overcome with *Qui est Alice Guy?*

At the same time, *Qui est Alice Guy?* includes original sequences that swing the entire film away from historical facts toward speculative fiction and ultimately reimagine Alice Guy as a feminist figure summoned from the belle époque into Paris in the mid-1970s. It is, indeed, paramount in my view that Karagheuz not only discusses Alice Guy in the third person but also brings her into the present time and place of the film by playing her in costume in five short scenes:

1. At a park somewhere in Paris, Karagheuz as Alice Guy buys a waffle from a male vendor, to whom she explains, "I invented the story film. Actresses, actors. It was maybe an idea in the air, but I had it first. I made a one-minute film. 17 meters of film. It was called *La Fée aux choux*. My name is Alice Guy." The vendor's indifference is palpable, especially when he says repeatedly: "Yes, yes, that's good," while making Alice Guy's waffle.

2. Lying down in a park, Karagheuz as Alice Guy comments on the early days of cinema, when cinema was a form of entertainment and a "fancy" (*désir*), a "spellbinding illusion" (*illusion féérique*), that made Léon Gaumont and Charles Pathé very rich. Then, standing next to an early camera, she explains that this camera was similar to the one she used for her first films.

3. Karagheuz as Alice Guy walks on the streets and then pauses to say, "A woman filmmaker [*cinéaste*]. Unbelievable. A woman filmmaker [*cinéaste*] since the very beginning of cinema. It wasn't a problem for anyone at first. Then, they didn't dare tell me anything. I was head

Figure 18. Hermine Karagheuz as Alice Guy buys a waffle in *Qui est Alice Guy?*, directed by Nicole-Lise Bernheim. *Source:* © INA 1976.

Figure 19. Hermine Karagheuz as Alice Guy lies down in a park in *Qui est Alice Guy?*, directed by Nicole-Lise Bernheim. *Source:* © INA 1976.

Figure 20. Hermine Karagheuz as Alice Guy reflects on her status as a woman filmmaker while walking up the street in *Qui est Alice Guy?*, directed by Nicole-Lise Bernheim. *Source:* © INA 1976.

of film production at Gaumont for eleven years. My longest film was *La Passion*, which I made in 1906, before my departure for the United States in 1907. I did superimpositions, which were new at the time. That film [*La Passion*] was thirty-minute long. Six hundred meters. I was both screenwriter and director."

4. Karagheuz as Alice Guy walks across the footbridge in the Parc des Buttes-Chaumont in Paris, near the location of the early Gaumont studios where Alice Guy worked between 1895 and 1907.[84] Karagheuz as Alice Guy explains that she got married and had two kids, lived in the United States, and made military pictures, dramas, and comedies with the best actors and actresses of the time. "I made a lot of films," she concludes. "A lot."

Figure 21. Hermine Karagheuz as Alice Guy walks across a footbridge in the Parc des Buttes-Chaumont in *Qui est Alice Guy?*, directed by Nicole-Lise Bernheim. *Source:* © INA 1976.

5. Karagheuz, still in costume, goes to Bois-d'Arcy, a French military fort that was transformed into a film archive by the Ministry of Cultural Affairs and the Centre National de la Cinématographie (now Centre National du Cinéma et de l'Image Animée, CNC) in 1969. Karagheuz asks a male archivist about Alice Guy's films, but the archivist does not know who Alice Guy is. Karagheuz then looks for those films herself, among piles of film canisters in an outdoor tunnel. Finally, Karagheuz as Alice Guy says: "I was forgotten. Yet I'm the one who had that great first idea."

These five scenes stand in sharp contrast to the archival documents (photographs, stills, and film excerpts) that populate the rest of the film,

Figure 22. Hermine Karagheuz as herself but in her Alice Guy costume searches for Alice Guy's films in an archive in *Qui est Alice Guy?*, directed by Nicole-Lise Bernheim. *Source:* © INA 1976.

mainly because of Alice Guy's different status as a first-person character in the five scenes and as a historical subject in the archival documents. In these scenes, the switch between the third and first persons is also significant, especially given that nothing else changes: Karagheuz does not change costumes or stop looking straight into the camera, and the setting remains Paris in the mid-1970s. There lies the difference between historical re-enactment, which is often employed in documentary filmmaking as a way to compensate for lack of archival documentation, and Karagheuz's performance in *Qui est Alice Guy?* Whereas historical re-enactment often relies on realism, whereby the performer *becomes* a character within that character's time and place, Karagheuz *plays* a character who remains distinct from and irreducible to her in the eyes of the audience. But if we the viewers are never led to believe that these scenes could have happened during Alice Guy's tenure at the Gaumont company, then what is at stake here? What does this performance do to Karagheuz, to Alice Guy, and to us? Karagheuz identifying with Alice Guy in this manner not only transforms Alice Guy into a feminist figure, that of the woman film pioneer; it also suggests that even though Alice Guy "wasn't a problem for anyone at first," a certain continuity or lineage exists from Alice Guy to contemporary women involved in French cinema. In the scene at Bois-d'Arcy, especially, the images of Karagheuz searching for Alice Guy's films in the archives function as a poignant reminder that only feminists care about women's contributions to film history. A counterpart to the historical figure the film also conjures up, the feminist figure in that scene is one more iteration of Alice Guy: not Gaumont's head of production in the 1900s, not Solax's president in the early 1910s, not the "old lady" of the 1950s and 1960s, but any French woman filmmaker speaking up for herself, breaking the historiographical silence, and coming out of oblivion on her own terms.

CONCLUSION: "REDUCED TO NOTHING" (AGAIN)

After the Musidora Festival and the publication of Guy Blaché's memoirs, the "Musidora" collective remained active—through various film programs and events—in the fight against women's exclusion from the French film industry, and they even influenced the creation of other women's film festivals (like the Festival International de Films de Femmes held in Créteil every year) and feminist groups in France. Yet "Musidora" also struggled to organize another festival, and the group was ultimately dissolved in the fall of 1977. Although the collective was short-lived, it certainly counted among the most passionate feminist film endeavors of the 1970s, not in the least because of its deep critical engagement with the gender politics of the film archive and because of its recovery of Guy Blaché.

Yet the legacy of "Musidora" is virtually unknown in France and in the United States, where Guy Blaché lives in a state of perpetual "recovery" that often masquerades as first-time "discovery" in popular culture. Since at least the outset of the #MeToo movement, a touchstone moment of feminist activism against sexual harassment and assault in film industries and beyond, there has been a renewed interest in historical French women filmmakers, including Guy Blaché. In addition to the Prix Alice Guy, which was founded by Véronique Le Bris and has rewarded one contemporary woman director every year since 2018, several comic books and graphic novels, children's books, podcasts, web series, and television documentaries about Guy Blaché have been released, often with the purpose of making visible women's accomplishments both in the past and the present. Since the premiere of Pamela B. Green's feature film *Be Natural: The Untold Story of Alice Guy-Blaché* at the Cannes Film Festival in May 2018, in particular, Guy Blaché has received so much attention from popular media that she has apparently come out of oblivion (again). Narrated by Jodie Foster and packed with archival photographs and documents; film excerpts; flashy visuals; and talking head interviews with movie stars, filmmakers, archivists, and academics, *Be Natural* presents itself as "a detective story, biopic, and feature documentary that rewrites film history, revealing for the first time the full scope of the life and work of cinema's first female director, screenwriter, and studio owner Alice Guy-Blaché."[85] Among other things, the film reconstructs Guy Blaché's French and US careers, gives an account of director Green's discovery of new personal materials and audio recordings, and questions why Guy Blaché was left out of many film history books and consequently forgotten by the general public. In hindsight, however, Green's most commendable accomplishment has been to contribute to the public rediscovery of Guy Blaché. In the context of the #MeToo movement in the United States, the timing of the release of *Be Natural* worked out quite nicely. In Green's words, "Now was the right time, more than ever, to step forward and help bring Alice's story to light, given all the current conversation about women's rights and how more often than not, women's stories are pushed to the shadows throughout history."[86]

Yet as Jay Weissberg rightly pointed out in his review of the film in *Variety*, "There's an alarming degree of disingenuousness, or perhaps merely naiveté, permeating" *Be Natural*.[87] The problem is not so much with the film's historical accuracy, or its claim that Guy Blaché was left out of early film history books because she was a woman and because many of her films remained unavailable for a very long time. Its fault, Weissberg wrote, is that it "ignores a number of earlier documentaries not to mention the significant amount of scholarship on pioneering filmmaker Alice Guy-Blaché. Also omitted is any mention of the 2009 Gaumont and Kino DVD box sets that made 66 of her films available. These are what can be called inconvenient truths, for Pamela B. Green . . . is on a mission to discover why—supposedly—no one has ever heard of Alice Guy-Blaché."[88] To be fair, the version of *Be Natural* released in the United States does mention the publications of several historians—Victor Bachy's *Alice Guy-Blaché (1873–1968): La Première Femme cinéaste du monde* (1993), Anthony Slide's *The Silent Feminists: America's First Women Directors* (1996), and Alison McMahan's *Alice Guy Blaché: Lost Visionary of the Cinema* (2002)—and it includes interviews with Slide, McMahan, Joan Simon, Jane Gaines, and others whose groundbreaking work in silent film history has already brought Guy Blaché out of the shadows. But Weissberg is right when he says that their voices are "drowned out by people with no ties to film history who all express amazement that they've never heard of Guy-Blaché."[89] Ultimately, we are left with the impression not that *the public* still does not know about Guy Blaché, which is somewhat true, but that *absolutely nobody* has ever cared to look for Guy Blaché as hard as Green does in *Be Natural*, which is certainly not true.

In France, where *Be Natural* was released online in 2019 and in movie theaters during the COVID-19 pandemic in 2020, the film was the topic of a fierce debate.⁹⁰ On one side, Laure Murat found it deplorable that such film historians as Georges Sadoul and G.-Michel Coissac had failed to recognize Guy Blaché's contributions to early cinema, and that France still remained "indifferen[t]" to Guy Blaché.⁹¹ Furthermore, Murat compared Guy Blaché to Méliès, who she argued was forgotten but "rediscovered" as early as 1925. For her, this proved that "a woman may very well be successful—and Alice Guy proved that brilliantly—but as soon as an amateur practice becomes a profession, an art form and a commercial enterprise, there's no place for her in history." Likewise, Emmanuelle Lequeux explained that Guy Blaché was "reduced to nothing" because of "incomplete archives, films without any credits or attributed to her assistants, the misogynistic laziness of film historians."⁹² "What if Méliès was a woman?" asked Lequeux. "Yes, a woman! This woman actually existed. Her name was Alice Guy. She would have made about a thousand films, many of which are apparently lost forever. Then she completely disappeared. The Lumière brothers, [F. W.] Murnau, [D. W.] Griffith: not one cinémathèque neglects her male counterparts."⁹³ Lequeux then credited Marquise Lepage's *Le Jardin oublié* (1995) and Pamela B. Green's *Be Natural* for preventing Guy Blaché from falling into complete oblivion.

On the other side, François Albera and Laurent Mannoni responded to Murat and Lequeux with a short text, "Are French Historians Against Alice Guy?," published in the film history journal *1895*.⁹⁴ Without having seen *Be Natural*, probably because of its delayed release in France, but after having read Weissberg's review, Albera and Mannoni took issue with Murat's claim that Guy Blaché was "literally erased by film historians" and with the importance given by Lequeux to *Le Jardin oublié* and *Be Natural* to the so-called discovery of Guy Blaché.⁹⁵ They argued that until the FIAF Conference in Brighton in 1978, film historians had very little evidence to discuss Guy Blaché at length, and that a plethora of books and articles had since remedied the oversight. In a similar vein, Frédéric Cavé called Murat's and Lequeux's articles, and by association, Green's film, "opportunistic (in the way that they ride the wave of #metoo) and offhanded (in the way that they pass over many films and works in silence)."[96] Jean-Michel Frodon was more generous toward *Be Natural*, but he still noted, "What's fascinating about Pamela Green's film is that, contrary to what it implies, Alice Guy isn't unknown. . . . But the existence and the importance of her work remain confidential."[97] Indeed, for Frodon, *Be Natural* tells not an "unknown" or "untold" story, but the story of a "denial" that has been used for "militant" purposes.[98]

Although this recent debate was sparked by the release and popular success of *Be Natural*, it rehashed many of the arguments used by (male) film historians and archivists and the "Musidora" collective during their confrontation in the 1970s. Whereas Albera, Mannoni, Cavé, and Frodon countered *Be Natural*'s claims with historical facts and historiographical considerations, Murat and Lequeux seemed more interested in expressing their frustration with what they considered yet another manifestation of French misogyny. Murat even cited the preface penned by Bernheim for the French edition of Guy Blaché's memoirs, in which Bernheim expressed similar ideas in almost identical terms. It also bears noting that *Be Natural* is comparable to Bernheim's *Qui est Alice Guy?* not only in subject matter but also in tone and execution. Like *Qui est Alice Guy?*, *Be Natural* begins with an excerpt from Guy Blaché's 1957 television interview with Chalais, which introduces Guy Blaché as a film pioneer whose career started before Hollywood in France in the 1890s. Although *Be Natural* relies on research and archival materials that were not available to Bernheim in the 1970s, the film proceeds to demonstrate that Guy Blaché remains forgotten, understudied, and unacknowledged by the public, which was what Bernheim had argued in *Qui est Alice Guy?* Finally, as Green herself admitted, *Be Natural* participated in a broader feminist project that aimed to shed light on "women's stories" in a similar way to "Musidora," whose interest in Guy Blaché was just as politically urgent in its time.

My point here is not that history repeats itself, or that today's feminists relate to Guy Blaché in exactly the same ways and for the same reasons as the "Musidora" collective in France fifty years ago. Instead, the comparison between these two moments reveals the long-standing currency of Guy Blaché as a feminist figure, as well as the complex ways in which French film historiography continues to marginalize women filmmakers and movie workers. This is not to say that the "Musidora" collective failed as feminist film activists committed to recovering women's work in the cinema. On the contrary, their defiance of the patriarchal impulses behind the writing and preservation of French film history lives on, more relevant than ever, in feminist scholars and critics today.

EPILOGUE

Toward Feminist Futures

IN 1950, about six years after she became involved with the CF, twenty-four years before a feminist film collective would take her name, and forty years before the academic field of feminist film history would develop in full, Musidora published an article about "Colette and the Silent Cinema," which included two letters she received from Colette during their decade-long friendship.[1] In the first letter, Colette complimented Musidora on her performance in *Johannes, fils de Johannes* (André Hugon, 1918), but suggested that she herself could better utilize Musidora's talents on screen. Colette wrote: "It seems to me—perhaps it is pure pride on my part—that (knowing you as I do, and knowing well the resources of your face and gestures) it seems to me that, just by giving you simple advice, and entirely disinterested observations, I would contribute, if need be, to maximum effects that no one has drawn from you."[2] We then learn that this letter convinced Musidora, who had already directed one film titled *Vicenta* (1920), to ask Colette to write the scenario of another film that Musidora would also direct.[3] But in addition to providing information about the collaboration between Musidora and Colette, and about each of these women's work as director and screenwriter, respectively, this article attests to yet another facet of Musidora. At the very end, Musidora reflected on the archival value of Colette's letters for cinema's history, as well as her own dedication to not only save but also archive these letters in a secure location. She wrote: "I thought it best to classify, with love, in my section of the historical research at the Cinémathèque française, these very perishable and invaluable treasures: letters from Colette and news clippings about Colette, one of the first great authors [*auteurs*] of cinema: Colette who loved [Cecil B.] De Mille."[4]

As we feminist film historians continue to write always more inclusive film histories, consider Musidora's words one last reminder for us to keep close Musidora and the other women from *Archiving the Past*. Now attuned to women's work in, and with, the film archive, I see it everywhere: in the activities of every institution—French and otherwise—dedicated to the preservation of cinema's global history; behind every new film restoration, publication, and curatorial project that women's work often underlies. *Archiving the Past* reveals only the tip of the iceberg, one small yet significant part of a larger whole; many more women besides Jeanne Moussinac, Laure Albin-Guillot, Musidora, Eve Francis, Marie Epstein, and the members of the "Musidora" collective have contributed to the production of film historical knowledge whose work remains invisible today. In France, I think of the many other female employees of the CF, including Françoise Carvillani (archivist), Françoise Jaubert (secretary), Renée Lichtig (editor), Léone Moreau (editor), and Giulia Veronesi (secretary), as well as the numerous female relatives of so-called male film pioneers, such as Maud Linder (daughter of comedian Max Linder), Luce Vigo (daughter of director Jean Vigo), and Madeline Malthête-Méliès (grand-daughter of director and producer Georges Méliès). The Centre audiovisuel Simone de Beauvoir, founded by videomakers and feminist activists Carole Roussopoulos, Delphine Seyrig, and Ioana Wieder in 1982, also comes to mind as a major player in the preservation of women's contributions to cinema in its broadest sense. I know now that French and global cinema's history would not exist without these women's tireless efforts to collect, recollect, and recover, both within and outside established institutions. As archivists, witnesses, activists, and more, they have also challenged the complex ways in which French and other film archives make invisible numerous non-male filmmakers and movie workers. My hope is that more scholars will see these women too, and that better feminist futures will become possible as a result of our looking for their work anywhere and everywhere all the time.

Notes

INTRODUCTION: ON WOMEN'S FILM HISTORY

1. Regarding Lotte Eisner, see Laurent Mannoni, *Histoire de la Cinémathèque française* (Paris: Gallimard, 2006); Julia Eisner, "Lotte Eisner: Pioneer of the Art and Craft of Collecting," *Screen* 62, no. 3 (Autumn 2021): 418–23; Julia Eisner, "In the Archive with Lotte Eisner: How She Solved the Problem of Maria (the Robot)" (presentation hosted by The Wiener Holocaust Library, November 18, 2021); Naomi DeCelles, *Recollecting Lotte Eisner: Cinema, Exile, and the Archive* (Oakland: University of California Press, 2022); and Janet Bergstrom, "Lotte Eisner, collectionneuse: De l'ombre à la lumière," in *Le Cinéma dans l'oeil du collectionneur*, ed. Charlotte Brady-Savignac et al. (Montréal: Les Presses de l'Université de Montréal, 2023), 103–42.

2. See Werner Sudendorf, "*Film-Kurier* 1919–1944," *Bulletin FIAF* 32 (September 1986): 15.

3. Lotte H. Eisner, *J'avais jadis une belle patrie*, trans. Marie Bouquet (Paris: Marest Editeur, 2022), 217.

4. During World War II, the Château de Béduer was owned by the lawyer, writer, and publisher Jeanne Loviton, also known as Jean Voilier, who was a friend and possibly even lover of Yvonne Dornès, one of the early supporters and administrators of the CF.

5. Eisner, *J'avais jadis une belle patrie*, 279. *Bonne à tout faire*, which could be translated as "jill of all trades" in English, has a more negative connotation in French. Here, I interpret it to mean that Eisner was responsible for much more than her official title of chief curator suggests, and that she rarely received credit, recognition, or even adequate compensation for that work.

6. Secondary sources often use the singular form (Commission de Recherche historique) to designate the commission led by Musidora. I employ the plural form (Commission de Recherches historiques) commonly found in primary sources from the CF.

7. Regarding women's and feminist archives, see, for example, Gerda Lerner, *The Creation of Feminist Consciousness: From the Middle Ages to Eighteen Seventy* (New York: Oxford University Press, 1993); and Joan Wallach Scott, "Women's Archives and Women's History" (keynote address, dedication at the Christine Dunlap Farnham Archives, Pembroke Center, Brown University, Providence, RI, October 10, 1986). Early examples include, among many others, the World Center for Women's Archives (1935–40) in the United States; the Women's Library (1926–), now housed by the London School of Economics and Political Science, in England; Marie-Louise Bouglé's feminist library (1921–42) and the Bibliothèque Marguerite Durand (1931–) in France; and the International Archives for the Women's Movement (1935–) in the Netherlands.

8. Kate Eichhorn, *The Archival Turn in Feminism: Outrage in Order* (Philadelphia: Temple University Press, 2013), 9.

9. Michel-Rolph Trouillot's work is particularly important for my conceptualization of the archive throughout this book. *Silencing the Past: Power and the Production of History* (Boston: Beacon Press, 1995).

10. Paula Amad, *Counter-Archive: Film, the Everyday, and Albert Kahn's Archives de la Planète* (New York: Columbia University Press, 2010); Katherine Groo, *Bad Film Histories: Ethnography and the Early Archive* (Minneapolis: University of Minnesota Press, 2019). "Colonial impulse" comes from Groo, *Bad Film Histories*, 49.

11. See, for example, Françoise Vergès, *Programme de désordre absolu: Décoloniser le musée* (Paris: La fabrique éditions, 2023).

12. Here I want to briefly acknowledge Kiki Loveday's article "The Pioneer Paradigm," *Feminist Media Histories* 8, no.1 (2022): 165–80. In it, Loveday demonstrates how the pioneer paradigm corresponds to "a nineteenth-century white supremacist imaginary" that contemporary feminist film historians should challenge and eventually move away from 166.

13. The following works have been particularly influential in feminist film historiography: Michel Foucault, *The Archaeology of Knowledge*, trans. A. M. Sheridan Smith (1972; New York: Vintage Books, 2010); Jacques Derrida, *Archive Fever: A Freudian Impression*, trans. Eric Prenowitz (Chicago: University of Chicago Press, 1996); Trouillot, *Silencing the Past*.

14. Kiki Loveday, "Do You Believe in Fairies? Cabbages, Victorian Memes, and the Birth of Cinema: Seeing Sapphic Sexuality in the Silent Era," in *Women Film Pioneers Project*, ed. Jane Gaines et al. (New York: Columbia University Libraries, 2019), https://wfpp.columbia.edu/2019/10/17/do-you-believe-in-fairies-cabbages-victorian-memes-and-the-birth-of-cinema-seeing-sapphic-sexuality-in-the-silent-era/.

15. I adapt "makers of meaning" and "bearers of meaning" from Laura Mulvey, "Visual Pleasure and Narrative Cinema," *Screen* 16, no. 3 (October 1, 1975): 6–18.

16. Hannah Frank, *Frame by Frame: A Materialist Aesthetics of Animated Cartoons* (Oakland: University of California Press, 2019).

17. Trouillot, *Silencing the Past*, 21.

18. Bonnie G. Smith, *The Gender of History: Men, Women, and Historical Practice* (Cambridge, MA: Harvard University Press, 1998).

19. Smith, *Gender of History*, 10.

20. Laura E. Helton, *Scattered and Fugitive Things: How Black Collectors Created Archives and Remade History* (New York: Columbia University Press, 2024), 27.

21. Among the scholarship on librarianship as gendered labor, the following works on French women librarians have been particularly important to my thinking throughout this book: Mary Niles Maack, "Women Librarians in France: The First Generation," *Journal of Library History* 18, no. 4 (Fall 1983): 407–49; Isabelle Antonutti, *Bâtisseurs de la lecture publique: Une histoire des premières bibliothécaires, 1900–1950* (Villeurbanne, France: Presses de l'ENSSIB, 2024).

22. As of March 2025. See "About the Project," in *Women Film Pioneers Project*, ed. Jane Gaines et al. (New York: Columbia University Libraries, 2015), https://wfpp.columbia.edu/about/.

23. Erin Hill, *Never Done: A History of Women's Work in Media Production* (New Brunswick, NJ: Rutgers University Press, 2016); Melanie Bell, *Movie Workers: The Women Who Made British Cinema* (Urbana: University of Illinois Press, 2021).

24. I borrow the term "constellation" from Monica Dall'Asta and Jane M. Gaines, "Prologue: Constellations: Past Meets Present in Feminist Film History," in *Doing Women's Film History: Reframing Cinemas, Past and Future*, ed. Christine Gledhill and Julia Knight (Urbana: University of Illinois Press, 2015), 12–25.

25. Robert Sitton, "Iris Barry," in *Women Film Pioneers Project*, ed. Jane Gaines et al. (New York: Columbia University Libraries, 2015), https://wfpp.columbia.edu/pioneer/iris-barry/; Robert Sitton, *Lady in the Dark: Iris Barry and the Art of Film* (New York: Columbia University Press, 2014); Bruce Henson, "Iris Barry: American Film Archive Pioneer," *Katharine Sharp Review* 4 (Winter 1997): 1–6; Rinella Cere, *An International Study of Film Museums* (London: Routledge, 2020); Kim Tomadjoglou, "A Love of Labor and a Cult of Fragments. Maria Adriana Prolo's Museo Nazionale del Cinema, Torino" (presentation at conference Dans l'oeil du collectionneur, Laboratoire CinéMédias/Technès, June 5, 2017).

26. For more information on these women and the institutions they founded, see Matoshi Ohba, "In Memoriam: Kashiko Kawakita," *Journal of Film Preservation* 22, no. 47 (October 1993): 69–70; Rinella Cere and Giovanna Santaera, "Fautrici dei musei del cinema nel mondo: Iris Barry, Lotte Eisner e Kashiko Kawakita," *Arabeschi* 19 (2021), http://www.arabeschi.it/23-fautrici-dei-musei-del-cinema-nel-mondo-iris-barry-lotte-eisner-e-kashiko-kawawita/; Karen Schwartzman et al., "An Interview with Margot Benacerraf: *Reverón, Araya*, and the Institutionalization of Cinema in Venezuela," *Journal of Film and Video* 44, nos. 3/4 (Fall 1992 and Winter 1993): 51–75; Eric Le Roy, "Entretien avec Lia Van Leer," *Journal of Film Preservation* 92 (2015): 29–35; "Aglaia Mitropoulou," *Variety*, January 28, 1991, 85; Patricia Torres San Martín, "Elena Sánchez Valenzuela," in *Women Film Pioneers Project*, ed. Jane Gaines et al. (New York: Columbia University Libraries, 2013), https://wfpp.columbia.edu/pioneer/ccp-elena-sanchez-valenzuela/; Patricia Torres San Martín, *Elena Sánchez Valenzuela* (Mexico City: Universidad Nacional Autónoma de México, 2018); and Sirine Pons, "La Cinémathèque tunisienne, Henri Langlois et la FIAF (1958–1963)" (presented at Cinémathèque française, Paris, France, February 12, 2015).

My gratitude goes to Leticia Berrizbeitia Añez, who first told me about Margot Benacerraf's connection to Langlois and her work toward the creation of the first national film archive in Venezuela, and to Enri Moreno Ceballos for sharing with me references about Elena Sánchez Valenzuela. It is also worth noting that the FIAF Symposium of 2023 on Women, Cinema, and Film Archives was partly dedicated to women's work as film archivists. But as Shelley Stamp reported, the symposium also demonstrated that "despite the profound impact of women's leadership curating key international film archives, the field of archiving remains male-dominated." Stamp, "Conference Report: FIAF Symposium: Women, Cinema, and Film Archives," *Feminist Media Histories* 10, nos. 2–3 (2024): 141. The FIAF Gender Observatory, launched as a result of the FIAF Symposium of 2023, aims to challenge the gender politics of global film archives today. See "FIAF Gender Observatory," FIAF, accessed August 4, 2025, https://www.fiafnet.org/pages/Community/fiaf-gender-observatory.html.

27. Feminist film historians form a vibrant international community whose scholarship, organizations, conferences, videographic criticism, databases, and curatorial programs are far too numerous to mention. In addition to the Women Film Pioneers Project, Cinema's First Nasty Women, and the books and articles cited throughout, *Archiving the Past* owes much to, for example, Jane Gaines, *Pink-Slipped: What Happened to Women in the Silent Film Industries?* (Urbana: University of Illinois Press, 2018); Maggie Hennefeld, *Specters of Slapstick and Silent Film Comediennes* (New York: Columbia University Press, 2018); and Shelley Stamp, *Lois Weber in Early Hollywood* (Oakland: University of California Press, 2015).

PREMIER ENTR'ACTE: COLLECTION

1. Lotte H. Eisner, "From One Who Went Forth to Learn What 'Cinema' Was: What the Prussian *Staatsbibliothek* Knows About Film," trans. Naomi DeCelles, *Screen* 62, no. 3 (Autumn 2021): 382.
2. Eisner, "From One Who Went Forth," 382.
3. Eisner, "From One Who Went Forth," 384.
4. Eisner, "From One Who Went Forth," 383.
5. Eisner, "From One Who Went Forth," 384.
6. Eisner, "From One Who Went Forth," 384.

CHAPTER 1. ARCHIVISTS

1. Lucienne Escoubé, "Sauvons les films de répertoire," *Pour Vous*, March 31, 1932, 3. Unless otherwise indicated, translations from the French are mine.

2. Lucie Derain, "Les Etoiles sous le microphone ... III.—le présent et l'avenir du film parlant et sonore," *Le Quotidien*, March 1, 1930, 1. Regarding sound cinema in France, see Colin Crisp, *The Classic French Cinema, 1930–1960* (Bloomington: Indiana University Press, 1993); and Dudley Andrew, *Mists of Regret: Culture and Sensibility in the Classic French Film* (Princeton, NJ: Princeton University Press, 1995). According to both of them, the so-called poetic realist films of the 1930s emerged in France as a way to counter the success of the first Hollywood sound films and "talkies" and to boost the slow emergence of a French national sound cinema.

3. Eric Smoodin, *Paris in the Dark: Going to the Movies in the City of Light, 1930–1950* (Durham, NC: Duke University Press, 2020), 23–24.

4. Langlois once admitted that it was Escoubé's article that "ultimately led to the creation of the Cinémathèque française." Henri Langlois, *Ecrits de cinéma: 1931–1977* (Paris: Flammarion, 2014), 226. Langlois mistakenly wrote that the article was published in *Pour Vous* in 1934.

5. In this chapter, "Moussinac" designates Jeanne Moussinac, whereas "L. Moussinac" designates her husband Léon. I employ this notation intentionally, as a way to focus attention on Jeanne and to decenter Léon.

6. As Elaine Burrows explains, a "system of statutory deposit" was also central to the British Film Institute (BFI) and its National Film Library in the 1930s. For practical and financial reasons, however, Ernest Lindgren, the BFI curator, recognized that a rigorous selection process was necessary to the good functioning of the BFI. Burrows, "A Historical Overview of NFTVA/BFI Collection Development Policies with Regard to Gender and Nation Questions," *Framework* 51, no. 2 (Fall 2010): 344–45.

7. Fonds Moussinac, Léon (cinéma, théâtre), COL-10. Bibliothèque nationale de France, Département des Arts du spectacle, Paris, France (hereafter FML).

8. "Dossiers divers: Correspondance, notes, décrets, statuts d'organisations et d'institutions, scénarios, projets et synopsis de films, rapports, coupures de presse, discours, documentation, 1932–1960," Archives de l'administration des Beaux-Arts. Politique du cinéma (années 1920–1950), F/21/8671, Archives Nationales, Pierrefitte-sur-Seine, France (hereafter AABA).

9. For the Roger-Viollet archive, see https://www.roger-viollet.fr/photographer/laure-albin-guillot-117.

10. Delphine Désveaux and Michaël Houlette, eds., *Laure Albin-Guillot: L'Enjeu classique* (Paris: Jeu de Paume, Editions de la Martinière, 2013), 24.

11. François Chapon, *C'était Jacques Doucet* (Paris: Fayard, 2006), 465.

12. RCOL-2(17,7), FML.

13. Christophe Gauthier, *La passion du cinéma: Cinéphiles, ciné-clubs et salles spécialisées à Paris de 1920 à 1929* (Paris: Ecole des Chartes, AFRHC [Association française de recherche sur l'histoire du cinéma], 1999).

14. My understanding of modern librarianship comes from, among others, Martine Poulain, ed., *Histoire des bibliothèques françaises: Les Bibliothèques au XXe siècle, 1914–1990* (Paris: Editions du Cercle de la Librairie, 1992). Before World War II, a number of different types of libraries existed in France: private libraries owned by wealthy collectors; popular libraries (*bibliothèques populaires*); school libraries; municipal libraries; and the Bibliothèque Nationale (BN), which was considered the world's largest library at the time. I am only concerned with the BN in this section.

15. Eugène Morel, *Bibliothèques: Essai sur le développement des bibliothèques publiques et de la librairie dans les deux mondes* (Paris: Mercure de France, 1908); *La Librairie publique* (Paris: Librairie Armand Colin, 1910). For more biographical details about Morel, see Gaëtan Benoît, *Eugène Morel: Pioneer of Public Libraries in France* (Duluth, MN: Litwin Books, 2008).

16. Morel, *Bibliothèques*, 216.

17. In a recent article about the BAA, the curator Marie-Anne Sarda explains, "Its [the BAA's] organization, which was unique in its time, resembled that of some art history departments in American universities, such as the Institute of Fine Arts at New York University (NYU), an ideal workplace, where one feels at home and has access to all the books." Sarda, "Rue Spontini (Partie 1)," Bibliothèque d'Art et d'Archéologie Jacques Doucet, July 30, 2021, https://baadoucet.hypotheses.org/1673. The comparison between the BAA and NYU brings to mind Eugène Morel's writings, in which Morel advocates for French public libraries to emulate the US model.

18. André Joubin, "La Bibliothèque d'art et d'archéologie de l'Université de Paris," *Actes du Congrès d'histoire de l'art* (1921), 138–39.

19. Joubin, "La Bibliothèque," 141.

20. 4-COL-10(6,1), 4-COL-10(6,2), 4-COL-10(6,3), FML.

21. 4-COL-10(6,1), FML.

22. Doucet most likely referred to the following: "Bibliographie du 'cinéma,'" *Le Crapouillot*, March 1927, 48. Although the bibliography is not signed, Doucet is probably right to assume it was written by L. Moussinac. The same issue of *Le Crapouillot* included an article by L. Moussinac about the history of cinema, "Etapes," *Le Crapouillot*, March 1927, 16–19.

23. 4-COL-10(6,2), FML. *L'Usine aux images* was apparently unobtainable for a long time. It was published in France in 1995.

24. 4-COL-10(8,13), FML.

25. 4-COL-10(8,7), FML. A one-page draft organizational document by Blaise Cendrars lists several sections dedicated to books, periodicals, manuscripts, photographs, and films. Despite being written in pencil, and without much detail (only nouns, nominal groups, and numbers), this document attests to a certain desire for rationalization that also manifests in the other sets of documents cited in this chapter. According to Christophe Gauthier, Doucet approached Blaise Cendrars about the BC before L. Moussinac in March 1928. Gauthier, "1927, Year One of the French Film Heritage," *Film History* 17, nos. 2/3 (2005): 298. Yet a letter from Cendrars to Jeanne Moussinac dated March 7, 1928, as well as the typed manuscript from 1927, clearly suggest something else. Although I have been unable to locate Moussinac's first letter to Cendrars, Cendrars's response indicates that Moussinac had reached out to Cendrars and requested his collaboration for the BC, not the other way around. Cendrars's letter reads: "Madame, it's with the greatest pleasure that I make myself available to constitute a cinema library for Mr. Doucet. If you think I can be useful to you, please come and see me next Friday from 3 to 5pm, at my place, 2 rue des Marronniers, in the 16th." The draft mentioned earlier was probably sent after a meeting between the two was arranged, of which there remains no apparent trace in the archives. It is unclear why Cendrars would discuss the organization of the BC after L. Moussinac had apparently sorted out the matter in the typed manuscript of 1927.

26. L. Moussinac sent the handwritten manuscript for "Sur la création d'une bibliothèque du cinématographe et son organisation" on April 14, 1927. R-COL-2(17,7), FML. The typed manuscript in the Fonds Léon Moussinac of the BnF is also dated 1927. 4-COL-10(7,3).

27. A copy of *Monde* from January 26, 1929, survives at the BnF, 4-COL10 (7,4), FML.

28. Léon Moussinac, *Panoramique du cinéma* (Paris: Au sans pareil, 1929), 118–19.

29. "Documentation: 1," *Dictionnaire de la langue française (Littré)*, Tome 2 (1873), https://artflsrv04.uchicago.edu/philologic4.7/publicdicos/navigate/15/4633; "Documentation: n. f.," *Dictionnaire de l'Académie française*, 8th ed., Tome 1 (1935), https://artflsrv04.uchicago.edu/philologic4.7/publicdicos/navigate/18/9788.

30. "Documentation: n. f."

31. 4-COL-10(8, 29), FML.

32. 4-COL-10(8, 29), FML.

33. Sharon Macdonald, "Collecting Practices," in *A Companion to Museum Studies*, ed. Sharon Macdonald (New York: John Wiley & Sons, 2010), 211.

34. Jeanne Moussinac mentioned Poulaille's article on German cinema in "La Bibliothèque cinématographique de M. Jacques Doucet," *Bulletin de la Société des amis de la Bibliothèque d'art et d'archéologie de l'Université de Paris, Fondation Jacques Doucet* 2 (1929), 12.

35. The exception would be Christophe Gauthier, who explains, in "1927," that Jeanne Moussinac did most of the legwork at the BC. Still, his final description of the BC slightly undermines Moussinac compared to her husband Léon. "Although prematurely interrupted," Gauthier writes, "this [the BC] was a serious effort at conserving film history. . . . One should speak of the prescience of the library begun by Jacques Doucet with Léon Moussinac as theoretician and Jeanne Moussinac as organizer, anticipating modern film-related conservation centers" (301).

36. Chapon, *C'était Jacques Doucet*, 467.

37. Due to COVID-19, and then to the forced administrative closure of the Bibliothèque littéraire Jacques-Doucet from 2022 through 2023, I was unable to access Moussinac's notebooks (supposedly) held in the Bibliothèque's collections and mentioned in Chapon's biography.

38. Respectively, 4-COL-10(5,4) and 4-COL-10(5,5), FML. Among the love letters a small dried flower has survived too.

39. Gaston Haustrate, "Jean Lods: Sa vie, son oeuvre," *Cinéma 74* 188 (June 1974): 119.

40. Valérie Vignaux, "Léon Moussinac intellectuel communiste," in *Léon Moussinac: Un intellectuel communiste*, ed. Valérie Vignaux and François Albera (Paris: AFRHC, 2014), 19.

41. Vignaux, "Léon Moussinac," 24.

42. Haustrate, "Jean Lods," 120.

43. Angela Kershaw, "The Journey to the USSR in the 1930s: Apology, Apocrypha, Apostasy," in *French Political Travel Writing in the Inter-War Years*, ed. Martyn Cornick et al. (New York: Routledge, 2017), 139.

44. Suzanne Briet, *Qu'est-ce que la documentation?* (Paris: EDIT [Editions documentaires industrielles et techniques], 1951). One of only three women to become a professional librarian at the BN in 1924, according to Sylvie Fayet-Scribe, Briet spent her career developing public access to the catalogs and bibliographies of the BN. Fayet-Scribe, "Connaissez-vous Suzanne Briet?," *Bulletin des bibliothèques de France (BBF)* 1 (2012): 40–44. Based on Suzanne Briet's employee file at the BN, which I have consulted at the BnF François-Mitterrand, Briet worked at the BN from 1924 until 1955. She first went by her husband's last name, Dupuy, until her divorce in 1933. When working on the catalogs and bibliographies of the BN, she was sometimes assisted by a "Mademoiselle Bigot." *Qu'est-ce que la documentation?* remains important to anyone interested in library sciences today.

45. Film professionals whose letters remain in the Fonds Léon Moussinac at the BnF are Claude Autant-Lara, Jacques de Baroncelli, Jean Benoit-Lévy, Raymond Bernard, Alberto Cavalcanti, Henri Chomette, René Clair, Germaine Dulac, Jean Epstein and his sister Marie Epstein, Abel Gance, Jean Grémillon, Jaque-Catelain, Dimitry Kirsanoff, Henry Krauss, Marcel L'Herbier, Léon Poirier, Jean Tedesco of the Vieux-Colombier, and Laurence Myrga of the Studio des Ursulines.

46. 4-COL-10(8, 18), FML.

47. 4-COL-10(8,14), FML. What Dulac meant by "negatives" is not entirely clear, but she most likely referred to camera negatives.

48. Regarding the historical importance of that scenario, see Alain Virmaux, "La Coquille et le clergyman, 'notes sur un film controversé,'" *Paris* 64, no. 681 (January 1, 1986): 158–68; and Jean-Paul Morel, "A la recherche de la coquille . . . ," *1895: Mille huit cent quatre-vingt-quinze* 91 (2020–22): 147–52.

49. 4-COL-10(8,28), FML.

50. 4-COL-10(8,28), FML.

51. 4-COL-10(8,15) and 4-COL-10(8,28), FML.

52. See 4-COL-10(8,27), 4-COL-10(8,10), and 4-COL-10(8,30), FML.

53. Briet, *Qu'est-ce que la documentation?*, 24–25.

54. 4-COL-10(9,1), FML.

55. Most of the film-related materials at the BN belonged to the Auguste Rondel collection, which then banker and collector Auguste Rondel donated to the state in 1920. The collection joined the Bibliothèque de l'Arsenal in 1925 and is now part of the BnF-Arts du spectacle. For more on that collection, see Rime Touil, "Les Sources du cinéma muet dans les collections du département des Arts du spectacle de la Bibliothèque nationale de France," in *A la recherche de l'histoire du cinéma en France (1908–1919): Lieux, sources, objets*, ed. Clément Puget and Laurent Véray (Pessac: Presses universitaires de Bordeaux, 2022), 89–106.

56. 4-COL-10(9,2), 4-COL-10(9,3), 4-COL-10(9,4), 4-COL-10(9,5), 4-COL-10(9,6), FML.

57. 4-COL-10(9,2), FML.

58. Léopold Delisle, *Catalogue général des livres imprimés de la Bibliothèque nationale* (Paris: Imprimerie Nationale, 1897), v–vi. The Clément classification divides the collections of the BN into twenty-three series.

59. BnF Catalogue général (title *Les Origines du cinématographe*, notice number FRBNF32014406), accessed April 27, 2022, https://catalogue.bnf.fr/ark:/12148/cb320144060; BnF Catalogue général (title *On tourne*, notice number FRBNF31116828), accessed April 27, 2022), https://catalogue.bnf.fr/ark:/12148/cb31116828x.

60. Gallica (title *On tourne*, notice number FRBNF31116828), accessed April 27, 2022, https://gallica.bnf.fr/ark:/12148/bd6t5368042c.

61. 4-COL-10(10,24), FML.

62. Interestingly enough, another letter from March 1928 suggests that Moussinac had also contacted Henry Poulaille to ask him to write an essay on Chaplin. Poulaille refused for reasons I have addressed previously; not only did he not wish to have his work be part of a library, but he was also already engaged in a study on German actress and film producer Henny Porten. (As far as I know, that study on Porten was never finished or published.) Whether Poulaille's study would have been a supplement to Soupault's remains unclear. Ultimately, Poulaille submitted an essay on German cinema.

63. 4-COL10/8(31), FML. In 1957, Soupault published a short book titled *Charlot*, which told the biography of Charlie Chaplin's famous screen character based on the films that character appeared in. *Charlot* (Paris: Librairie Plan, 1957). Regarding the popularity of Chaplin with Soupault and other members of the Parisian avant-garde in the 1920s, see François Albera, "'L'Ecole comique française', une avant-garde posthume?," in "Aux sources du burlesque cinématographique: Les Comiques français des premiers temps," ed. Laurent Guido and Laurent Le Forestier, special issue of *1895: Mille huit cent quatre-vingt-quinze* 61 (September 1910): 77–114; and Jennifer Wild, *The Parisian Avant-Garde in the Age of Cinema, 1900–1923* (Oakland: University of California Press, 2015).

64. 4-COL-10(10,24), 36–37, FML.

65. Moussinac, "La Bibliothèque."

66. Moussinac, "La Bibliothèque," 14.

67. R-COL-2(17,7), FML.

68. Touil, "Les Sources du cinéma," 92.

69. Touil, "Les Sources du cinéma," 92.

70. "Ministère de l'Education Nationale," *Journal officiel de la République française*, March 24, 1934, 2979.

71. To learn more about these other preservation efforts, see Gauthier, *La Passion du cinéma* and "1927"; and Béatrice de Pastre-Robert and Emmanuelle Devos, "La Cinémathèque de la Ville de Paris," *1895: Mille huit cent quatre-vingt-quinze* 18 (Summer 1995): 107–21.

72. Eugène Morel, *La Loi sur le dépôt légal (19 mai 1925)* (Paris: Librairie Ancienne Honoré Champion, 1925).

73. Morel, *La Loi*, 17.

74. "Loi sur le dépôt légal," *Journal officiel de la République française*, May 27, 1925, 4934–35.

75. Frédéric Saby, "Approche historique du dépôt légal en France," *Sociétés & Représentations* 35 (2013): 15–26.

76. According to BnF librarian Rime Touil's estimations, Pathé deposited six thousand scripts between 1907 and 1922, and Gaumont deposited four hundred between 1906 and 1926. "Les Sources du cinéma," 99.

77. R. D'Ast, "Notre enquête: Vers une cinémathèque nationale," *La Liberté*, May 18, 1932, 2.

78. F/21/8671, AABA.

79. "Ministère de l'Education Nationale," 2979.

80. René Chavance, "Pour la conservation de nos films: Une cinémathèque au Palais du Trocadéro," *La Liberté*, April 11, 1932, 1.

81. F/21/8671, AABA.

82. F/21/8671, AABA.

83. F/21/8671, AABA.

84. As was fairly common at the time, Laure Albin-Guillot used her husband's first and last names as her last name. Her husband, Albin Célestin Louis Guillot (1875–1929), had studied medicine but worked as an industrialist and music composer.

85. Christian Bouquet, *Laure Albin-Guillot ou la volonté d'art* (Paris: Marval, 1996), 6.

86. Désveaux and Houlette, *Laure Albin-Guillot*, 12.

87. "La Cinémathèque Nationale," *Le Cinéopse*, February 1933, 9.

88. Raymond Borde, *Les Cinémathèques* (Paris: L'Age d'homme, 1983), 57–58.

89. See Catherine Gonnard, "Une carrière au féminin," in *Laure Albin-Guillot: L'Enjeu classique*, ed. Delphine Désveaux and Michaël Houlette (Paris: Jeu de Paume, Editions de la Martinière, 2013), 27–31.

90. "Exposition de photographies tirées de films scientifiques," *Le Parisien*, April 4, 1933, 2.

91. René Micquel, "Avec les cinéastes amateurs," *L'Image*, January 1, 1934, 23–27.

92. Gilles Ollivier, "Histoire des images, histoire des sociétés: L'Exemple du cinéma d'amateur," *1895: Mille huit cent quatre-vingt-quinze* 17 (1994), 118.

93. Albin-Guillot's nomination at the SAP was announced in "Service des archives photographiques des beaux-arts," *Journal officiel de la République française*, May 15, 1932, 5090. Based on extant documents from the Archives Nationales, administrators of the Beaux-Arts had discussed the idea of a national cinematheque since at least the end of 1929, when Albin-Guillot's predecessor, Paul Ratouis de Limay, was still the head of the service.

94. See SPCA's official website, https://www.ecpad.fr/collections/premiere-guerre-mondiale/.

95. Paul Ratouis de Limay, "Les Archives photographiques des Beaux-Arts," in *Congrès archéologique de France, XCVIIe Session, Tenue à PARIS en 1934* (Paris: A. Picard, 1935), 289.

96. Henriette Chandet, "Palmarès féminin," *L'Echo de Paris*, June 19, 1932, 4; "Directrice des archives photographiques des Beaux-Arts," *La Française*, September 24, 1932, 2.

97. "Les Archives du cinéma," *La Volonté*, January 23, 1933, 2.

98. These administrators include Georges Huismans, Emile Bollaert, and René Gadave.

99. Albin-Guillot was also a member of the Association des Amis de la CN, which organized public fundraising events and lobbied for more government financing.

100. F/21/8671, AABA.

101. F/21/8671, AABA.

102. F/21/8671, AABA.

103. Documents in the Archives Nationales suggest that "R. Dupoux" was the only film technician employed at the CN. He was a former employee of Kodak Pathé.

DEUXIEME ENTR'ACTE: RECOLLECTION

1. Lotte Eisner, "Comment écrire l'histoire du cinéma," *Positif* 6 (April 1953): 38.

2. Eisner, "Comment écrire l'histoire du cinéma," 38.

3. See Eisner, *J'avais jadis une belle patrie*.

4. Lotte Eisner, "Preface to English-Language Edition," in *F. W. Murnau* (London: Secker & Warburg, 1973), 6.

5. "The Making of F. W. Murnau's 'Tabu'—The Outtakes Edition," Deutsche Kinemathek, accessed August 4, 2025, https://www.deutsche-kinemathek.de/en/collections-archives/digital-collection/murnau-tabu.

6. Eisner, "Comment écrire l'histoire du cinéma," 38.

CHAPTER 2. WITNESSES

1. Between the 1920s and 1940s, the castle served as a retirement home for the Mutuelle du Cinéma. It was later acquired by the city of Orly. Today, the castle still stands in what is now called the Parc Méliès and hosts the Ecole Georges Méliès, which offers educational programs in animation, digital special effects, and video games.

2. Madeleine Malthête-Méliès, *Georges Méliès l'enchanteur* (Grandvilliers: La Tour Verte, 2011), 478–79. The Cercle du Cinéma was probably founded at the end of 1935. Its first screening took place on January 17, 1936, in Paris.

3. Lucien Patry, "Entretien avec Georges FRANJU: Directeur artistique de la Cinémathèque Française," *Films & Documents: Revue des techniques audiovisuelles* 332 (October–December 1980): 38.

4. "La Cinémathèque française est créée," *La Cinématographie française*, September 26, 1936, 97.

5. Mannoni, *Histoire de la Cinémathèque française*.

6. "Des jeunes sauvent les vieux films," *Comoedia*, January 17, 1936, 6.

7. Henri Langlois, "Classiques de l'écran muet," *La Cinématographie française* 876–77 (August 24, 1935): 17.

8. "On tourne," *Le Jour*, May 21, 1936, 6. Members of the "first French avant-garde" were Louis Delluc, Abel Gance, Marcel L'Herbier, Germaine Dullac, Jean Epstein, and René Clair.

9. Richard Abel, *French Cinema: The First Wave, 1915–1929* (Princeton, NJ: Princeton University Press, 1984), 251.

10. For example, the CRH often claimed that it was Léonce Perret, not D. W. Griffith, who invented the close-up. According to Bernard Bastide, "the creation of the Commission on that date isn't a coincidence. This is happening five years after the creation of the Cinémathèque française, [and] two years before the celebrations of the fiftieth anniversary of the first public projection of the Lumière cinématographe, which is to say at a time when the notion of cinematographic heritage [*patrimoine cinématographique*] became legitimate." "La Commission de recherches historiques de la Cinémathèque française," in *Histoire du cinéma: Problématique des sources*, ed. Irène Bessière and Jean A. Gili (Paris: Institut National d'Histoire de l'Art, 2004), 113.

11. Laurent Mannoni, "Henri Langlois and the Musée du Cinéma," *Film History* 18, no. 3 (2006): 274–87.

12. As I explain later, I borrow the concept of "shared authority" from Michael Frisch, *A Shared Authority: Essays on the Craft and Meaning of Oral and Public History* (Albany: State University of New York Press, 1990).

13. While most CRH transcripts are currently filed in the CRH collection of the CF, some may be found elsewhere, in the CF's Fonds Georges Sadoul, for example. In the chapter on the "French comic school" (école comique française) in

the third volume of his *Histoire générale du cinéma* (1951), Sadoul cites an interview with director Jean Durand and actors Gaston Modot and Jeanne Marie-Laurent from 1944, which appears nowhere in the CRH collection. Georges Sadoul, *Histoire générale du cinéma: 3, le cinéma devient un art 1909–1920, vol. 1, l'avant-guerre* (Paris: Denoël, 1951), 159, 162. Instead, the CRH collection includes a transcript for the interview organized with Durand's nephew—name unknown, possibly Philippe Durand—after Durand's death in 1946. CRH55-B3, Fonds de la Commission de Recherches historiques, La Cinémathèque française, Paris, France (hereafter CRHCF). All credits go to Bernard Bastide for recently locating Durand's interview in the Fonds Georges Sadoul.

14. Bastide, "La Commission de recherches historiques," 120.

15. I am aware of only a few other oral history projects dedicated to the cinema in the United States: the George Pratt Cinema Oral History (1958) at the George Eastman Museum in Rochester, NY; the Popular Arts Project (1958–60) at Columbia Center for Oral History; Kevin Brownlow's published book of interviews, *The Parade's Gone By . . .* (New York: Ballantine Books, 1968); the Oral History Program at the Academy of Motion Picture Arts and Sciences (1989–); and Women in Film Oral History (1989–2007). In the preface to *Women Filmmakers in Early Hollywood* (Baltimore, MD: Johns Hopkins University Press, 2006), ix, Karen Ward Mahar explains that working for the oral history project sponsored by the Women in Film Foundation had influenced her research into early US cinema.

16. In the years before the CRH, several industrialists, filmmakers, and actors published their memoirs, including Félix Mesguich (*Tours de manivelle*, 1933), Ivan Mosjoukine (*Quand j'étais Michel Strogoff*, 1927), and Charles Pathé (*Souvenirs et conseils d'un parvenu*, 1926; *De Pathé Frères à Pathé Cinéma*, 1940). In 1925, G.-Michel Coissac also acknowledged that he had met with Léon Gaumont, Charles Pathé, Jules Demaria, and Edmont Benoît-Lévy, whom he thanked in the note to the reader in his book *Histoire du cinématographe* (1925). Henri Fescourt had also interviewed the stage and film actress Aimée Tessandier in 1912, as well as Emile Cohl, Ladislas Starevitch, Boris Bilinsky, Raoul Grimoin-Sanson, and possibly others for his edited collection, *Le Cinéma, des origines à nos jours* (1932). Finally, as they were working on their book, Maurice Bardèche and Robert Brasillach frequently visited Georges Méliès in Orly. Several French radio shows also featured early filmmakers and movie workers,

which certainly speaks to the broader public interest in French film history in the interwar years.

17. "OHA Core Principles," Oral History Association, accessed April 27, 2022, https://www.oralhistory.org/oha-core-principles/#_edn1.

18. "OHA Core Principles."

19. "Born in Slavery: Slave Narratives from the Federal Writers' Project, 1936 to 1938," Library of Congress, accessed April 27, 2022, https://www.loc.gov/collections/slave-narratives-from-the-federal-writers-project-1936-to-1938/about-this-collection/.

20. "Born in Slavery."

21. "Oral Histories," John F. Kennedy Presidential Library and Museum, accessed April 27, 2022, https://www.jfklibrary.org/archives/about-archival-collections/oral-histories.

22. "Oral Histories."

23. Florence Descamps, *L'Historien, l'archiviste et le magnétophone: De la constitution de la source orale à son exploitation* (Paris: Comité pour l'histoire économique et financière de la France, 2001).

24. Descamps, *L'Historien, l'archiviste et le magnétophone*, n.p.

25. Ronald J. Grele, "Oral History as Evidence," in *Handbook of Oral History*, ed. Thomas L. Charlton et al. (Lanham, MD: AltaMira Press, 2006), 53.

26. Grele, "Oral History as Evidence," 53.

27. Grele, "Oral History as Evidence," 63; Trouillot, *Silencing the Past*, 26.

28. Grele, "Oral History as Evidence," 75.

29. That kind of suspicion is arguably still there among historians of early cinema.

30. CRH1-B1, CRHCF; emphasis added. These documents probably included a mix of primary and secondary sources, such as original film catalogs (for Méliès, Gaumont, and Pathé) (CRH89-B4), early film newspapers and magazines, Charles Pathé's memoirs (CRH54-B3), *Histoire du cinéma* (1935, 1943, 1948) by Maurice Bardèche and Robert Brasillach (CRH39-B2), and publications by René Jeanne and Georges Sadoul.

31. Annette Förster, *Women in the Silent Cinema: Histories of Fame and Fate* (Amsterdam: Amsterdam University Press, 2017), 139.

32. Förster, *Women in the Silent Cinema*, 162–63.

33. Förster, *Women in the Silent Cinema*, 166.

34. Francis Lacassin claimed that Musidora participated in the adaptation of *La Vagabonde* and in the direction of *Minne,* but Förster explains that she remains unable to confirm these two credits. Förster, *Women in the Silent Cinema*, 237.

35. Förster explains that Les Films Musidora were mentioned only once in the press, in *Filma* in December 1919. According to Förster, *Soleil et ombre* was probably codirected by Musidora and Jacques Lasseyne, even though only Lasseyne was credited in contemporary publicity material. *Women in the Silent Cinema*, 270. Furthermore, Förster indicates that *La Terre des taureaux* was "not intended to be presented as a film, but the film parts were meant to be screened along with and between live performances by Musidora and Cañero" (271).

36. The film was apparently titled *La Magique image* and is considered lost today. I have also found that a film called *Photogénie 50* was mentioned in 1950. See J.-F. Devay, "Le Festival d'Antibes," *Combat*, September 2, 1950, 2.

37. Förster, *Women in the Silent Cinema*, 210.

38. See, for example, Léa Buisson, "De Musidora à Mad Souri: L'Influence du cinéma sur *Le Trésor des Jésuites* de Breton et Aragon," *L'Annuaire théâtral* 59 (Spring 2016): 31–47.

39. Förster, *Women in the Silent Cinema*, 211.

40. CRH89-B4, CRHCF.

41. CRH89-B4, p. 2, CRHCF.

42. In several interviews, the narrators also mentioned that they were there as a personal favor to Musidora. See, for instance, CRH54-B3, p. 5, CRHCF.

43. See, for example, CRH71-B3, p. 5, CRHCF, in which Musidora remembered seeing *L'Ange bleu* (*The Blue Angel*, Josef von Sternberg, 1930) at the Studio des Ursulines; and CRH70-B3, p. 1, CRHCF, in which Musidora explained that she would start the meeting by reading Henri Langlois's questions out loud.

44. CRH29-B1, CRHCF.

45. CRH29-B1, CRHCF.

46. CRH29-B1, p. 6, CRHCF. The handwritten additions to the typed transcript are indicated between asterisks (*).

47. CRH51-B2, CRHCF.

48. CRH51-B2, p. 14, CRHCF.

49. Francis Lacassin, "Musidora," *Anthologie du cinéma* 6 (1971): 441–504.

50. CRH4-B1, CRHCF. As of July 2021, I have been unable to identify who wrote this report by hand.

51. Förster, *Women in the Silent Cinema*, 211.

52. Förster, *Women in the Silent Cinema*, 211. In addition to Lacassin, "Musidora," see, for example, Henri Fescourt, *La Foi et les montagnes; ou, le septième art au passé* (Paris: P. Montel, 1959), 93–96; Patrick Cazals, *Musidora, la dixième muse* (Paris: Editions Henri Veyrier, 1978). In his book, Fescourt cites the interview with Renée Sylvaire. He probably also had conversations with Musidora.

53. Sandy Flitterman-Lewis, *To Desire Differently: Feminism and the French Cinema* (Urbana: University of Illinois Press, 1990). According to Flitterman-Lewis, Marie Epstein wrote her first script, "Les Mains qui meurent," in 1923, for a scenario competition sponsored by Pathé-Consortium. Although Epstein won the first prize, the film was never made (145). Flitterman-Lewis also explains that Epstein and Benoit-Lévy's films, which are "strongly rooted in their time and typical of the national cinematic identity that French filmmakers of the thirties sought," offer representations of women and female sexuality that are nonetheless unique to Epstein's oeuvre (184). See also: Flitterman-Lewis and Astrid Burnod, "Marie Epstein," in *Women Film Pioneers Project*, ed. Jane Gaines et al. (New York: Columbia University Libraries, 2016), https://wfpp.columbia.edu/pioneer/marie-epstein/.

54. CRH74-B4; CRH75-B4, CRHCF.

55. CRH47-B2, pp. 11–12, CRHCF.

56. CRH62-B3, p. 13, CRHCF.

57. CRH23-B1, CRH70-B3, CRHCF. According to Gilles Delluc, Francis and Delluc met in 1913, married in 1918, and separated in 1922. *Louis Delluc, 1890–1924: L'Eveilleur du cinéma français au temps des années folles* (Périgueux, France: Pilote 24 édition, 2002).

58. CRH23-B1, p. 5, CRHCF. Francis mentioned that the dress was designed by a woman named Jo.

59. CRH70-B3, CRHCF.

60. CRH71-B3, p. 21, CRHCF.

61. Francis's pen name became the title for Delluc's 1922 film, in which she played the leading part.

62. Paula Amad, "'Objects Became Witnesses': Eve Francis and the Emergence of French Cinephilia and Film Criticism," *Framework: The Journal of Cinema and Media* 46, no. 1 (Spring 2005): 60.

63. Amad, "'Objects Became Witnesses,'" 47.

64. See Delluc, *Louis Delluc*, 377, 381–82.

65. Janine Bouissounouse was apparently close to Jeanne Moussinac's husband Léon, with whom she attended the Congrès International du Cinéma Indépendant in Switzerland in 1929. Like L. Moussinac, Bouissounouse was featured in *Tempête sur la Sarraz*, the film Sergei Eisenstein supposedly shot at the Congrès.

66. Louise Escoffier was the name Lotte Eisner used while in hiding during World War II and for some time after the war ended.

67. In the CRH collection and elsewhere, Nora Jonuxi's last name is sometimes spelled "Januxi." Her real name was apparently Pauline Durand, and she might have been from Marseilles.

68. CRH66-B3, CRHCF.

69. CRH65-B3, p. 3, CRHCF.

70. CRH24-B1, CRHCF.

71. CRH30-B1, CRHCF.

72. CRH41-B2, p. 3, CRHCF.

73. CRH41-B2, p. 8, CRHCF. Although claims of being "first" are generally dubious and ill-conceived, they often function to valorize individuals or national cinemas whose contributions to cinema's history have been forgotten, underestimated, or contested. In feminist film history, the emphasis on Alice Guy Blaché being the "first" woman filmmaker and Dorothy Arzner the "first" filmmaker to use a boom microphone, among many others, serves a similar purpose.

74. Alain Carou, "Le Scénario français en quête d'auteurs (1908–1918)," *1895: Mille huit cent quatre-vingt-quinze* 65 (2011): 28–51. According to Carou, "some businessmen, who had been selling literary or dramatic texts for a long time, tried to diversify with film scripts" that they bought from young writers—like Jonuxi and Abel Gance, for example—without direct access to film studios (39).

75. CRH41-B2, p. 10, CRHCF.

76. Carou suggests that the scenarios deposited at the BnF in the 1910s sometimes included the names of the writers. "Le Scénario français en quête d'auteurs," 30. But I have not been able to verify if Jonuxi's name appeared anywhere in that collection. In addition to "104 or 105 plays," and "more than 2,000 articles," Jonuxi claimed to have written a total of 145 scripts until 1922.

77. CRH41-B2, p. 1, CRHCF. Musidora claims that it was only after she requested that Louis Feuillade talk to Léon Gaumont that the actors' names started to appear on film posters. CRH41-B2, pp. 7–8, CRHCF.

78. "Le Concours de scénarios," *L'Oeuvre*, January 20, 1923, 2.

79. "Le Concours de scénarios," 2.

80. CRH1-B1, CRHCF.

81. Tom Gunning, "Systematizing the Electric Message: Narrative Form, Gender, and Modernity in *The Lonedale Operator*," in *American Cinema's Transitional Era: Audiences, Institutions, Practices*, ed. Charlie Keil and Shelley Stamp (Los Angeles: University of California Press, 2004), 15–50.

82. Delphine Gardey, "Mécaniser l'écriture et photographier la parole: Utopies, monde du bureau et histoire de genre et de techniques," *Annales* 54–53 (1999): 594.

83. Although Alice Guy Blaché was (and remains) known as Alice Guy in France, she expressed the desire later in life to retain both her maiden and married names in retrospective accounts of her career.

84. Alice Guy Blaché, *The Memoirs of Alice Guy Blaché*, trans. Roberta and Simone Blaché (Metuchen, NJ: Scarecrow Press, 1986), 11.

85. It is not impossible that other women worked at the same company. They were perhaps stationed in other departments, which would explain why Guy Blaché said she was the only woman in the "great room."

86. Later, and as a result of feminization, offices became slightly more hospitable to women than what Guy Blaché experienced at the Marais factory; at the very least, women were rarely "alone among a dozen men" anymore.

87. Hill, *Never Done*, 27.

88. Hill, *Never Done*, 26.

89. Hill, *Never Done*, 25.

90. CRH19-B1, p. 34, CRHCF. Two identical versions of the same document exist in the CRH collection.

91. CRH20-B1, CRHCF.

92. CRH71-B3, CRHCF.

93. CRH74-B4, CRHCF.

94. CRH46-B2, p. 2, CRHCF.

95. CRH89-B4, p. 2, CRHCF.

96. CRH30-B1, p. 13, CRHCF.
97. CRH33-B2, p. 24, CRHCF.
98. CRH69-B3, CRHCF.
99. CRH47-B2, CRHCF.
100. Bastide, "La Commission de recherches historiques," 120.
101. CRH69-B3, CRH51-B2, CRH50-B2, CRHCF.
102. I borrow the term "unhistoricized" from the Women Film Pioneers Project. See "Unhistoricized Women Film Pioneers," in *Women Film Pioneers Project*, ed. Jane Gaines et al. (New York: Columbia University Libraries, 2015), https://wfpp.columbia.edu/resources/unhistoricized-women-film-pioneers/.
103. CRH26-B1, 5, CRHCF.
104. CRH41-B2, p. 3, p. 8, CRHCF.
105. CRH30-B1, p. 13, CRHCF.

TROISIEME ENTR'ACTE: RECOVERY

1. For more on the reception of *The Cabinet of Dr. Caligari* in France, see Marc Lavastrou, "De Louis Delluc à *Caligari* . . .: L'Introduction du cinéma allemand en France," *Trajectoires* 5 (2011), https://doi.org/10.4000/trajectoires.685.
2. Lotte H. Eisner, *The Haunted Screen: Expressionism in the German Cinema and the Influence of Max Reinhardt*, trans. Roger Greaves (1973; Berkeley: University of California Press, 2008).
3. Eisner, *Haunted Screen*, 39.
4. Eisner, *Haunted Screen*, 39.
5. Eisner, *Haunted Screen*, 17.

CHAPTER 3. ACTIVISTS

1. Dana Sardet, phone conversation with author, March 27, 2025. Many thanks to Dana Sardet for her time and generosity. Her memories of the "Musidora" collective were crucial during this book's final stage of revisions. For a brief overview of Sardet's life, see Louisa Ourrad, "Portrait—Dana Sardet," *Les Femmes s'animent*, April 7, 2023, https://lesfemmessaniment.fr/portrait-dana-sardet-louisa-ourrad/.

2. To avoid any confusion here and throughout this chapter, "Musidora" designates the collective, and Musidora is the filmmaker.

3. An abridged and slightly different version of this chapter was published as "My Name Is Alice Guy: The 'Musidora' Collective and Women's Film History," *Feminist Media Histories* 8, no. 3 (Summer 2022): 155–77. I have since been able to get in touch with Dana Sardet, whose memories of the "Musidora" collective have helped me better comprehend its engagement with the film archive.

4. Among the founders of "Musidora," Nicole-Lise Bernheim was a writer, journalist, radio producer, and filmmaker with at least one acting credit at the time, in *Mon coeur est rouge* (Michèle Rosier, 1976); Françoise Flamant was a sociologist; Dana Sardet a filmmaker, videomaker, and photographer; Claudine Serre (also known as Claudine Monteil) a writer, historian, and close friend of Simone de Beauvoir, her sister Hélène, and Jean-Paul Sartre; Claire Clouzot a photographer, film critic, and the first cousin once removed of Henri-Georges Clouzot; and Danie Dubos a comic book colorist and the wife of set photographer and film director Pierre Zucca.

5. Allyson Nadia Field, "Editor's Introduction: Sites of Speculative Encounter," *Feminist Media Histories* 8, no. 2 (2022): 3.

6. Christine Garnier, "Comment réussissent les femmes: VI, Jacqueline Audry 'Travailler plus vite que les hommes,'" *Revue des deux mondes*, February 15, 1961, 666–73.

7. Garnier, "Comment réussissent les femmes," 668–69.

8. Garnier, "Comment réussissent les femmes," 673.

9. Garnier, "Comment réussissent les femmes," 673. Regarding gender in the films made by the French New Wave in the 1950s and 1960s, see Geneviève Sellier, *Masculine Singular: French New Wave Cinema,* trans. Kristin Ross (Durham, NC: Duke University Press, 2008).

10. Regarding Jacqueline Audry's career, see Brigitte Rollet, *Jacqueline Audry: La Femme à la caméra* (Rennes: Presses universitaires de Rennes, 2015).

11. "Musidora" chose Jacqueline Audry as their president, which was most likely an honorary title used to promote and legitimize the group's activities, especially the women's film festival they organized in April 1974.

12. "Les Femmes et le cinéma," *La Revue du cinéma: Image et son* 283 (April 1974): n.p.

13. Christine Delphy, "Les Origines du Mouvement de libération des femmes en France," *Nouvelles questions féministes* 16/18 (1991): 137–48. May 1968 refers to a major moment of political unrest in France, when mostly factory workers and students organized mass strikes and protests against President Charles de Gaulle's government.

14. Delphy, "Les Origines du Mouvement," 142.

15. These demands were written on the poster announcing the rally that took place in New York City's Bryant Park. The Women's Strike for Equality also advocated for other, more general rights for women.

16. As a system of oppression supported by capitalism, sexism functions to exploit women's labor, undermine their contributions to the national economy, exclude them from positions of power, exploit them sexually, control their bodies and sexualities, and ultimately maintain their subaltern position. The MLF, which included women only, thus intended to fight sexism collectively by speaking up and taking control of their own means of emancipation from the patriarchal tyranny. Then, until the early 1980s, the MLF worked to address women's issues (gender pay gap, stereotypical gender roles, marriage, vaginal orgasm, unwanted pregnancies, etc.) during large general assemblies every two weeks, and also formed smaller working groups that gathered more frequently, participated in female workers' strikes, organized protests, wrote articles for the press, and campaigned for the right to free and accessible abortion and contraception, which the "Veil law" put forward by then French health minister Simone Veil decriminalized in 1975. Another victory for the movement was the adoption of the "Roudy law" of 1983, named after the women's rights minister Yvette Roudy, which guaranteed women equal access and salaries in private businesses that had government contracts.

17. Films and videos shown during meetings of the women's movement included *Y'a qu'à pas baiser* (Carole Roussopoulos, 1971) and *Histoires d'A* (Charles Belmont and Marielle Issartel, 1973).

18. Françoise Picq, *Libération des femmes: Les Années-Mouvement* (Editions du Seuil, 1993), 156–57.

19. Hélène Fleckinger, "De la contribution des féministes aux expérimentations techniques, sociales et formelles de la 'vidéo des premiers temps' (France, 1968–1981)," in *Genre et techniques, XIXe–XXIe siècle*, ed. Fabien Knittel and Pascal Raggi (Rennes: Presses universitaires de Rennes, 2013), 253–66.

20. Fleckinger, "De la contribution des féministes," 258.

21. One indicator that the issue of women's representation in mass media was global is that, in 1968, the Commission on the Status of Women at the United Nations appointed a special rapporteur whose assignment was "to report on ways to eliminate stereotypes in the mass media's portrayal and coverage of women and girls." UN Women, *A Short History of the Commission on the Status of Women* (New York: Intergovernmental Support Division UN Women, 2019). See also Dee Boersma, "A Report on the United Nations Commission on the Status of Women and Mass Media," *Journal of the University Film Association* 26, nos. 1/2 (1974): 3–4.

22. Barbara Confino, "An Interview with Agnès Varda," *Saturday Review*, August 12, 1972, 35. That this interview appeared in an American publication is certainly no coincidence, given the importance of the feminist debate in the United States.

23. Molly Haskell, *From Reverence to Rape: The Treatment of Women in the Movies* (Chicago: University of Chicago Press, 1987), xiii.

24. Haskell, *From Reverence to Rape*, 33.

25. Brigitte Rollet, "Femmes cinéastes en France: L'Après-Mai 68," *Clio: Femmes, Genre, Histoire* 10 (1999): 2.

26. Eric Rhode, cited in *Cahiers du Cinéma: The 1950s: Neo-Realism, Hollywood, New Wave*, ed. Jim Hillier (Cambridge, MA: Harvard University Press, 1985), 5. See also François Truffaut, "Une certaine tendance du cinéma français," *Cahiers du cinéma* 6, no. 31 (January 1, 1954): 15.

27. Andrew Sarris, "The American Cinema," *Film Culture* (Spring 1963): 46. Several years later, in 1976, Sarris wrote a short article titled "The Ladies' Auxiliary" that revised his position about women filmmakers. As he himself acknowledged, "The new feminist perspectives on the cinema in the past decade (particularly in Molly Haskell's *From Reverence to Rape*, 1974) have refocused attention on the real and potential roles of woman directors." Andrew Sarris, "The Ladies' Auxiliary, 1976," in *Women and the Cinema: A Critical Anthology*, ed. Karyn Kay and Gerald Peary (New York: E. P. Dutton, 1977), 384–85.

28. "Editorial," *Women and Film* 1 (1972): 5–6. The "auteur theory" is the fourth problem cited by the journal's editors, after "a closed and sexist industry whose survival is precisely based on discrimination," woman's image on screen, and the objectification of women in advertising, and before the "elitist

hierarchy, destructive competition, and vicious international politics" that characterize the film industry today and "the prejudice on the part of film departments in universities and film institutes in accepting women in the faculty or as production students."

29. Regarding women's film festivals in the 1970s, see, for example, B. Ruby Rich, *Chick Flicks: Theories and Memories of the Feminist Film Movement* (Durham, NC: Duke University Press, 1998); and Katharina Kamleitner, "On Women's Film Festivals: Histories, Circuits, Futures" (PhD diss., University of Glasgow, 2020). The First International Festival of Women's Films took place at the Fifth Avenue Cinema in New York City between June 13 and 21, 1972. The festival Films by Women/Chicago '74, organized by Rich, Patricia Erens, Laura Mulvey, Julia Least, Virginia Wright Wexman, and others, was held at the Film Center of the School of the Art Institute (now the Gene Siskel Film Center) from September 3 to 17, 1974.

30. Françoise Flamant, "Des femmes organisent un festival," *La Revue du cinéma: Image et son* 283 (April 1974): n.p.

31. Marie-Jo Bonnet, "Musidora," in *Mon MLF* (Paris: Albin Michel, 2018), 174–75.

32. A twenty-six-minute video shot by Catherine Lahourcade and Anne-Marie Faure during the Musidora Festival gives us an insight into postscreening discussions and debates. Titled *Musidora: Festival international de films de femmes* and currently edited by the Centre audiovisual Simone de Beauvoir, it shows a majority of young white women reflecting on the presence of men at the festival, the relationship between women's cinema and politics, and so forth. Among the participants, one may recognize the actress and screenwriter Marie-France Pisier and a few French Canadian filmmakers from the National Film Board of Canada.

33. For a more detailed list of women's film festivals in the 1970s, see Clarissa K. Jacobs, "Women's Film Festival Timeline," *The Women and Film Project* (blog), accessed January 25, 2021, https://womenandfilmproject.wordpress.com/resources/festival-timeline/.

34. B. Ruby Rich, "The Crisis of Naming in Feminist Film Criticism," *Jump Cut* 19 (December 1978), https://www.ejumpcut.org/archive/onlinessays/JC19folder/RichCrisisOfNaming.html.

35. Antoine Damiens, "Film Festivals of the 1970s and the Subject of Feminist Film Studies: Collaborations and Regimes of Knowledge Production," *Journal of Film and Video* 72, nos. 1–2 (Spring/Summer 2020): 21–32.

36. Damiens, "Film Festivals of the 1970s," 24.

37. Damiens, "Film Festivals of the 1970s," 25; Mandy Merck, "Mulvey's Manifesto," *Camera Obscura* 22, no. 3 (2007): 1–23. See also Lynn Spigel, "Theorizing the Bachelorette: 'Waves' of Feminist Media Studies," *Signs* 30, no. 1 (Autumn 2004): 1209–21.

38. Rich, "Crisis of Naming." As a result of their emphasis on the film apparatus over "woman's image," Johnston and Mulvey were also much more skeptical than their US counterparts about the films by contemporary women filmmakers featured at women's film festivals. This shouldn't undermine the impact of these festivals on feminist film criticism and theory, however. The British approach became popular among US feminists via *Camera Obscura* later in the 1970s.

39. Ginette Vincendeau, "Women's Cinema, Film Theory and Feminism in France: Reflections After the 1987 Créteil Festival," *Screen* 28, no. 4 (Autumn 1987): 5.

40. Vincendeau, "Women's Cinema," 6.

41. Vincendeau, "Women's Cinema," 7.

42. Colette Godard, "Femmes entre elles," *Le Monde*, April 15, 1974, https://www.lemonde.fr/archives/article/1974/04/15/femmes-entre-elles_2525577_1819218.html. A few weeks before the Musidora Festival began, *Le Monde* had also published a brief announcement by Godard, "Festival Musidora," *Le Monde*, March 23, 1974, https://www.lemonde.fr/archives/article/1974/03/23/festival-musidora_2515592_1819218.html.

43. Barbara Halpern Martineau, "Paris/Chicago: Women's Film Festivals 1974," *Women and Film* 7 (1975): 10–27.

44. Halpern Martineau, "Paris/Chicago," 13.

45. See "La Revue du cinéma," *SubStance* 3, no. 9 (Spring 1974): 147–51.

46. Marcelle Fonfreide, "Introduction," *La Revue du cinéma: Image et son* 283 (April 1974): 18.

47. Nelly Kaplan, "A nous l'histoire d'une de nos folies," *La Revue du cinéma: Image et son* 283 (April 1974): n.p.; Nicole-Lise Bernheim, "Réactions," *La Revue du cinéma: Image et son* 283 (April 1974): n.p.

48. Françoise and Bénédicte, "Les Femmes et la technique du cinéma," *La Revue du cinéma: Image et son* 283 (April 1974): n.p.; Edith Vergne, "Les Métiers du cinéma: La Script-girl," *La Revue du cinéma: Image et son* 283 (April 1974): n.p.

49. Nicole-Lise Bernheim, "Entretien avec Jeanne Moreau," *La Revue du cinéma: Image et son* 283 (April 1974): n.p.

50. Viviane Forrester, "Le Regard des femmes," *La Revue du cinéma: Image et son* 283 (April 1974): n.p.

51. Des femmes de Musidora, *Paroles . . . elles tournent!* (Paris: Editions des femmes, 1976). The title of this book is difficult to translate into English. First, it is a play on the command "Silence . . . action!," or "Silence . . . ça tourne!" in French, which signals that women are finally speaking up for themselves. It might also have been a reference to Annie Leclerc's book *Parole de femmes* (1974), whose conceptions of feminism and femininity caused controversy upon publication. Finally, in using not the singular but the plural of the noun "parole," it emphasizes the collective dimension of the "Musidora" project.

52. Aurore Turbiau, "Musidora—Paroles . . . Elles tournent ! (1976)," *Littératures engagées*, June 2, 2019, https://engagees.hypotheses.org/83. Regarding the "Musidora" collective and feminist film criticism and theory in France, Alexandre Moussa also argues that, while the collective's writings are complex, varied, and close to Marjorie Rosen's and Molly Haskell's foundational works, they failed "when it comes to establishing principles for a feminist film theory." Alexandre Moussa, "'Paroles . . . elles tournent!': Musidora and the Rise and Fall of Feminist Film Criticism in France, 1973–1981" (presented at conference of Society for Cinema and Media Studies, Denver, CO, April 13, 2023).

53. Regarding Musidora's career behind the camera, see Förster, *Women in the Silent Cinema*.

54. According to Flamant in *La Revue du cinéma*, "Musidora lived from 1889 until 1957. She was first a famous silent film actress who then started directing films at a time when very few women had the chance to do so. . . . This 'femme fatale' knew how to express herself in her own works." "Des femmes organisent un festival," n. pag.; see also Françoise Flamant, *A tire d'elles: Itinéraires de féministes radicales des années 1970* (Rennes: Presses universitaires de Rennes, 2007).

55. Flamant, "Des femmes organisent un festival," n. pag.

56. Flamant, *A tire d'elles*, 40.

57. Nicole-Lise Bernheim, preface to *Autobiographie d'une pionnière du cinéma*, by Alice Guy (Paris: Denoël/Gonthier, 1976), 9. In the American edition of Alice Guy Blaché's memoirs, titled *The Memoirs of Alice Guy Blaché*, Anthony Slide explained that he "first became aware of the existence of Alice Guy Blaché's memoirs on April 10, 1973, when I visited her daughter, Simone, at her then-home in Mahwah, New Jersey." Alice Guy Blaché, *Memoirs*, vi. In our phone conversation on March 27, 2025, Sardet explained that Slide had mailed Guy Blaché's memoirs to her parents' house on the East Coast while she was visiting them from France. She then brought the manuscript back to France with her.

58. As I have argued elsewhere, Alice Guy Blaché's trajectory in and out of French and US film histories is quite complex. This chapter mostly focuses on how the "Musidora" collective perceived Guy Blaché as largely forgotten after the 1920s. See Aurore Spiers, "Rediscovered Again: The Nonlinear Path of Alice Guy Blaché into US Film History," in *The Routledge Companion to American Film History*, ed. Paula Massood and Pamela Robertson Wojcik (New York: Routledge, 2025). 378–88.

59. Bernheim, preface, 8.

60. Documents in the Alice Guy-Blaché collection at the Museum of Modern Art (MoMA) show that Guy Blaché had contacted several publishers in France about her memoirs, including Payot, Flammarion, Hachette, and Seuil, between 1961 and 1963. My gratitude goes to Clara Auclair for sharing her findings from the MoMA with me.

61. Regarding Alice Guy Blaché's memoirs, see Amelie Hastie, *Cupboards of Curiosity: Women, Recollection, and Film History* (Durham, NC: Duke University Press, 2007).

62. Colette Audry was a teacher, writer, and screenwriter who collaborated with her sister Jacqueline Audry on four of Jacqueline's films, mainly *Les Malheurs de Sophie* (1946), *Olivia* (1951), *Fruits amers* (1967), and *Le Lis de mer* (1969). In 1964, Colette Audry became the editor of the "Collection Femme" at Denoël Gonthier, which was apparently the first French collection to publish titles written by women only. In addition to Guy Blaché's memoirs, Audry published French translations of Betty Friedan's *The Feminine Mystique* (*La Femme mystifiée*) and *The Autobiography of Eleanor Roosevelt* (*Ma vie*), and works by Charlotte Delbo and others. See Séverine Liatard, "Colette Audry: Une intellectuelle

dans la sphère littéraire en 1962," in *Femmes de pouvoir: Mythes et fantasmes*, ed. Odile Krakovitch et al. (Paris: L'Harmattan, 2001), 135–42.

63. "Pionnier: n.m.," *Dictionnaire de l'Académie française*, 8th ed. (1935), https://www.dictionnaire-academie.fr/article/A8P1541; "Pionnier, Pionnière nom et adjectif," *Dictionnaire de l'Académie française*, 9th ed. (2011), https://www.dictionnaire-academie.fr/article/A9P2487. The woman pioneer cited as an example in 2011 was Marie Curie, whose work on radioactivity "made her a pioneer." For the date of publication of the volume that included the entries beginning with P, see "La 9e edition," Académie française, accessed April 28, 2022, https://www.academie-francaise.fr/le-dictionnaire/la-9e-edition.

64. Charles Ford, *Femmes cinéastes; ou le triomphe de la volonté* (Paris: Denoël, 1972), 9, 16. Ford also described Lotte Reiniger and Lucie Derain as pioneers. 84, 182.

65. In her memoirs, Guy Blaché also suggested that she had made her first fiction film, *La Fée aux choux*, in 1896, when the Lumière brothers and Léon Gaumont were still only interested in manufacturing motion picture cameras and making demonstration films in order to promote these cameras. Guy, *Autobiographie*, 61–62.

66. Francis Lacassin, "Out of Oblivion: Alice Guy Blaché," *Sight and Sound* (Summer 1971): 151.

67. Ford, *Femmes cinéastes*, 13.

68. Ford, *Femmes cinéastes*, 13, 16, 22.

69. Bernheim, preface, 10, 11.

70. "Qui est Alice Guy?," featuring Claire Clouzot, Nicole-Lise Bernheim, Daniel Toscan du Plantier, Charles Ford, Henri Langlois, Francis Lacassin, Jacques Deslandes, André Zwobada, Liliane de Kermadec, Colette Audry, and Delphine Seyrig, aired on July 2, 1975. https://www.radiofrance.fr/franceculture/podcasts/les-nuits-de-france-culture/qui-est-alice-guy-5694320.

71. Delphine Seyrig's presence during that radio program is fascinating. According to Sardet, Seyrig was a big supporter of the "Musidora" collective, whose festival in April 1974 she attended.

72. Ford, *Femmes cinéastes*, 9, 16.

73. Langlois's dismissive statement and tone strike me as rather strange here, given that Guy Blaché herself sometimes credited Langlois for helping to rehabilitate her work in France in the 1950s.

74. Dall'Asta and Gaines, "Prologue."
75. Bernheim, preface, 7–8.
76. Bernheim, preface, 9.
77. Bernheim, preface, 9.
78. Flamant, *A tire d'elles*, 43.
79. Flamant, *A tire d'elles*, 43.
80. The television show *Hiéroglyphes* might have been entirely dedicated to cinema. As of March 2025, however, I have not been able to find any more information about this program. At the time of writing, *Qui est Alice Guy?* is available on INA's website at https://www.ina.fr/video/CPC7606810102. According to Hélène Fleckinger in her conference presentation "Le Collectif Musidora, entre cinéma et féminisme: Variations autour d'une photographie de Pierre Zucca," *Qui est Alice Guy?* might also have been shown in a screening program dedicated to "Images of Women in the Cinema" in 1977.
81. Based on my email conversation with Monique Renault on February 8, 2021, Renault met Nicole-Lise Bernheim in 1973, on the steps of the Grand Palais in Paris, where Bernheim was giving out flyers about the "Musidora" collective. Renault, whose feminist animated films weren't always met with approval within the film industry, found "Musidora" incredibly supportive. She was involved in the organization of the Musidora Festival, and she is listed in the "First Index of French Women Filmmakers" published by Dana Sardet and Claire Clouzot in *La Revue du cinéma* (April 1974). According to Renault's website, she had already directed three animated films by 1975: *Psychoderche* (1972), *A la vôtre* (1973), and *Swiss Graffitti* (1975). Monique Renault, accessed April 28, 2022, https://www.moniquerenault.nl/bio.html.
82. Guy Blaché tells the same story in her memoirs: "Daughter of an editor, I had read a good deal and retained quite a bit. I had done a little amateur theatricals and I thought that one might do better than these demonstration films. Gathering my courage, I timidly proposed to Gaumont that I might write one or two title scenes and have a few friends perform in them. If the future development of motion pictures had been foreseen at this time, I should never have obtained his consent. My youth, my inexperience, my sex, all conspired against me." *Memoirs of Alice Guy Blaché*, 24.
83. A copy of a film was identified as *La Fée aux choux* by Jan Olsson and Tom Gunning in Stockholm in 1997. While McMahan considers that film to be

the one from 1896 that Guy Blaché often discussed, recent scholarship has argued that it was likely made in 1900. See Alison McMahan and Sabine Lenk, "A la recherche d'objets filmiques non identifiés: Autour de l'oeuvre d'Alice Guy-Blaché," *Archives* 81 (August 1999): 1–19.

84. Many early Gaumont films were shot in the Parc des Buttes-Chaumont, including Alice Guy's *Une héroïne de 4 ans* (1907).

85. Adrian Curry, "*Be Natural* Press Kit," Kino Lorber/Zeitgeist Films, [p. 3], accessed October 1, 2020, https://www.dropbox.com/sh/70efct8ilbrkjsr/AAC96wELUljpmKGUjgbpRMHGa?dl=0&preview=BE+NATURAL+-+Press+Kit+-+revised.pdf. This press kit has since been revised.

86. Curry, *Be Natural* Press Kit, [p. 5].

87. Jay Weissberg, "'Be Natural: The Untold Story of Alice Guy-Blaché,'" *Variety*, May 30, 2018, https://variety.com/2018/film/reviews/be-natural-the-untold-story-of-alice-guy-blache-review-2-1202826198/.

88. Weissberg, "Be Natural."

89. Weissberg, "Be Natural."

90. The release of *Be Natural*, which was retitled *L'Histoire cachée d'Alice Guy-Blaché* in France, was delayed several times and then scheduled for March 18, 2020. But because of the shutdown due to COVID-19, the film opened in French movie theaters on June 22, 2020. Véronique Le Bris, "*Be Natural*: L'Histoire cachée d'Alice Guy-Blaché," *Cine-Woman*, June 11, 2020, https://www.cine-woman.fr/be-natural-alice-guy-blache/.

91. Laure Murat, "La Pellicule invisible d'Alice Guy," *Libération*, June 5, 2019, https://www.liberation.fr/debats/2019/06/05/la-pellicule-invisible-d-alice-guy_1731901/.

92. Emmanuelle Lequeux, "La Cinéaste Alice Guy, près de mille films et cent ans d'oubli," *Le Monde*, August 12, 2019, https://www.lemonde.fr/festival/article/2019/08/12/la-cineaste-alice-guy-pres-de-mille-films-et-cent-ans-d-oubli_5498658_4415198.html.

93. Lequeux, "La cinéaste Alice Guy."

94. François Albera and Laurent Mannoni, "Polémique: Les Historiens français contre Alice Guy?," *1895: Mille huit cent quatre-vingt-quinze* 88 (Summer 2019): 221–24.

95. Albera and Mannoni, "Polémique," 221–24.

96. Frédéric Cavé, "Autour d'Alice Guy: Sexe, mensonges et omission?," *Nonfiction.fr*, November 1, 2019, https://www.nonfiction.fr/article-10090-autour-dalice-guy-sexe-mensonges-et-omissions.htm.

97. Jean-Michel Frodon, "'Be Natural', une histoire mal entendue," *Slate.fr*, May 22, 2020, http://www.slate.fr/story/188574/cinema-critique-be-natural-alice-guy-oubliee-feministe.

98. Frodon, "'Be Natural.'" One senses in Frodon's use of the word "militant" a disdain for feminism that is often characteristic of public discourses in France.

EPILOGUE: TOWARD FEMINIST FUTURES

1. Musidora, "Colette et le cinéma muet: Souvenirs de Musidora," in *Musidora, la dixème muse*, by Patrick Cazals (Paris: H. Veyrier, 1978), 195–99. Regarding Colette and Musidora's friendship, see Annette Förster, *Women in the Silent Cinema*, 141.

2. Musidora, "Colette et le cinéma muet," 197.

3. While Musidora claims that she directed *Vicenta* before working with Colette on *La Flamme cachée* (1918), *Vicenta* might have been released after this other film, in 1919 or 1920. For Colette's film reviews and screenplays translated into English, see Colette, *Colette at the Movies: Criticism and Screenplays*, ed. Alain Virmaux and Odette Virmaux, trans. Sarah W. R. Smith (1975; New York: Frederick Ungar, 1980).

4. Musidora, "Colette et le cinéma muet," 199.

Bibliography

Abel, Richard. *French Cinema: The First Wave, 1915–1929*. Princeton, NJ: Princeton University Press, 1984.

"About the Project." In *Women Film Pioneers Project*, edited by Jane Gaines, Radha Vatsal, and Monica Dall'Asta. New York: Columbia University Libraries, 2015. https://wfpp.columbia.edu/about/.

"Aglaia Mitropoulou." *Variety*, January 28, 1991, 85.

Albera, François. "'L'Ecole comique française', une avant-garde posthume?" In "Aux sources du burlesque cinématographique: Les Comiques français des premiers temps," edited by Laurent Guido and Laurent Le Forestier. Special issue, *1895: Mille huit cent quatre-vingt-quinze* 61 (September 1910): 77–114.

Albera, François, and Laurent Mannoni. "Polémique: Les Historiens français contre Alice Guy?" *1895: Mille huit cent quatre-vingt-quinze* 88 (Summer 2019): 221–24.

Amad, Paula. *Counter-Archive: Film, the Everyday, and Albert Kahn's Archives de la Planète*. New York: Columbia University Press, 2010.

Amad, Paula. "'Objects Became Witnesses': Eve Francis and the Emergence of French Cinephilia and Film Criticism." *Framework: The Journal of Cinema and Media* 46, no. 1 (Spring 2005): 56–73.

Andrew, Dudley. *Mists of Regret: Culture and Sensibility in the Classic French Film*. Princeton, NJ: Princeton University Press, 1995.

Antonutti, Isabelle. *Bâtisseurs de la lecture publique: Une histoire des premières bibliothécaires, 1900–1950*. Villeurbanne, France: Presses de l'ENSSIB, 2024.

Audé, Françoise. *Ciné-modèles, cinéma d'elles*. Paris: L'Age d'homme, 1990.

Bachy, Victor. *Alice Guy-Blaché (1873–1968): La Première Femme cinéaste du monde*. Perpignan: Institut Jean Vigo, 1993.

Bardèche, Maurice, and Robert Brasillach. *Histoire du cinéma*. Givors: A. Martel, 1953–54.

Bastide, Bernard. "La Commission de recherches historiques de la Cinémathèque française." In *Histoire du cinéma: Problématique des sources*, edited by Irène Bessière and Jean A. Gili, 113–24. Paris: Institut National d'Histoire de l'Art, 2004.

Bell, Melanie. *Movie Workers: The Women Who Made British Cinema*. Urbana: University of Illinois Press, 2021.

Benoît, Gaëtan. *Eugène Morel: Pioneer of Public Libraries in France*. Duluth, MN: Litwin Books, 2008.

Bergstrom, Janet. "Lotte Eisner, collectionneuse: De l'ombre à la lumière." In *Le Cinéma dans l'oeil du collectionneur*, edited by Charlotte Brady-Savignac, André Habib, Louis Pelletier, and Jean-Pierre Sirois-Trahan, 103–42. Montréal: Les Presses de l'Université de Montréal, 2023.

Bernheim, Nicole-Lise. "Entretien avec Jeanne Moreau." *La Revue du cinéma: Image et son* 283 (April 1974): n.p.

Bernheim, Nicole-Lise. Preface to *Autobiographie d'une pionnière du cinéma*, by Alice Guy, 7–12. Paris: Denoël/Gonthier, 1976.

Bernheim, Nicole-Lise. "Réactions." *La Revue du cinéma: Image et son* 283 (April 1974): n.p.

"Bibliographie du 'cinéma.'" *Le Crapouillot*, March 1927, 48.

Boersma, Dee. "A Report on the United Nations Commission on the Status of Women and Mass Media." *Journal of the University Film Association* 26, nos. 1/2 (1974): 3–4.

Bonnet, Marie-Jo. "Musidora." In *Mon MLF*, 173–79. Paris: Albin Michel, 2018.

Borde, Raymond. *Les Cinémathèques*. Paris: L'Age d'homme, 1983.

"Born in Slavery: Slave Narratives from the Federal Writers' Project, 1936 to 1938." Library of Congress. Accessed April 27, 2022. https://www.loc.gov

/collections/slave-narratives-from-the-federal-writers-project-1936-to-1938/about-this-collection/.

Bouquet, Christian. *Laure Albin-Guillot ou la volonté d'art.* Paris: Marval, 1996.

Branchut-Gendron, Véronique. "Rencontre avec Isabelle Antonutti, directrice de l'ouvrage 'Figures de bibliothécaire.'" Presses de l'ENSSIB, September 24, 2020. https://presses.enssib.fr/temoignages/interview-isabelle-antonutti.

Breton, Émile. *Femmes d'images.* Paris: Éditions Messidor, 1984.

Briet, Suzanne. *Qu'est-ce que la documentation?* Paris: EDIT (Editions documentaires industrielles et techniques), 1951.

Brownlow, Kevin. *The Parade's Gone By . . .* New York: Ballantine Books, 1968.

Buisson, Léa. "De Musidora à Mad Souri: L'Influence du cinéma sur *Le Trésor des Jésuites* de Breton et Aragon." *L'Annuaire théâtral* 59 (Spring 2016): 31–47.

Burrows, Elaine. "A Historical Overview of NFTVA/BFI Collection Development Policies with Regard to Gender and Nation Questions." *Framework* 51, no. 2 (Fall 2010): 344–45.

Carou, Alain. "Le Scénario français en quête d'auteurs (1908–1918)." *1895: Mille huit cent quatre-vingt-quinze* 65 (2011): 28–51.

Cauquy, Emilie, and Marie Frappat. "L'idea di conservare il cinema: Marie Epstein alla Cinémathèque française." YouTube video. June 16, 2016. Posted by Cineteca Bologna on June 27, 2016. https://www.youtube.com/watch?v=_KhGMwXDsmg.

Cavé, Frédéric. "Autour d'Alice Guy: Sexe, mensonges et omission?" *Nonfiction.fr*, November 1, 2019. https://www.nonfiction.fr/article-10090-autour-dalice-guy-sexe-mensonges-et-omissions.htm.

Cazals, Patrick. *Musidora, la dixième muse.* Paris: Editions Henri Veyrier, 1978.

Cere, Rinella. *An International Study of Film Museums.* London: Routledge, 2020.

Cere, Rinella, and Giovanna Santaera. "Fautrici dei musei del cinema nel mondo: Iris Barry, Lotte Eisner e Kashiko Kawakita." *Arabeschi* 19 (2021). http://www.arabeschi.it/23-fautrici-dei-musei-del-cinema-nel-mondo-iris-barry-lotte-eisner-e-kashiko-kawawita/.

Chandet, Henriette. "Palmarès féminin." *L'Echo de Paris,* June 19, 1932, 4.

Chapon, François. *C'était Jacques Doucet.* Paris: Fayard, 2006.

Chavance, René. "Pour la conservation de nos films: Une cinémathèque au Palais du Trocadéro." *La Liberté,* April 11, 1932, 1.

Coissac, G-Michel. *Histoire du cinématographe: Des origines jusqu'à nos jours*. Paris: Editions du "Cinéopse," 1925.

Colette. *Colette at the Movies: Criticism and Screenplays*. Edited by Alain Virmaux and Odette Virmaux. Translated by Sarah W. R. Smith. New York: Frederick Ungar Publishing, Co., 1980. Originally published 1975.

Confino, Barbara. "An Interview with Agnès Varda." *Saturday Review*, August 12, 1972, 35.

Crisp, Colin. *The Classic French Cinema, 1930–1960*. Bloomington: Indiana University Press, 1993.

Curry, Adrian. "*Be Natural* Press Kit." Kino Lorber/Zeitgeist Films. Accessed October 1, 2020. https://www.dropbox.com/sh/7oefct8ilbrkjsr/AAC96wEL UljpmKGUjgbpRMHGa?dl=0&preview=BE+NATURAL+-+Press+Kit+-+revised.pdf.

Dall'Asta, Monica, and Jane M. Gaines. "Prologue: Constellations: Past Meets Present in Feminist Film History." In *Doing Women's Film History: Reframing Cinemas, Past and Future*, edited by Christine Gledhill and Julia Knight, 13–25. Urbana: University of Illinois Press, 2015.

Damiens, Antoine. "Film Festivals of the 1970s and the Subject of Feminist Film Studies: Collaborations and Regimes of Knowledge Production." *Journal of Film and Video* 72, nos. 1–2 (Spring/Summer 2020): 21–32.

D'Ast, R. "Notre enquête: Vers une cinémathèque nationale." *La Liberté*, May 18, 1932, 2.

de Pastre-Robert, Béatrice, and Emmanuelle Devos. "La Cinémathèque de la Ville de Paris." *1895: Mille huit cent quatre-ving-quinze* 18 (Summer 1995): 107–21.

DeCelles, Naomi. *Recollecting Lotte Eisner: Cinema, Exile, and the Archive*. Oakland: University of California Press, 2022.

Delisle, Léopold. *Catalogue général des livres imprimés de la Bibliothèque nationale*. Paris: Imprimerie Nationale, 1897.

Delluc, Gilles. *Louis Delluc, 1890–1924: L'Eveilleur du cinéma français au temps des années folles*. Périgueux, France: Pilote 24 édition, 2002.

Delphy, Christine. "Les Origines du Mouvement de libération des femmes en France." *Nouvelles questions féministes* 16/18 (1991): 137–48.

Derain, Lucie. "Les Etoiles sous le microphone . . . III.—le présent et l'avenir du film parlant et sonore." *Le Quotidien*, March 1, 1930, 1–2.

Derrida, Jacques. *Archive Fever: A Freudian Impression*. Translated by Eric Prenowitz. Chicago: University of Chicago Press, 1996.

Des femmes de Musidora. *Paroles . . . elles tournent!* Paris: Editions des femmes, 1976.

"Des jeunes sauvent les vieux films." *Comoedia*, January 17, 1936, 6.

Descamps, Florence. *L'Historien, l'archiviste et le magnétophone: De la constitution de la source orale à son exploitation*. Paris: Comité pour l'histoire économique et financière de la France, 2001.

Désveaux, Delphine, and Michaël Houlette, eds. *Laure Albin-Guillot: L'Enjeu classique*. Paris: Jeu de Paume, Editions de la Martinière, 2013.

Devay, J.-F. "Le Festival d'Antibes." *Combat*, September 2, 1950, 2.

Dictionnaire de la langue française (Littré). Tome 2. "Documentation: 1." 1873. https://artflsrv04.uchicago.edu/philologic4.7/publicdicos/navigate/15/4633.

Dictionnaire de l'Académie française. 8th ed. Tome 1. "Documentation: n. f." 1935. https://artflsrv04.uchicago.edu/philologic4.7/publicdicos/navigate/18/9788.

Dictionnaire de l'Académie française. 8th ed. "Pionnier: n. m." 1935. https://www.dictionnaire-academie.fr/article/A8P1541.

Dictionnaire de l'Académie française. 9th ed. "Pionnier, Pionnière nom et adjectif." 2011. https://www.dictionnaire-academie.fr/article/A9P2487.

"Directrice des archives photographiques des Beaux-Arts." *La Française*, September 24, 1932, 2.

"Editorial." *Women and Film* 1 (1972): 5–6.

Eichhorn, Kate. *The Archival Turn in Feminism: Outrage in Order*. Philadelphia: Temple University Press, 2013.

Eisner, Julia. "In the Archive with Lotte Eisner: How She Solved the Problem of Maria (the Robot)." Online presentation hosted by The Wiener Holocaust Library, November 18, 2021.

Eisner, Julia. "Lotte Eisner: Pioneer of the Art and Craft of Collecting." *Screen* 62, no. 3 (Autumn 2021): 418–23.

Eisner, Lotte. "Comment écrire l'histoire du cinéma." *Positif* 6 (April 1953): 37–40.

Eisner, Lotte. "Preface to English-Language Edition." In *F. W. Murnau*, 5–12. London: Secker & Warburg, 1973.

Eisner, Lotte H. "From One Who Went Forth to Learn What 'Cinema' Was: What the Prussian *Staatsbibliothek* Knows About Film." Translated by Naomi DeCelles. *Screen* 62, no. 3 (Autumn 2021): 382–85.

Eisner, Lotte H. *The Haunted Screen: Expressionism in the German Cinema and the Influence of Max Reinhardt.* Translated by Roger Greaves. Berkeley: University of California Press, 2008. Originally published 1973.

Eisner, Lotte H. *J'avais jadis une belle patrie.* Translated by Marie Bouquet. Paris: Marest Editeur, 2022.

Escoubé, Lucienne. "Sauvons les films de répertoire." *Pour Vous,* March 31, 1932, 3.

"Exposition de photographies tirées de films scientifiques." *Le Parisien,* April 4, 1933, 2.

Fayet-Scribe, Sylvie. "Connaissez-vous Suzanne Briet?" *Bulletin des bibliothèques de France (BBF)* 1 (2012): 40–44.

Fescourt, Henri. *La Foi et les montagnes; ou, le septième art au passé.* Paris: P. Montel, 1959.

Fescourt, Henri. *Le Cinéma, des origines à nos jours.* Paris: Éditions du Cygne, 1932.

"FIAF Gender Observatory." FIAF. Accessed August 4, 2025. https://www.fiafnet.org/pages/Community/fiaf-gender-observatory.html.

"FIAF Members." FIAF. Accessed April 28, 2022. https://www.fiafnet.org/pages/Community/Members.html.

Field, Allyson Nadia. "Editor's Introduction: Sites of Speculative Encounter." *Feminist Media Histories* 8, no. 2 (2022): 1–13.

Flamant, Françoise. *A tire d'elles: Itinéraires de féministes radicales des années 1970.* Rennes: Presses universitaires de Rennes, 2007.

Flamant, Françoise. "Des femmes organisent un festival." *La Revue du cinéma: Image et son* 283 (April 1974): n.p.

Fleckinger, Hélène. "De la contribution des féministes aux expérimentations techniques, sociales et formelles de la 'vidéo des premiers temps' (France, 1968–1981)." In *Genre et techniques, XIXe–XXIe siècle,* edited by Fabien Knittel and Pascal Raggi, 253–66. Rennes: Presses universitaires de Rennes, 2013.

Fleckinger, Hélène. "Le Collectif Musidora, entre cinéma et féminisme: Variations autour d'une photographie de Pierre Zucca." Presentation at the conference Musidora, qui êtes-vous?, November 2020.

Flitterman-Lewis, Sandy. *To Desire Differently: Feminism and the French Cinema.* Urbana: University of Illinois Press, 1990.

Flitterman-Lewis, Sandy, and Astrid Burnod. "Marie Epstein." In *Women Film Pioneers Project,* edited by Jane Gaines, Radha Vatsal, and Monica Dall'Asta.

New York: Columbia University Libraries, 2016. https://wfpp.columbia.edu/pioneer/marie-epstein/.

Fonfreide, Marcelle. "Introduction." *La Revue du cinéma: Image et son* 283 (April 1974): 18.

Ford, Charles. *Femmes cinéastes; ou le triomphe de la volonté.* Paris: Denoël, 1972.

Forrester, Viviane. "Le Regard des femmes." *La Revue du cinéma: Image et son* 283 (April 1974): n.p.

Förster, Annette. *Women in the Silent Cinema: Histories of Fame and Fate.* Amsterdam: Amsterdam University Press, 2017.

Foucault, Michel. *The Archaeology of Knowledge.* Translated by A. M. Sheridan Smith. New York: Vintage Books, 2010. Originally published 1972.

Françoise and Bénédicte. "Les Femmes et la technique du cinéma." *La Revue du cinéma: Image et son* 283 (April 1974): n.p.

Frank, Hannah. *Frame by Frame: A Materialist Aesthetics of Animated Cartoons.* Oakland: University of California Press, 2019.

Frappat, Marie. *Cinémathèques à l'italienne: Conservation et diffusion du patrimoine cinématographique en Italie.* Paris: L'Harmattan, 2006.

Frisch, Michael. *A Shared Authority: Essays on the Craft and Meaning of Oral and Public History.* Albany: State University of New York Press, 1990.

Frodon, Jean-Michel. "'Be Natural', une histoire mal entendue." *Slate.fr*, May 22, 2020. http://www.slate.fr/story/188574/cinema-critique-be-natural-alice-guy-oubliee-feministe.

Gaines, Jane. *Pink-Slipped: What Happened to Women in the Silent Film Industries?* Urbana: University of Illinois Press, 2018.

Gardey, Delphine. "Mécaniser l'écriture et photographier la parole: Utopies, monde du bureau et histoire de genre et de techniques." *Annales* 54, no. 3 (1999): 587–614.

Garnier, Christine. "Comment réussissent les femmes: VI, Jacqueline Audry 'Travailler plus vite que les hommes.'" *Revue des deux mondes*, February 15, 1961, 666–73.

Gauthier, Christophe. *La Passion du cinéma: Cinéphiles, ciné-clubs et salles spécialisées à Paris de 1920 à 1929.* Paris: AFRHC (Association française de recherche sur l'histoire du cinéma), Ecole des Chartes, 1999.

Gauthier, Christophe. "1927, Year One of the French Film Heritage." *Film History* 17, nos. 2/3 (2005): 289–306.

Godard, Colette. "Femmes entre elles." *Le Monde*, April 15, 1974. https://www.lemonde.fr/archives/article/1974/04/15/femmes-entre-elles_2525577_1819218.html.

Godard, Colette. "Festival Musidora." *Le Monde*, March 23, 1974. https://www.lemonde.fr/archives/article/1974/03/23/festival-musidora_2515592_1819218.html.

Gonnard, Catherine. "Une carrière au féminin." In *Laure Albin-Guillot: L'Enjeu classique*, edited by Delphine Désveaux and Michaël Houlette, 27–31. Paris: Jeu de Paume, Editions de la Martinière, 2013.

Grele, Ronald J. "Oral History as Evidence." In *Handbook of Oral History*, edited by Thomas L. Charlton, Lois E. Myers, and Rebecca Sharpless, 43–101. Lanham, MD: AltaMira Press, 2006.

Groo, Katherine. *Bad Film Histories: Ethnography and the Early Archive*. Minneapolis: University of Minnesota Press, 2019.

Gunning, Tom. "Systematizing the Electric Message: Narrative Form, Gender, and Modernity in *The Lonedale Operator*." In *American Cinema's Transitional Era: Audiences, Institutions, Practices*, edited by Charlie Keil and Shelley Stamp, 15–50. Los Angeles: University of California Press, 2004.

Guy Blaché, Alice. *The Memoirs of Alice Guy Blaché*. Translated by Roberta and Simone Blaché. Metuchen, NJ: Scarecrow Press, 1986.

Halpern Martineau, Barbara. "Paris/Chicago: Women's Film Festivals 1974." *Women and Film* 7 (1975): 10–27.

Haskell, Molly. *From Reverence to Rape: The Treatment of Women in the Movies*. Chicago: University of Chicago Press, 1987.

Hastie, Amelie. *Cupboards of Curiosity: Women, Recollection, and Film History*. Durham, NC: Duke University Press, 2007.

Haustrate, Gaston. "Jean Lods: Sa vie, son œuvre." *Cinéma 74* 188 (June 1974): 114–23.

Helton, Laura E. *Scattered and Fugitive Things: How Black Collectors Created Archives and Remade History*. New York: Columbia University Press, 2024.

Hennefeld, Maggie. *Specters of Slapstick and Silent Film Comediennes*. New York: Columbia University Press, 2018.

Henson, Bruce. "Iris Barry: American Film Archive Pioneer." *Katharine Sharp Review* 4 (Winter 1997): 1–6.

Hill, Erin. *Never Done: A History of Women's Work in Media Production*. New Brunswick, NJ: Rutgers University Press, 2016.

Hillier, Jim, ed. *Cahiers du Cinéma: The 1950s; Neo-Realism, Hollywood, New Wave*. Cambridge, MA: Harvard University Press, 1985.

Jacobs, Clarissa K. "Women's Film Festival Timeline." *The Women and Film Project* (blog). Accessed January 25, 2021. https://womenandfilmproject.word press.com/resources/festival-timeline/.

Joubin, André. "La Bibliothèque d'art et d'archéologie de l'Université de Paris." *Actes du Congrès d'histoire de l'art* (1921): 138–45.

Kamleitner, Katharina. "On Women's Film Festivals: Histories, Circuits, Futures." PhD diss., University of Glasgow, 2020.

Kaplan, Nelly. "A nous l'histoire d'une de nos folies." *La Revue du cinéma: Image et son* 283 (April 1974): n.p.

Kershaw, Angela. "The Journey to the USSR in the 1930s: Apology, Apocrypha, Apostasy." In *French Political Travel Writing in the Inter-War Years*, edited by Martyn Cornick, Martin Hurcombe, and Angela Kershaw, 134–69. New York: Routledge, 2017.

"La Cinémathèque française est créée." *La Cinématographie française*, September 26, 1936, 97.

"La Cinémathèque Nationale." *Le Cinéopse*, February 1933, 9.

"La 9e edition." Académie française. Accessed April 28, 2022. https://www.academie-francaise.fr/le-dictionnaire/la-9e-edition.

"La Revue du cinéma." *SubStance* 3, no. 9 (Spring 1974): 147–51.

Lacassin, Francis. *A la recherche de Jean Durand*. Paris: AFRHC (Association française de recherche sur l'histoire du cinéma), 2004.

Lacassin, Francis. "Musidora." *Anthologie du cinéma* 6 (1971): 441–504.

Lacassin, Francis. "Out of Oblivion: Alice Guy Blaché." *Sight and Sound* (Summer 1971): 151–54.

Langlois, Henri. "Classiques de l'écran muet." *La Cinématographie française* 876–77 (August 24, 1935): 17–18.

Langlois, Henri. *Ecrits de cinéma: 1931–1977*. Paris: Flammarion, 2014.

Lavastrou, Marc. "De Louis Delluc à *Caligari* . . .: L'Introduction du cinéma allemand en France." *Trajectoires* 5 (2011). https://doi.org/10.4000/trajectoires.685.

Le Bris, Véronique. "*Be Natural*: L'Histoire cachée d'Alice Guy-Blaché." *Cine-Woman*, June 11, 2020. https://www.cine-woman.fr/be-natural-alice-guy-blache/.

"Le Concours de scenarios." *L'Oeuvre*, January 20, 1923, 2.

Le Roy, Eric. "Entretien avec Lia Van Leer." *Journal of Film Preservation* 92 (2015): 29–35.

Lejeune, Elodie. "Suzanne Bidault: Une pionnière oubliée." *Relations Internationales* 118 (Summer 2004): 139–54.

Lejeune, Paule. *Le Cinéma des femmes: 105 femmes d'expression française (France, Belgique, Suisse), 1895–1987*. Paris: Éditions Atlas, 1987.

Lequeux, Emmanuelle. "La Cinéaste Alice Guy, près de mille films et cent ans d'oubli." *Le Monde*, August 12, 2019. https://www.lemonde.fr/festival/article/2019/08/12/la-cineaste-alice-guy-pres-de-mille-films-et-cent-ans-d-oubli_5498658_4415198.html.

Lerner, Gerda. *The Creation of Feminist Consciousness: From the Middle Ages to Eighteen Seventy*. New York: Oxford University Press, 1993.

"Les Archives du cinéma." *La Volonté*, January 23, 1933, 2.

"Les Femmes et le cinéma." *La Revue du cinéma: Image et son* 283 (April 1974): n.p.

Liatard, Séverine. "Colette Audry: Une intellectuelle dans la sphère littéraire en 1962." In *Femmes de pouvoir: Mythes et fantasmes*, edited by Odile Krakovitch, Geneviève Sellier, and Eliane Viennot, 135–42. Paris: L'Harmattan, 2001.

"Loi sur le dépôt legal." *Journal officiel de la République française*, May 27, 1925, 4935–36.

Loveday, Kiki. "Do You Believe in Fairies? Cabbages, Victorian Memes, and the Birth of Cinema: Seeing Sapphic Sexuality in the Silent Era." In *Women Film Pioneers Project*, edited by Jane Gaines, Radha Vatsal, and Monica Dall'Asta. New York: Columbia University Libraries, 2019. https://wfpp.columbia.edu/2019/10/17/do-you-believe-in-fairies-cabbages-victorian-memes-and-the-birth-of-cinema-seeing-sapphic-sexuality-in-the-silent-era/.

Loveday, Kiki. "The Pioneer Paradigm." *Feminist Media Histories* 8, no. 1 (2022): 165–80.

Macdonald, Sharon. "Collecting Practices." In *A Companion to Museum Studies*, edited by Sharon Macdonald, 207–42. New York: John Wiley & Sons, 2010.

"The Making of F. W. Murnau's 'Tabu'—The Outtakes Edition." Deutsche Kinemathek. Accessed August 4, 2025. https://www.deutsche-kinemathek.de/en/collections-archives/digital-collection/murnau-tabu.

Malthête-Méliès, Madeleine. *Georges Méliès l'enchanteur*. Grandvilliers: La Tour Verte, 2011.

Mannoni, Laurent. "Henri Langlois and the Musée du Cinéma." *Film History* 18, no. 3 (2006): 274–87.

Mannoni, Laurent. *Histoire de la Cinémathèque française*. Paris: Gallimard, 2006.

McMahan, Alison. *Alice Guy Blaché: Lost Visionary of the Cinema*. London: Bloomsbury, 2014.

McMahan, Alison, and Sabine Lenk. "A la recherche d'objets filmiques non identifiés: Autour de l'oeuvre d'Alice Guy-Blaché." *Archives* 81 (August 1999): 1–19.

Merck, Mandy. "Mulvey's Manifesto." *Camera Obscura* 22, no. 3 (2007): 1–23.

Mesguich, Félix. *Tours de manivelle: Souvenirs d'un chasseur d'images*. Paris: Grasset, 1933.

Micquel, René. "Avec les cinéastes amateurs." *L'Image*, January 1, 1934, 23–27.

"Ministère de l'Education Nationale." *Journal officiel de la République française*, March 24, 1934, 2978–79.

Monique Renault. Accessed April 28, 2022. https://www.moniquerenault.nl/bio.html.

Morel, Eugène. *Bibliothèques: Essai sur le développement des bibliothèques publiques et de la librairie dans les deux mondes*. Paris: Mercure de France, 1908.

Morel, Eugène. *La Librairie publique*. Paris: Librairie Armand Colin, 1910.

Morel, Eugène. *La Loi sur le dépôt légal (19 mai 1925)*. Paris: Librairie Ancienne Honoré Champion, 1925.

Morel, Jean-Paul. "A la recherche de la coquille . . . ." *1895: Mille huit cent quatre-ving-quinze* 91 (2020–22): 147–52.

Mosjoukine, Ivan. *Quand j'étais Michel Strogoff*. Paris: La Renaissance du Livre, 1927.

Moussa, Alexandre. "'Paroles . . . elles tournent!': Musidora and the Rise and Fall of Feminist Film Criticism in France, 1973–1981." Presented at conference of Society for Cinema and Media Studies, Denver, CO, April 13, 2023.

Moussinac, Jeanne. "La Bibliothèque cinématographique de M. Jacques Doucet." *Bulletin de la Société des amis de la Bibliothèque d'art et d'archéologie de l'Université de Paris, Fondation Jacques Doucet* 2 (1929): 11–14.

Moussinac, Léon. "Étapes." *Le Crapouillot*, March 1927, 16–19.

Moussinac, Léon. *Panoramique du cinéma*. Paris: Au sans pareil, 1929.

Mulvey, Laura. "Visual Pleasure and Narrative Cinema." *Screen* 16, no. 3 (October 1, 1975): 6–18.

Murat, Laure. "La Pellicule invisible d'Alice Guy." *Libération*, June 5, 2019. https://www.liberation.fr/debats/2019/06/05/la-pellicule-invisible-d-alice-guy_1731901.

Musidora. "Colette et le cinéma muet: Souvenirs de Musidora." In *Musidora, la dixème muse*, by Patrick Cazals, 195–99. Paris: H. Veyrier, 1978.

Niles Maack, Mary. "Women Librarians in France: The First Generation." *Journal of Library History* 18, no. 4 (Fall 1983): 407–49.

"Notre référendum sur les films du répertoire." *Pour Vous*, May 5, 1932, 2.

"OHA Core Principles." Oral History Association. Accessed April 27, 2022. https://www.oralhistory.org/oha-core-principles/#_edn1.

Ohba, Matoshi. "In Memoriam: Kashiko Kawakita." *Journal of Film Preservation* 22, no. 47 (October 1993): 69–70.

Ollivier, Gilles. "Histoire des images, histoire des sociétés: L'Exemple du cinéma d'amateur." *1895: Mille huit cent quatre-ving-quinze* 17 (1994): 115–32.

"On tourne." *Le Jour*, May 21, 1936, 6.

"Oral Histories." John F. Kennedy Presidential Library and Museum. Accessed April 27, 2022. https://www.jfklibrary.org/archives/about-archival-collections/oral-histories.

Ourrad, Louisa. "Portrait—Dana Sardet." *Les Femmes s'animent*, April 7, 2023. https://lesfemmessaniment.fr/portrait-dana-sardet-louisa-ourrad/.

Pathé, Charles. *De Pathé Frères à Pathé Cinéma*. Nice: Imprimerie de l'Eclaireur de Nice, 1940.

Pathé, Charles. *Souvenirs et conseils d'un parvenu*. Paris: n.p., 1926.

Patry, Lucien. "Entretien avec Georges FRANJU: Directeur artistique de la Cinémathèque Française." *Films & Documents: Revue des techniques audio-visuelles* 332 (October–December 1980): 37–39.

Patry, Lucien. "Entretien avec Marie EPSTEIN (février 1980)." *Films & Documents: Revue des techniques audio-visuelles* 332 (October–December 1980): 32–37.

Picq, Françoise. *Libération des femmes: Les Années-Mouvement*. Paris: Éditions du Seuil, 1993.

Pons, Sirine. "La Cinémathèque tunisienne, Henri Langlois et la FIAF (1958–1963)." Presented at Cinémathèque française, Paris, France, February 12, 2015.

Poulain, Martine, ed. *Histoire des bibliothèques françaises: Les Bibliothèques au XXe siècle, 1914–1990*. Paris: Éditions du Cercle de la Librairie, 1992.

"Qui est Alice Guy?" Interview with Claire Clouzot, Nicole-Lise Bernheim, Delphine Seyrig, Daniel Toscan du Plantier, Charles Ford, Henri Langlois, Francis Lacassin, Jacques Deslandes, André Zwobada, Liliane de Kermadec, and Colette Audry. *France Culture*, July 2, 1975. Radio recording, 51 minutes. https://www.franceculture.fr/emissions/les-nuits-de-france-culture/qui-est-alice-guy-1ere-diffusion-02071975.

Ratouis de Limay, Paul. "Les Archives photographiques des Beaux-Arts." In *Congrès archéologique de France, XCVIIe Session, Tenue à PARIS en 1934*, 287–99. Paris: A. Picard, 1935.

Reynaud, Bérénice. "Hommage—Cinémathèque: Une muse disparaît." *Cahiers du cinéma*, no. 471 (September 1, 1993): 6.

Rich, B. Ruby. *Chick Flicks: Theories and Memories of the Feminist Film Movement*. Durham, NC: Duke University Press, 1998.

Rich, B. Ruby. "The Crisis of Naming in Feminist Film Criticism." *Jump Cut* 19 (December 1978). https://www.ejumpcut.org/archive/onlinessays/JC19folder/RichCrisisOfNaming.html.

Rollet, Brigitte. "Femmes cinéastes en France: L'Après-Mai 68." *Clio: Femmes, Genre, Histoire* 10 (1999): 1–13.

Rollet, Brigitte. *Jacqueline Audry: La Femme à la caméra*. Rennes: Presses universitaires de Rennes, 2015.

Roud, Richard. *A Passion for Films: Henri Langlois and the Cinémathèque française*. New York: Viking Press, 1983.

Saby, Frédéric. "Approche historique du dépôt légal en France." *Sociétés & Représentations* 35 (2013): 15–26.

Sadoul, Georges. *Histoire générale du cinéma: 3, le cinéma devient un art 1909–1920. Volume 1, l'avant-guerre*. Paris: Denoël, 1951.

Sarda, Marie-Anne. "Rue Spontini (Partie 1)." Bibliothèque d'Art et d'Archéologie Jacques Doucet, 30 July 2021. https://baadoucet.hypotheses.org/1673.

Sarris, Andrew. "The American Cinema." *Film Culture* (Spring 1963): 1–51.

Sarris, Andrew. "The Ladies' Auxiliary, 1976." In *Women and the Cinema: A Critical Anthology*, edited by Karyn Kay and Gerald Peary, 384–87. New York: E. P. Dutton, 1977.

Schwartzman, Karen, Harel Calderon, and Julianne Burton-Carvajal. "An Interview with Margot Benacerraf: *Reverón, Araya,* and the Institutionalization of Cinema in Venezuela." *Journal of Film and Video* 44, nos. 3/4 (Fall 1992/Winter 1993): 51–75.

Scott, Joan Wallach. "Women's Archives and Women's History." Keynote address for the dedication of the Christine Dunlap Farnham Archives, Pembroke Center, Brown University, Providence, RI, October 10, 1986.

Sellier, Geneviève. *Masculine Singular: French New Wave Cinema.* Translated by Kristin Ross. Durham: Duke University Press, 2008.

"Service des archives photographiques des beaux-arts." *Journal officiel de la République française,* May 15, 1932, 5090.

Sitton, Robert. "Iris Barry." In *Women Film Pioneers Project,* edited by Jane Gaines, Radha Vatsal, and Monica Dall'Asta. New York: Columbia University Libraries, 2015. https://wfpp.columbia.edu/pioneer/iris-barry/.

Sitton, Robert. *Lady in the Dark: Iris Barry and the Art of Film.* New York: Columbia University Press, 2014.

Slide, Anthony. *The Silent Feminists: America's First Women Directors.* Lanham, MD: Rowman & Littlefield, 2022. Originally published 1996.

Smith, Bonnie G. *The Gender of History: Men, Women, and Historical Practice.* Cambridge, MA: Harvard University Press, 1998.

Smoodin, Eric. *Paris in the Dark: Going to the Movies in the City of Light, 1930–1950.* Durham, NC: Duke University Press, 2020.

Soupault, Philippe. *Charlot.* Paris: Librairie Plon, 1957.

Spiers, Aurore. "My Name Is Alice Guy: The 'Musidora' Collective and Women's Film History." *Feminist Media Histories* 8, no. 3 (Summer 2022): 155–77.

Spiers, Aurore. "Rediscovered Again: The Nonlinear Path of Alice Guy Blaché into US Film History." In *The Routledge Companion to American Film History,* edited by Paula Massood and Pamela Robertson Wojcik, 378–88. New York: Routledge, 2025.

Spigel, Lynn. "Theorizing the Bachelorette: 'Waves' of Feminist Media Studies." *Signs* 30, no. 1 (Autumn 2004): 1209–21.

Stamp, Shelley. "Conference Report: FIAF Symposium: Women, Cinema, and Film Archives." *Feminist Media Histories* 10, nos. 2–3 (2024): 140–44.

Stamp, Shelley. *Lois Weber in Early Hollywood.* Oakland: University of California Press, 2015.

Sudendorf, Werner. "Film-Kurier 1919–1944." *Bulletin FIAF* 32 (September 1986): 15.
Tomadjoglou, Kim. "A Love of Labor and a Cult of Fragments: Maria Adriana Prolo's Museo Nazionale del Cinema, Torino." Presentation at conference Dans l'oeil du collectionneur, Laboratoire CinéMédias/Technès, June 5, 2017.
Torres San Martín, Patricia. "Elena Sánchez Valenzuela." In *Women Film Pioneers Project*, edited by Monica Dall'Asta, Jane Gaines, and Radha Vatsal. New York: Columbia University Libraries, 2013. https://wfpp.columbia.edu/pioneer/ccp-elena-sanchez-valenzuela/.
Torres San Martín, Patricia. *Elena Sánchez Valenzuela*. Mexico City: Universidad Nacional Autónoma de México, 2018.
Touil, Rime. "Les sources du cinéma muet dans les collections du département des Arts du spectacle de la Bibliothèque nationale de France." In *A la recherche de l'histoire du cinéma en France (1908–1919): Lieux, sources, objets*, edited by Clément Puget and Laurent Véray, 89–106. Pessac: Presses universitaires de Bordeaux, 2022.
Trouillot, Michel-Rolph. *Silencing the Past: Power and the Production of History*. Boston: Beacon Press, 1995.
Truffaut, François. "Une certaine tendance du cinéma français." *Cahiers du cinéma* 6, no. 31 (January 1, 1954): 15.
Turbiau, Aurore. "Musidora—Paroles . . . Elles tournent! (1976)." *Littératures engagées*, June 2, 2019. https://engagees.hypotheses.org/83.
UN Women. *A Short History of the Commission on the Status of Women*. New York: Intergovernmental Support Division UN Women, 2019.
"Unhistoricized Women Film Pioneers." In *Women Film Pioneers Project*, edited by Jane Gaines, Radha Vatsal, and Monica Dall'Asta. New York: Columbia University Libraries, 2015. https://wfpp.columbia.edu/resources/unhistoricized-women-film-pioneers/.
Vergès, Françoise. *Programme de désordre absolu: Décoloniser le musée*. Paris: La fabrique éditions, 2023.
Vergne, Edith. "Les Métiers du cinéma: La Script-girl." *La Revue du cinéma: Image et son* 283 (April 1974): n.p.
Vignaux, Valérie. "Léon Moussinac intellectuel communiste." In *Léon Moussinac: Un intellectuel communiste*, edited by Valérie Vignaux and François Albera, 13–33. Paris: AFRHC (Association française de recherche sur l'histoire du cinéma), 2014.

Vincendeau, Ginette. "Women's Cinema, Film Theory and Feminism in France: Reflections After the 1987 Créteil Festival." *Screen* 28, no. 4 (Autumn 1987): 14–18.

Virmaux, Alain. "La Coquille et le clergyman, 'notes sur un film controversé.'" *Europe* 64, no. 681 (January 1, 1986): 158–68.

Ward Mahar, Karen. *Women Filmmakers in Early Hollywood*. Baltimore, MD: Johns Hopkins University Press, 2006.

Weissberg, Jay. "'Be Natural: The Untold Story of Alice Guy-Blaché.'" *Variety*, May 30, 2018. https://variety.com/2018/film/reviews/be-natural-the-untold-story-of-alice-guy-blache-review-2-1202826198/.

Wild, Jennifer. *The Parisian Avant-Garde in the Age of Cinema, 1900–1923*. Oakland: University of California Press, 2015.

ARCHIVAL COLLECTIONS

"Dossiers divers: Correspondance, notes, décrets, statuts d'organisations et d'institutions, scénarios, projets et synopsis de films, rapports, coupures de presse, discours, documentation, 1932–1960." Archives de l'administration des Beaux-Arts (AABA). Politique du cinéma (années 1920–1950), Archives Nationales, Pierrefitte-sur-Seine, France.

Fonds de la Commission de Recherches historiques (CRHCF). La Cinémathèque française, Paris, France.

Fonds Moussinac, Léon (FML) (cinéma, théâtre). Bibliothèque nationale de France, Département des Arts du spectacle, Paris, France.

Index

Abel, Richard, 69
Académie française, 28, 128
activists, 1, 151; engagement in recovery work, 107–9; Guy Blaché as subject of *Qui est Alice Guy?*, 135–43; Guy Blaché as woman film pioneer, 127–35; legacy of "Musidora" collective, 143–48; "Musidora" collective in context, 114–27; Sardet anecdote, 111–13. *See also* Guy Blaché, Alice; "Musidora" collective
Affiche, L' (film), 89
Akerman, Chantal, 119
Albera, François, 146–47
Albert-Birot, Pierre, 27
Albin-Guillot, Laure, 5, 13, 20, 150, 165n84; advocacy of, 54–55; as amateur filmmaker, 51; commitment of, 45; contributions of, 53–54; drawing on discourses about, 22–23; early career of, 47–48; frustration of, 56; legacy of, 57–61; nomination of, 165n93; photograph of, 53*fig.*; photomontage by, 48*fig.*; reconstructing career of, 50; as SAP employee, 51–53; serving as CN director, 48–50; studio portrait of, 45*fig. See also* Cinémathèque Nationale; Service des Archives photographiques
Alice Guy Blaché: Lost Visionary of the Cinema (McMahan), 145
Alice Guy-Blaché (Bachy), 145
Alice Guy. *See* Guy Blaché, Alice
Amad, Paula, 7, 91
amateur filmmaker, portrait of, 51

American approach (film theory), 120, 122
American Cinema, The (Sarris), 118
American Film Institute, 127
Âmes de fous (film), 90
Amis de Spartacus, Les (ciné-club), 24, 31
Amis du cinéma, 69
Andréyor, Yvette, 92
Andriot, Josette, 105
Anik, Djemil, 93
Annales School, 77
archive. *See* film archive
Archives de la Planète, 7
Archives françaises du film, 111
Archives Nationales (National Archives), 9, 22, 45, 49, 56, 166n103
archivists, 1, 151; Bibliothèque du Cinéma as site of, 23–41; Cinémathèque Nationale as site of, 42–61; legacies of, 57–61; preserving silent cinema, 19–20; at Prussian State Library, 15–18. *See also* Bibliothèque du Cinéma; Cinémathèque Nationale
"Are French Historians Against Alice Guy?" (Albera and Mannoni), 146–47
Arzner, Dorothy, 100, 172n73
Asselin, Mme, 93
Audé, Françoise, 112
Audry, Colette, 128–29, 181n62
Audry, Jacqueline, 114, 119, 175n11
Autant-Lara, Claude, 162n45
auteurism, 4–5, 112; "auteur theory," 118, 177n28
Autobiographie d'une pionnière du cinéma (Guy Blaché), 127

BAA. *See* Bibliothèque d'art et d'archéologie
Bachy, Victor, 145
Baignoire des Langlois, La, 58–60, 59*fig.*
Balzac, Honoré de, 98
Bardèche, Maurice, 168n16, 169n30
Bardinon, Mme, 93
Barnard Zine Library, 7
Baroncelli, Jacques de, 162n45
Barry, Iris, 11–12
Bartleby (Melville), 98
Bastide, Bernard, 167n10
bathtub, film canisters piled up in, 58–60, 59*fig.*
BC. *See* Bibliothèque du Cinéma
Bean, Jennifer M., 13
Beard, Mary Ritter, 10
Beauvoir, Simone de, 178n32
Béduer, Château de, 154n4
Bell, Melanie, 11
Bellon, Denise, 58, 59*fig.*
Belmont, Charles, 116
Benacerraf, Margot, 12
Be Natural: The Untold Story of Alice Guy-Blaché (film), 144–47, 184n90
Benoît-Lévy, Edmond, 95, 168n16
Benoit-Lévy, Jean, 89, 162n45, 171n53
Bergson, Henri, 39
Bernard, Raymond, 162n45
Bernheim, Nicole-Lise, 112, 113, 119, 147, 175n4, 183n81; conversation with Flamant, 126–27; and Guy Blaché debate, 127–28, 130–35; and *Qui est Alice Guy?*, 135–43; recounting instances of misogyny, 124. *See also* *Qui est Alice Guy?*
BFI. *See* British Film Institute
biases, questioning, 6, 106, 113, 125, 131, 134
bibliography, 21, 26, 28, 33, 36, 79, 160n22

Bibliothèque d'art et d'archéologie (BAA), 23, 25–27, 159n17
Bibliothèque de l'Arsenal, 40–41, 163n55
Bibliothèque du Cinéma (BC), 2, 5, 20–22, 31, 160n25, 161n35; accounting for labor at, 33; acquisition of, 40; afterlife of, 40–41; bibliographic work at, 33–34; blueprint for, 27–28; classifying collections from, 39–40; conception of, 23–24; concerns over collection management and public access, 26–27; contempt for, 29; contributions to, 33–35; extant documents produced by, 38–39; index cards of, 36–38; legacy of, 57–61; main secondary documents produced by, 36; manifesto of, 27–28; overemphasizing roles in organizing collections of, 29–30; praising, 35; secondary documents produced by, 36; Seguin hearing about, 36; shaping work of Albin-Guillot, 41; threatening independence of authors, 28–29; unpacking term used for, 24–25
Bibliothèque du Film (BiFi), 24, 60–61. *See also* Cinémathèque française
Bibliothèque Marguerite Durand, 154n7
Bibliothèque Nationale (BN), 159n14, 162n44; and Auguste Rondel collection, 163n55; complete chaos at, 24–25; *dépôt légal* system of, 21, 42–45; designing classification system for, 37–38; emergence of, 2; index cards for titles available at, 36–38; "rough bibliography" assembled by, 36; shaping work of Albin-Guillot, 41; as training ground for library sciences, 20–21

Bibliothèque nationale de France (BnF), 9, 41, 58, 162n44; BnF-Arts du spectacle, 21, 40, 163n55; depositing scripts into, 164n76; digital collection of, 22; donating to, 21; extant archives from, 31–32; Fonds Léon Moussinac of, 26, 34, 160n26, 162n45; index cards at, 37; letters remaining in, 162n45; online catalog of, 38
Bidault, Suzanne, 3
BiFi. *See* Bibliothèque du Film
Bilinsky, Boris, 168n16
BIRHC. *See* Bureau International de la Recherche Historique Cinématographique
BN. *See* Bibliothèque Nationale
BnF. *See* Bibliothèque nationale de France
Bo, Sonika, 105
Bon, Suzanne, 94
Bonnet, Marie-Jo, 119
Bora, Mademoiselle, 93
Borde, Raymond, 49
Borel, Suzanne, 80
Born in Slavery: Slavery Narratives from the Federal Writers' Project, 1936 to 1938, 76
Boudrioz, Robert, 90
Bouglé, Marie-Louise, 154n7
Bouissounouse, Janine, 93, 172n65
Bouqueret, Christian, 47
Bourgeois, Bernadette, 93–94
Bourgeois, Gérard, 94
Brasillach, Robert, 168n16, 169n30
Braunberger, Pierre, 67
Breton, Emile, 112
Brière, La (film), 34
Briet, Suzanne, 33, 35–36, 162n44
British approach (film theory), 120, 122

British Film Institute (BFI), 158n6
Brownlow, Kevin, 168n15
Bruno, Giuliana, 13
Bureau International de la Recherche Historique Cinématographique (BIRHC), 104
Bureaucrats, The. See *Employés, Les*
Burrows, Elaine, 158n6
Burton, Antoinette, 6

Cabinet of Dr. Caligari, The (film), 107–9
Cahiers du cinéma, 113, 118
call numbers. *See* index cards
Camera Obscura, 179n38
Canada, 119–20, 178n32
Cannes Film Festival, 144
Canudo, Ricciotto, 27, 69
Carl, Renée, 92, 126
Carou, Alain, 172n74, 172n76
Carré, Michel, 93–94, 100
Carré, Mme M., 93
cartoons, "frame-by-frame" examination of, 9
Carvillani, Françoise, 150
CASA. *See* Club des amis du septième art
Catelain, Jaque, 162n45
Cavalcanti, Alberto, 162n45
Cavani, Liliana, 119
Cavé, Frédéric, 146–47
Cazals, Patrick, 88
Ceballos, Enri Moreno, 157n26
Cendrars, Blaise, 29, 160n25
Centre audiovisuel Simone de Beauvoir, 151
Centre national du cinéma et de l'image animée (CNC), 2, 141
Cercle du Cinéma, Le (ciné-club), 67–69

CF. *See* Cinémathèque française
Chalais, François, 135–36
Champreux, Isabelle, 93–94
Chandet, Henriette, 52
Chaplin, Charlie, 38–39, 69, 164n63
Chapon, François, 23–24, 30
Charlot (Delluc), 26
Charlot (Soupault), 164n63
Chavance, René, 44–45
Cheat, The (film), 91
Chevaux du Vercors, Les (film), 114
Chomette, Henri, 162n45
Chopra, Joyce, 119
Chytilová, Vera, 119
ciné-club, 24, 67–69, 90, 101, 108
Cinéma (Albert-Birot), 27
Cinéma, des origines à nos jours, Le (Fescourt), 168n16
cinema, women in production and preservation of. *See* collection; recollection; recovery
cinema library, defining, 24, 160n25. *See also* Bibliothèque du Cinéma
Cinéma 71, 129
Cinema's First Nasty Women, 13, 157n27
Cinemateca Nacional de Venezuela, 12
Cinémathèque de Toulouse, 22, 49, 111
Cinémathèque française (CF), 4–5, 9, 20, 22, 24, 67, 75, 78, 154n4; CRH collection of, 84, 167n13; emergence of, 2, 80; employment at, 3, 88–89, 98, 101, 150, 154n4; enlisting help from, 119; and erasure of women's film history, 104–5; film preservation practices of, 68; Fonds Georges Sadoul, 167n13; general preference for, 49, 56; institutional history of, 68; and

legitimization of recollection, 63–65; many moves of, 72; organizing Guy Blaché homage, 132; preserving cinema at, 56; primary sources from, 154n6; recovery work, 107–9; resemblances, 60–61; Sardet anecdote, 111–13, 126; vision for, 68–71; during World War II, 58–60, 59*fig*.

Cinémathèque Nationale (CN), 5, 20–21, 41; advocating for, 54–56; Albin-Guillot contributing to, 48–54; architectural ideas for, 54–55; budget of, 54; creation of, 22–23; and *dépôt légal* system, 42–45; describing, 45–46; employment at, 166n103; extant photographs of, 58–59; inauguration of, 42; legacy of, 57–61; as novel enterprise, 42; photograph of, 60*fig*.; photography of, 47–48, 50; relocation of, 45–46; SAP and, 51–53; supporting, 48–49; system established by, 45–46

Cinémathèque tunisienne, 12

Cinématographie, La, 35

Cinématographie française, 68, 101

Cinéopse, Le, 49

Clair, René, 40, 67, 162n45

Clarke, Shirley, 119

Clément, Nicolas, 37–38

Clouzot, Claire, 112, 124–25, 127–28, 131–32, 134, 175n4, 183n81

Club des amis du septième art (CASA), 69

CN. *See* Cinémathèque Nationale

CNC. *See* Centre national du cinéma et de l'image animée

Cohen, David William, 9

Cohl, Emile, 75, 168n16

Coissac, G.-Michel, 146, 168n15

"Colette and the Silent Cinema" (Musidora), 149

Colette (friend of Musidora), 81–82, 149–51, 185n3

collection, 11; afterlife of, 40–41; Albin-Guillot contributing to, 42–61; Bibliothèque du Cinéma as, 23–41; book collections, 23, 33–34; Cinémathèque Nationale as, 42–61; "collecting film history" as scientific practice of, 20–21; collections management, 12, 20, 24, 26, 42, 45, 57, 60; concerns over collections management and public access, 26–27; dividing, 25; and "documentation," 28; establishing precision, 22; film collection, 3, 17, 54, 58, 63; index cards and, 37–38; legacies, 57–61; library collections, 16–17, 42–43; and modern principles, 25–26; Moussinac contributing to, 23–41; overview, 15–18; preserving silent cinema, 19–20; primary materials from, 21–22; theoretical reflections on, 11. *See also* Bibliothèque du Cinéma; Cinémathèque Nationale

Collection Femme, 129

Collector, The (Fowles), 29

Colson-Malleville, Marie-Anne, 70–71, 78, 94–95, 103, 106, 126. *See also* Commission de Recherches historiques

Columbia University, 77

"Comment écrire l'histoire du cinéma" (Eisner), 64

"Comment on fait un film" (exhibition), 90

commercial cinema, criticism of, 117

Commission de Recherches historiques (CRH), 5–6, 13, 68, 167n10, 172n66;

Commission de Recherches historiques (CRH) *(continued)* collection, 71–72, 75, 78, 84, 91, 100–101, 103, 167n13; contextualizing involvement of women in, 100–101; difficulties encountered with narrators, 101, 103; digitizing collection of, 71–72; equal contributions to, 94–95; Eve Francis interview, 90–91; finding transcripts, 167n13; focus on French national cinema, 70; incompleteness of, 72, 75; inspiration from, 104; interviews, 69–71, 78–79, 81, 84, 88, 91, 94, 98, 104–5; Jean Epstein interview, 88–90; key issue for, 96–97; motives behind, 70; narrators for, 91–95; Nora Jonuxi interview, 96–97, 106, 172n67; objectives of, 69; as oral history, 75–79; organizing meetings of, 70–71; patriarchal impulses of, 104–5; reconstruction through interviews, 96–97; Renée Sylvaire interview, 84, 86; stenographer typists of, 97–101, 103; unpolished state of collection at, 78; witness interviewers, 80–82, 84–91; women of, 80–103; as women's film history, 103–6; years before, 168n16

Commission of Historical Research. *See* Commission de Recherches historiques

Commission on the Status of Women (UN), 177n21

Comoedia, 81

Coquille et le clergyman, La (film), 34

COVID-19, 145, 161n37, 184n90

Crapouillot, Le, 26–27, 34, 160n22

CRH. *See* Commission de Recherches historiques

Dagmar, Berthe, 104, 105
d'Alcy, Jehanne, 67, 100, 102*fig.*
Dall'Asta, Monica, 156n24
Damiens, Antoine, 120
Delluc, Louis, 26, 69, 90–91, 108
Delphy, Christine, 115
Demaria, Jules, 168n16
Demenÿ, Georges, 37, 136
DeMille, Cecil B., 100
Denoël Gonthier, 128, 181n57, 181n62
Denola, Georges, 98
dépôt légal, 58; associating with modern librarianship, 42–43; Cinémathèque Nationale and, 43–45; concerns regarding, 54; *double dépôt légal*, 43; expanding list of documents covered by, 43; importance of, 21; and systematization, 41
Derain, Lucie, 19, 126, 181n62
Descamps, Florence, 76–77
Deslandes, Jacques, 131, 132, 133–34
Destiny (film), 107–9
Désveaux, Delphine, 47–48
Detective's Dog, The (film), 136
Dewey Decimal Classification, 25
Dictionnaire de la langue française, 28
Dieckmann, Eva, 65
directing (as men's work), 117–18, 180n54
documentaliste, 33, 35–36, 39, 41, 50
documentary production, 33, 35–36
documentation, 5, 21, 26, 28, 33–36, 40–41, 55, 142
"document production," 35–36, 39
Dormoy, Marie, 40

Dornès, Yvonne, 3, 80, 154n4
Doucet, Jacques, 23–27, 30–31, 33–35, 39–41, 57, 160n22, 160n25
Dubos, Danie, 112, 175n4
Duhamel, Sarah, 105
Dulac, Germaine, 2, 34, 40, 50, 67, 69, 71, 80, 90, 94–95, 103, 105–6, 119, 126, 162n45
Durand, Jean, 2, 94, 168n13
Durand, Philippe, 168n13
Duras, Marguerite, 119, 134

early cinema, 116, 127–28, 136, 146, 169n29
early video, 116–17
Echo de Paris, L', 52
Ecole Georges Méliès, 166n1
ECPAD. *See* Etablissement de Communication et de Production Audiovisuelle de la Défense
Ecran démoniaque, L' (Eisner), 4, 63, 80, 108
Edinburgh International Film Festival (EFF), 120
EFF. *See* Edinburgh International Film Festival
Eichhorn, Kate, 6–7
Eisner, Lotte, 3–5, 11–12, 61, 154n5, 172n66; contributions of, 3–4; engaging in recovery work, 107–9; and Lousie Escoffier, 93, 172n66; visiting the Prussian State Library, 15–18; as woman of the CRH, 80; writing about Weimar cinema, 63–65. *See also* Cinémathèque française
El Dorado (film), 90
Employés, Les (Balzac), 98
Epstein, Jean, 2, 35, 40, 61, 80, 162n45; interview with, 88–90; and

stenographers, 103. *See also* Cinémathèque française
Epstein, Marie, 3, 64, 70, 71, 80, 88, 90, 97, 101, 150, 162n45, 171n53. *See also* Cinémathèque française; Commission de Recherches historiques
Escoffier, Louise, 93, 172n66. *See also* Eisner, Lotte
Escoubé, Lucienne, 19, 158n4
Espagnole, L' (Star), 82
"Essai sur Charlie Chaplin" (Soupault), 38–39
Etablissement de Communication et de Production Audiovisuelle de la Défense (ECPAD), 52
extant films, 50, 63–64, 68–69, 97, 113, 130–31

F. W. Murnau (Eisner), 4, 63, 65
Fantasio, 81
Faure, Anne-Marie, 178n32
Fayet-Scribe, Sylvie, 162n44
Fédération Internationale des Archives du Film (FIAF): activities of, 104; Conference Brighton, 146; emergence of, 2–3; Gender Observatory, 157n26; Symposium of 2023 on Women, Cinema, and Film Archives, 157n26
Fée aux choux, La (film), 92, 129, 132, 136, 182n65, 183n83
feminist futures, moving toward, 149–51
Femmes cinéastes; ou le triomphe de la volonté (Ford), 132
Ferro, Marc, 9
Fescourt, Henri, 88, 168n16, 171n52
Festival International de Films de Femmes, 143

Fête espagnole, La (film), 34, 90
Feuillade, Louis, 2, 173n77
FIAF. See Fédération Internationale des Archives du Film
fiction film, 92, 127, 129, 132, 182n65
film archive, 148, 150–51, 157n26; collaboration between historians and, 71; collection, 15–61; competition, 56; consequences of creation of, 21; emergence of, 2; engagement with, 1–5; erasing women's film history, 104–5; establishing women as agents of historical knowledge production, 3–4; feminist and postcolonial theories of, 5–8; legacies of, 57–61; masculinist practices in, 4–5; and "Musidora" collective, 126–27, 130–31, 135; and *Qui est Alice Guy?*, 136–43; recollection, 60–106; recovery, 107–48; reimagining as site of women's intervention, 8–14; researching women's film history at, 111–13; using to transform Guy Blaché into feminist figure, 113; women's engagement in, 105–6
film criticism, 28–29, 40, 91, 120–22, 124, 179n38, 180n52
film festival, 6, 12, 113, 115, 119–20, 122, 143, 175n11, 178n29, 178n33, 179n38. *See also* Musidora Festival
film historian, 9, 64, 80, 82, 88, 107–8; and Alice Guy, 130, 133–34, 146–47; bias of, 131–32; expressing frustration toward, 133–34; feminist, 1, 8, 13–14, 126, 131, 150, 155n12; French, 75, 104, 108, 127–29, 131; "laziness" of, 146
film historiography, 1–2, 6, 9–10, 12, 14, 30, 49, 64, 72, 108, 113, 126, 135

film history (*about* and *by* women): collection, 15–61; contributions outside established institutions, 4–5; emergence of film archive, 2; feminist and postcolonial archive theories, 5–8; overview, 1–14; recollection, 60–106; recovery, 107–48; reimagining archives as sites of women's intervention, 8–14
Film-Kurier, 3
Film Library. See Bibliothèque du Film
Filmoteca Nacional de México, 12
film pioneers, 6, 69, 71, 75, 78–79, 84, 105, 118, 127–28, 132, 136, 143, 147, 150
Films Albatros, Les, 67, 89
film theory, 120, 122, 180n52
"first French avant-garde," 69, 167n8
Flamant, Françoise, 112, 119, 124, 126, 175n4
Flamme cachée, La (film), 81–82, 185n3
Fleckinger, Hélène, 116–17
Flitterman-Lewis, Sandy, 89, 171n53
Fonds Léon Moussinac, 21–22, 36
Fonfreide, Marcelle, 124
Fontaine, Madeleine, 67
Ford, Charles, 82, 112, 128–30, 131–32
Forrester, Viviane, 125
Förster, Annette, 81, 88, 170n34–35
Fowles, John, 29
Française, La, 52
France, 22, 30, 37, 39–40, 49, 51, 80, 113, 173n83, 181n57, 181n60; Alice Guy as woman film pioneer in, 127–35; *Cabinet of Dr. Caligari* release in, 107–9; cinema as serious historical knowledge in, 20–21; CN discourses in, 52; commercial successes in, 114; debating *Be Natural* in, 145–47; *dépôt*

légal in, 42–45; discussing discrimination in, 115–18; feminist film theory in, 122; film preservation in, 1–14, 42, 56–60, 111–12; film theory in, 122; Great Depression hitting, 54; growing success of male filmmakers in, 114–15; legacy of "Musidora" collective in, 143–48; library sciences in, 21; oral sources in, 75–79; poetic realist films, 158n2; political unrest in, 176n13; precursors to women's film history in, 112–13; preserving silent cinema in, 19–20; *Qui est Alice Guy?* in, 135–43; rationalizing film knowledge in, 41; *Revue du cinéma* discourse in, 123–27; steno-typists in, 98–101; toward feminist future in, 149–51; transforming librarianship in, 28; Weimar cinema in, 63–65, 107–9. *See also* collection; recollection; recovery

Francis, Eve, 64, 70–71, 88, 90–91, 95, 150. *See also* Cinémathèque française; Commission de Recherches historiques

Franju, Georges, 3, 67
Frank, Hannah, 9
Friedan, Betty, 115
Frisch, Michael, 78
Fritz Lang (Eisner), 4, 63, 65
Frodon, Jean-Michel, 147
From Reverence to Rape: The Treatment of Women in the Movies (Haskell), 117
Fuller, Margaret, 10

Gaines, Jane M., 11, 13, 145, 156n24
Gance, Abel, 90, 162n45
Gardey, Delphine, 98
Gaulle, Charles de, 176n13
Gaumont, Léon, 75, 97, 128, 132, 168n16, 173n77, 182n65
Gaumont (studio), 96, 99, 133, 140
Gauthier, Christophe, 24, 160n25, 161n35
Gender of History, The (Smith), 9–10
George Pratt Cinema Oral History, 168n15
Gibory, Alphonse, 90
Godard, Colette, 123
Goulli, Sophie El, 12
Grand Souffle, Le (film), 96
Great Britain, 37, 119–20, 122, 126
Great Depression, 20, 54
Greek Film Archive, 12
Green, Pamela B., 144–47
Grele, Ronald J., 77–78
Grémillon, Jean, 162n45
Griffith, D. W., 98, 167n10
Grimoin-Sanson, Raoul, 168n16
Gronotayski, Georges, 51
Groo, Katherine, 7
Gunning, Tom, 98, 183n82
Guy Blaché, Alice, 2, 8, 105, 112, 119, 172n73, 173n85–86, 182n65, 183n82; "Alice Guy" in context of the women's liberation movement, 130–31; conversation about, 131–35; excerpts in *La Revue du cinéma*, 125–26; learning typing and stenography, 99–100; and legacy of "Musidora" collective, 143–48; main point of historical debate on, 129–30; MoMA collection of, 181n60; as narrator of personal history, 91–92; questioning biases of, 113; recovery project focused on, 128–29; retaining maiden and married

Guy Blaché, Alice (*continued*)
    names, 173n83; as subject of *Qui est Alice Guy?*, 135–43; trajectory of, 181n58; US edition of memoirs of, 181n57; as woman film pioneer, 127–35

Haskell, Molly, 117, 180n52
Haunted Screen, The. See *Ecran démoniaque, L'*
Helton, Laura E., 10
Hennefeld, Maggie, 13
Henri-Robert, Jacques, 51
Hepburn, Audrey, 117
héroïne de 4 ans, Une (film), 184n84
Herzog, Werner, 109
Hessling, Catherine, 105
Hiéroglyphes (series), 135, 183n80
Hill, Erin, 11, 100
Hillel-Erlanger, Irène, 105
Histoire comparée du cinéma (Deslandes), 132
Histoire de la Cinémathèque française (Mannoni), 68
Histoire du cinéma (Bardèche and Brasillach), 169n30
Histoire du cinématographe (Coissac), 168n16
Histoire générale du cinéma (Sadoul), 168n13
Histoires d'A (film), 116, 176n17
historical knowledge production, establishing women as agents of, 3–4
Hollywood, 11, 65, 68–69, 70, 100, 117–18, 147, 158n2
Homunculus (film), 108
Houlette, Michaël, 47–48
House Without a Door, The (film), 108
Hugon, André, 81
Huismans, Georges, 22

INA. See Institut national de l'audiovisuel
index cards, 33, 36–38, 40
India Song (film), 134
Institute of Communication and Audiovisual Production of Defense. See Etablissement de Communication et de Production Audiovisuelle de la Défense
Institut national de l'audiovisuel (INA), 135, 137*fig*., 139*fig*., 140*fig*., 141*fig*., 142*fig*.
International Archives for the Women's Movement, 154n7
International Federation of Film Archives. See Fédération Internationale des Archives du Film
International Festival of Women's Films, 121*fig*., 178n29
interviews, 6, 31, 64–65, 72; CRH interviews, 68–71, 78–79, 81, 84, 88, 91, 94, 98, 104–5; equal contributions, 94–95; narrators and, 91–97; and oral history, 75–79; stenographer typists and, 97–103; witness interviewers and, 80–91. See also recollection
Iribe, Marie-Louise, 105, 126
Irma Vep (character). See Musidora; *Vampires, Les*
Issartel, Marielle, 116

Jardin oublié, Le (film), 146
Jaubert, Françoise, 150
Jazz Singer, The (film), 19
Jeanne, René, 82
Jerusalem Cinematheque–Israel Film Archive, 12
Jocelyn (film), 34
Johannes, fils de Johannes (film), 149

John F. Kennedy Oral History
    Collection, 76
John F. Kennedy Presidential Library, 76
Johnston, Claire, 120, 179n38
Joly, Henri, 73*fig.*
Joly, Jeanne, 94
Jonuxi, Nora, 81, 93, 96–97, 106, 172n66,
    172n67, 172n74, 172n76
Joubin, André, 25–26
Journal de Moscou, Le, 31
Judex (serial), 81

Kahn, Albert, 7
Kamenka, Alexandre, 89
Kaplan, Nelly, 119, 124
Karagheuz, Hermine, 135–36, 138–43,
    139*fig.*, 140*fig.*, 141*fig.*, 142*fig.*
Karl, Roger, 90
Karman, Harvey, 116
Kawakita, Kashiko, 12
Keaton, Buster, 69
Kelly, Grace, 117
Kennedy, John F., 76
Kermadec, Liliane de, 119, 131, 133–34
Kirsanoff, Dimitry, 162n45
Krauss, Henry, 162n45
Krauss, Werner, 16

Lacassin, Francis, 88, 104, 112, 129, 131,
    133–34, 170n34
"ladies' auxiliary," 118
"Ladies' Auxiliary, The" (Sarris), 177n27
Lahourcade, Catherine, 178n32
Lang, Fritz, 4, 63–65, 108
Langlois, Henri, 2–3, 5, 20, 61, 72, 103–4,
    106, 108, 111, 157n26, 158n4, 170n43,
    182n73; acquiring films, 67–70; and

Alice Guy debate, 131–33; correcting
    interview transcripts, 79; and CRH
    interviews, 82, 84, 88, 90; and extant
    films, 97; general preference for, 49,
    56; interviewing, 64; leadership of,
    58–60, 59*fig.*; writing in *Cinématographie française*, 68
Lasseyne, Jacques, 170n35
Le Bris, Véronique, 144
Leclerc, Annie, 180n51
Lejeune, Paule, 112
Leni, Paul, 63
Lepage, Marquise, 146
Lequeux, Emmanuelle, 146–47
Lerner, Gerda, 6
Leyraud, Anne, 101, 102*fig.*
L'Herbier, Marcel, 90–91, 162n45
librarianship, scholarship on, 155n21
libraries, 9, 12, 16, 21, 24–25, 29, 41–42,
    159n14, 159n17
library, term, 24–25
Library of Alexandria, 17
Library of Congress, 76
library sciences, 21, 162n44
Lichtig, Renée, 150
Liézer, Janine, 92
Linder, Maud, 150
Lindgren, Ernest, 158n6
Lloyd, Harold, 69
Lods, Jean, 20, 30–31. *See also* Moussinac,
    Jeanne
Lods, Sabine, 21
London School of Economics and
    Political Science, 154n7
Lonedale Operator, The (film), 98
Loveday, Kiki, 8, 13, 155n12
Loviton, Jeanne, 154n4

Lubitsch, Ernst, 3
Lumière brothers, 2, 92–94, 96, 128, 132, 146, 182n65
Lupino, Ida, 118
Lynn, Emmy, 90, 94

Macdonald, Sharon, 29
Macpherson, Jeanie, 100
Magique image, La (film), 82, 170n36
Mahar, Karen Ward, 168n15
Malheurs de Sophie, Les (film), 114, 181n62
Mallet-Stevens, Robert, 54–55
Malthête-Méliès, Madeleine, 150
Manès, Gina, 93, 101
Mannoni, Laurent, 68, 70, 146–47
Manuel, Jacques, 90
Marchal, Arlette, 90, 94
Marie-Laurent, Jeanne, 93, 168n13
Marken, Jane, 93
Martineau, Barbara Halpern, 123
Mathieu, Julienne, 105
McMahan, Alison, 145, 183n82
Meerson, Mary, 3, 80, 93, 111, 119. *See also* Cinémathèque française
Méfaits d'une tête de veau, Les (film), 129
Méliès, Georges, 2, 67–68, 75, 128, 168n16
Méliès, Mme. *See* d'Alcy, Jehanne
Méliès, Paul, 85*fig.*
Melville, Herman, 98
Ménessier, Henri, 70
men's gaze, 125
Merck, Mandy, 120
Mesguich, Félix, 168n16
#MeToo movement, 144
Metro-Goldwyn Company, 40
Micquel, René, 51
microfilms, 36, 76

militant cinema, 116
Milowanoff, Sandra, 93
Ministère de l'Education et des Beaux-Arts, 22, 51–52, 56
Ministry of Education and Fine Arts. *See* Ministère de l'Education et des Beaux-Arts
Minne (film), 81
misogyny, 104–5, 119, 132, 147
Mistler, Jean, 53
Mitropoulou, Aglaia, 12
Mitry, Jean, 70
MLAC. *See* Mouvement pour la liberté de l'avortement et de la contraception
MLF. *See* Mouvement de Libération des Femmes
Modot, Gaston, 67, 168n13
Monca, Blanche, 92, 94
Monca, Georges, 94
Mon coeur est rouge (film), 175n4
Monde, Le, 27, 123
Monroe, Marilyn, 117
Moreau, Jeanne, 124, 125
Moreau, Léone, 150
Morel, Eugène, 24–25, 29, 33–34, 42–43
Mort du soleil, La (film), 95
Motion Picture Magazine, 27
Moussa, Alexandre, 180n52
Moussinac, Jeanne, 13, 150, 158n5, 160n25, 161n34–35, 172n65; and afterlife of the BC, 40–41; analysis of labor of, 41; biographical information about, 31; on cinema as art form, 24; considering activism of, 20–23; donations to, 33–35; Henry Poulaille writing to, 28–29; index cards of, 36–38; legacy of, 57–61; photo booth portrait of, 33*fig.*; praising

project of, 35; "rough bibliography" assembled by, 36; searching for details about, 30–31; seeking expertise of, 36; spearheading the BC, 31, 33–34; writing about BC classification, 39–40. *See also* Bibliothèque du Cinéma

Moussinac, Léon, 5, 24, 31, 33–35, 40, 50, 69, 90, 158n5, 160n25–26, 172n65; film library manifesto of, 27–28; letters between Doucet and, 26–27; overemphasizing role of, 29–30; on rapid development of film criticism, 27–28

Mouvement de Libération des Femmes (MLF), 115–17, 176n16

Mouvement pour la liberté de l'avortement et de la contraception (MLAC), 116

Mulvey, Laura, 120, 122, 126, 155n15, 179n38

Murat, Laure, 146–47

Murnau, F. W., 63, 65

Murnau, Robert Plumpe, 65

Musée du Cinéma, 24, 61, 70

Musée du Jeu de Paume, 47

Museo Nazionale del Cinema, 12

Museum of Cinema. *See* Musée du Cinéma

Museum of Modern Art (MoMA), 12, 181n60

Musidora: Festival international de films de femmes (film), 178n32

"Musidora" collective, 13, 150, 181n58, 183n81; aim of, 112; archival materials related to, 113; choosing president of, 175n11; complex relationship with cinema, 114–15; in context, 114–27; contradictory positions of, 115; emergence of, 112–13; emphasizing collective dimension of, 180n51; failure of, 180n52; film festival poster of, 121*fig.*; founding, 112, 175n4; and Guy Blaché recovery project, 127–35; legacy of, 143–48; major historical "discovery" by, 126–27; memories of, 174n1, 175n3; perception of "Alice Guy," 130–31; questioning film archive biases, 113; and *Qui est Alice Guy?*, 135–43; reactivating debates about French film historical narrative, 131–35; in *La Revue du cinéma*, 123–27; Sardet anecdote, 111–13; women's film festival organized by, 119–25; and women's liberation movement, 115–18

Musidora Festival, 170n35; and critical cinema discourses, 123–27; distinguishing from other women's film festivals, 120, 122; poster for, 121*fig.*; press coverage for, 123; program of, 119–20

Musidora (filmmaker), 3, 6, 64, 70–71, 78–79, 94, 105, 170n34, 173n77, 180n54, 185n3; acting career of, 81–82; considering words of, 149–51; discussing *Soleil et ombre*, 87–88; Eve Francis interview, 90–91; handwritten letter dictated to, 73*fig.*; interview transcripts corrected by, 74*fig.*, 86*fig.*, 88*fig.*; Jean Epstein interview, 88–90; leading Commission de Recherches historiques, 5–6; meeting Langlois, 88; and narrators, 91–97; Nora Jonuxi interview, 96–97, 106; as oral historian and narrator, 80–81; publicity photograph of, 83*fig.*; Renée Sylvaire interview, 84, 86; role in CRH interviews, 81–82, 84, 86–88; and stenographer typists, 97–101, 103.

Musidora (filmmaker) *(continued)*
　See also Cinémathèque française;
　Commission de Recherches
　historiques
Musidoras, Las, 13
Mutuelle du Cinéma, 166n1
Myles, Lynda, 120
Myrga, Laurence, 162n45

Naissance du cinéma (Moussinac), 26
Napierkowska, Stacia, 105
narrators, 170n42; Commission de
　Recherches historiques and, 91–95;
　difficulties encountered with, 101, 103
National Archives. *See* Archives
　Nationales
National Audiovisual Institute. *See*
　Institut national de l'audiovisuel
National Film Archive of Japan, 12
National Film Board of Canada, 178n32
National Organization for Women
　(NOW), 115
negatives, 34, 162n47
Never Done (Hill), 100
New Vision Photography, 47
New Wave. *See* Nouvelle Vague
New York Festival of Women's Films, 120
Nineteenth Amendment (US Constitu-
　tion), 115–16
Nosferatu (film), 65, 107–9
Nouvelle Vague (New Wave), 114–15, 118
NOW. *See* National Organization for
　Women

Office de Documentation bibliogra-
　phique (Office of Bibliographic
　Documentation), 36

Ollivier, Gilles, 51
Olsson, Jan, 183n82
On tourne (Pirandello), 37–38
Ophüls, Max, 114
oral history: accepting as valid source for
　historical research, 76–77; as archival
　practice, 77–78; defining, 75–76;
　emphasizing women as oral historians,
　80–81; projects related to, 168n15;
　standards for projects of, 76
Oral History Association, 75
Oral History Program (Academy of
　Motion Picture Arts and Sciences),
　168n15
Origines du cinématographe, Les (Demenÿ),
　37–38

Pabst, G. W., 63, 114
Painlevé, Jean, 50
Palais de Chaillot, 70
Palais du Trocadéro, 54
Panoramique du cinéma, 27
Parade's Gone By . . ., The (Brownlow),
　168n15
Paramount, 35, 40
Parc Méliès, 166n1
Parole de femmes (Leclerc), 180n51
Paroles . . . elles tournent! (Musidora), 125,
　180n51
Passion, La (film), 136, 140
past, archiving. *See* collection; recollec-
　tion; recovery
Pathé, Antoinette, 93–94
Pathé, Charles, 75, 128, 168n15
Pathé Frères (studio), 43, 67, 97, 164n76
Pearlman, Karen, 13
Peiss, Kathy, 6

Penseur, Le (film), 34
Perret, Léonce, 167n10
Perret, Valentine, 104
Perrot, Michelle, 6
Perrot, Victor, 90
Photographic and Cinematographic Section of the Army. *See* Section photographique et cinématographique de l'armée
"photographic documentation," 28, 34
Picq, Françoise, 116
Pied Piper of Hamelin, The (film), 108
pioneer, term, 7–8. *See also* film pioneers
"Pioneer Paradigm, The" (Loveday), 155n12
Pirandello, Luigi, 37–38
Pisier, Marie-France, 178n32
Plantier, Daniel Toscan du, 131, 133
Plumpe, Ursula, 65
poetic realist films, 158n2
Poirier, Léon, 35, 162n45
Pommer, Erich, 3
Pompidou, Georges, 123
Popular Arts Project, 168n15
Porchez, Marie, 81
Porten, Henny, 163n62
Positif (magazine), 64
Poulaille, Henry, 28–29, 163n62
Pour Don Carlos (film), 82
Pour une contre-histoire du cinéma (Lacassin), 112, 132
preservation (of cinema), 2, 7, 23, 42, 45, 49, 56, 58, 87, 150–51. *See also* film archive
primary sources, 6, 24, 30–31, 154n6
Prince, Gabrielle, 93
Prix Alice Guy, 144
Prolo, Maria Adriana, 12

Prussian State Library, 15–18, 63
Pupier, Madame (Lumière factory worker), 93, 96

Qu'est-ce que la documentation? (Briet), 33
Qui est Alice Guy? (film), 113, 134, 137*fig.*, 147; animation by Monique Renault in, 137*fig.*; availability of, 183n80; building monument to Alice Guy, 136, 138; central claim in, 135–36; contents of, 135; original sequences in, 138–43, 139*fig.*, 140*fig.*, 141*fig.*, 142*fig.*

Ravel, Gaston, 96–97
Ray, Man, 50
recollection: creating Le Cercle du Cinéma, 67–68; CRH as women's film history, 103–6; CRH interviews, 69–70; CRH women, 80–103; forms of, 63–64; legitimization of, 64–65; narrators, 91–97; oral history, 75–79; stenographer typists, 97–101, 103; theoretical reflections on, 11; witness interviewers, 80–91
recovery: engaging in recovery work, 107–9; Guy Blaché as subject of *Qui est Alice Guy?*, 135–43; Guy Blaché as woman film pioneer, 127–35; legacy of "Musidora" collective, 143–48; "Musidora" collective in context, 114–27; reconstruction through interviews, 96–97; Sardet anecdote, 111–13; theoretical reflections on, 11
Reiniger, Lotte, 119, 181n62
Renault, Monique, 135–36, 137*fig.*, 183n81
Renoir, Jean, 35
Revue du cinéma, La: Image et son, 115, 123–27, 134, 183n81

Rich, B. Ruby, 120
Richard, Jacques, 104, 132
Riot Grrrl Collection, 7
"Rire, Le" (Bergson), 39
Robinne, Gabrielle, 93
Rollet, Brigitte, 117–18
Rondel, Auguste, 40–41
Roques, Jacques, 81
Roques, Jeanne. *See* Musidora (filmmaker)
Rosen, Marjorie, 180n52
Roudy, Yvette, 176n16
Roussel, Melle, 100
Roussopoulos, Carole, 119, 151
"Ruse de guerre" (Guy Blaché), 131

Saccone, Kate, 11, 13
Sadoul, Georges, 70, 72, 94, 146, 168n13
SAP. *See* Service des Archives photographiques
Sarda, Marie-Anne, 159n17
Sardet, Dana, 111–13, 124–26, 174n1, 175n4, 181n57, 183n81
Sarris, Andrew, 118, 177n27
Saturday Review, 117
Schémas, 26
Scott, Joan Wallach, 6
Screen, 120, 122
Seashell and the Clergyman, The. *See Coquille et le clergyman, La*
secondary sources, 24, 30–31, 84, 97, 154n6, 169n30
Section photographique et cinématographique de l'armée (SPCA), 52
Seguin, Michelle, 21, 36–38. *See also* Bibliothèque Nationale
Sellier, Geneviève, 112

Serre, Claudine, 112, 124, 175n4
Service des Archives photographiques (SAP), 49, 51–53, 58
Service of the Photographic Archives. *See* Service des Archives photographiques
sexism, MLF combatting, 176n16
Seyrig, Delphine, 131, 151
"shared authority," 167n12; narrators and, 91–97; oral history and, 78; reliance on, 71; stenographer typists and, 97–103; witness interviewers and, 80–91
Shoot!. *See On tourne*
Sight and Sound, 129
silent cinema, 72, 88; dedication to preserving, 67–68; interviewing so-called pioneers of, 64; practices for crediting in, 96–97; preserving, 19–20
Silent Feminists, The (Slide), 145
Simon, Joan, 145
Slave Narratives: A Folk History of Slavery in the United States from Interviews with Former Slaves, 76
Slide, Anthony, 127, 145, 181n57
Smiling Madame Beudet, The. *See Souriante Madame Beudet, La*
Smith, Bonnie G., 6, 9–10
Société française de Photographie, 51
"sociological" approach (film theory), 120, 122
Solax, 130, 135–36, 143
Soleil et ombre (film), 82, 87–88, 126, 170n35
Soroptimist Club, 50
sound cinema, emergence of, 19–20
Soupault, Philippe, 36, 38–39, 164n63
Souriante Madame Beudet, La (film), 34
SPCA. *See* Section photographique et cinématographique de l'armée

Staël, Germaine de, 10
Stamp, Shelley, 13, 157n26
Starevitch, Ladislas, 168n16
stenographer typists (steno-typists): associations between stenography and domestic activities, 98–99; contextualizing involvement of women, 100–101; development of role of, 98–99; foregrounding as feminized labor, 100–101; tasks of, 97–98; uneasy position of, 101, 103; valuable contributions of, 98
Stigmate, Le (film), 94
Stucker (camera operator), 87–88
Student of Prague, The (film), 108
"Sur la création d'une bibliothèque du cinématographe et son organisation" (Moussinac), 27, 160n26
Sylvaire, Renée, 74*fig.*, 84, 86, 93

talkies, 68, 158n1
Taylor, Elizabeth, 117
Tedesco, Jean, 162n45
Temps héroïques, Les (film), 91
Terre des taureaux, La (film), 82, 126, 170n35
"theoretical" approach (film theory), 120, 122
Thompson, Paul, 9
Tissot, Alice, 92
To Desire Differently: Feminism and the French Cinema (Flitterman-Lewis), 89
Toronto Women & Film, 120
Touil, Rime, 41, 164n76
Tourneur, Louise, 89, 93–94
Tourneur, Maurice, 101
Trouillot, Michel-Rolph, 7, 9, 78, 154n7
Trousers, The (film), 16

Turbiau, Aurore, 125
typewriter, 98. *See also* stenographer typists

UFOLEIS. *See* Union Française des Oeuvres Laïques d'Education par l'Image et le Son
Union Française des Oeuvres Laïques d'Education par l'Image et le Son (UFOLEIS), 123
United Artists, 40
United States, 7, 10, 37–38, 40, 76, 98, 100, 111, 115, 117, 119–20, 123, 126–28, 130, 140, 144–45, 154n7, 168n15, 177n22, 179n38
University of Chicago, 77
Usine aux images, L' (Canudo), 27

Vagabonde, La (film), 81, 83*fig.*
Valenzuela, Elena Sánchez, 12, 157n26
Vampires, Les (serial), 81–82, 123–24
Van Leer, Lia, 12
Varda, Agnès, 117, 119
Védrès, Nicole, 93
Veil, Simone, 176n16
Verdun, visions d'histoire (film), 34–35
Vergne, Edith, 125
Veronesi, Giulia, 150
Vicenta (film), 82, 150, 185n3
Vignaux, Valérie, 30–31
Vigo, Luce, 150
Village Voice, 118
Ville de Madame Tango, La (film), 81
Vincendeau, Ginette, 122
visual media, education utilizing, 116–17
"Visual Pleasure and Narrative Cinema" (Mulvey), 120, 122
Volonté, La, 52, 53*fig.*

Walter, Jeanne, 40–41
Wang, Yiman, 13
Wegener, Paul, 63
Weill, Claudia, 119
Weimar cinema, 4, 63–65, 80, 108–9
Weissberg, Jay, 145–46
Wenders, Wim, 109
Wertmüller, Lina, 119
Wieder, Ioana, 151
Wieland, Joyce, 119
witnesses, 1, 151; creating Le Cercle du Cinéma, 67–68; CRH interviews, 69–70; CRH women, 80–103; forms of recollection, 63–64; legitimizing recollection, 63–64; narration services, 91–95; narrators, 91–97; oral history, 75–79; reconstruction through interviews, 96–97; stenographer typists, 97–101, 103; witness interviewers, 80–91
witness interviewers, 71, 80–81, 89, 91–92, 97, 100–101, 103. *See also* "shared authority"
Women and Film, 123
Women Filmmakers in Early Hollywood (Mahar), 168n15
Women Film Pioneers Project, 11, 13, 157n27
Women in Film Oral History, 168n15

Women's Event (Edinburgh International Film Festival), 120
women's film history: collection, 15–61; contributions outside established institutions, 4–5; CRH as, 103–6; emergence of film archive, 2; erasing, 104–5; feminist and postcolonial theories of archive, 5–8; missed opportunity for, 104–6; overview, 1–14; recollection, 63–106; recovery, 107–48; reimagining archive as site of women's intervention, 8–14
women's gaze, 125
women's liberation movement, 115–18
Women's Library, 154n7
Women's Strike for Equality, 115, 176n15
World Center for Women's Archives, 154n7
World War I, 108
World War II, 3, 16, 109, 118, 154n4, 159n14, 172n66

Y'a qu'à pas baiser (film), 176n17

Zecca, Ferdinand, 129
Zetterling, Mai, 119, 125
Zucca, Pierre, 123, 175n4
Zwobada, André, 131, 133–34

Founded in 1893,
UNIVERSITY OF CALIFORNIA PRESS
publishes bold, progressive books and journals
on topics in the arts, humanities, social sciences,
and natural sciences—with a focus on social
justice issues—that inspire thought and action
among readers worldwide.

The UC PRESS FOUNDATION
raises funds to uphold the press's vital role
as an independent, nonprofit publisher, and
receives philanthropic support from a wide
range of individuals and institutions—and from
committed readers like you. To learn more, visit
ucpress.edu/supportus.

www.ingramcontent.com/pod-product-compliance
Lightning Source LLC
Chambersburg PA
CBHW020813230426
43666CB00007B/986